THE GREAT LAKES

WAYNE GRADY

PRINCIPAL PHOTOGRAPHY BY BRUCE LITTELJOHN

ILLUSTRATIONS BY EMILY S. DAMSTRA

THE

GREAT

LAKES

THE NATURAL HISTORY
OF A CHANGING REGION

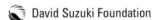 David Suzuki Foundation

GREYSTONE BOOKS

DOUGLAS & MCINTYRE PUBLISHING GROUP

VANCOUVER/TORONTO/BERKELEY

Text copyright © 2007 by Wayne Grady
Photographs copyright © 2007 by the
photographers credited

07 08 09 10 11 5 4 3 2 1

Greystone Books
A division of Douglas & McIntyre Ltd.
2323 Quebec Street, Suite 201
Vancouver, British Columbia
Canada V5T 4S7
www.greystonebooks.com

David Suzuki Foundation
219-2211 West 4th Avenue
Vancouver, British Columbia
Canada V6K 4S2

Library and Archives Canada Cataloguing in Publication
Grady, Wayne
The Great Lakes : the natural history of a changing region /
Wayne Grady ; principal photography by Bruce Litteljohn ;
illustrations by Emily S. Damstra.

Co-published by the David Suzuki Foundation.
Includes bibliographical references and index.

ISBN 978-1-55365-197-0

1. Natural history—Great Lakes Region (North America).
2. Great Lakes (North America)—History. 3. Great Lakes
(North America)—Environmental conditions.
4. Lake ecology—Great Lakes (North America). I. Litteljohn,
Bruce M., 1935- II. Damstra, Emily S. III. David Suzuki
Foundation IV. Title.

QH104.5.G7G723 2007   508.77   C2007-903889-1

Grateful acknowledgment is made to the following for
permission to reproduce or quote from their works:

Margaret Atwood for "Lichen and Reindeer Moss on
Granite," © Margaret Atwood, 2007. Used by permission
of the author.

Diana Beresford-Kroeger for a quotation from *Arboretum
America: A Philosophy of the Forest*, University of Michigan
Press, Ann Arbor, Michigan, 2003.

Robert Finch for lines from "Lake," included in *Sail-boat and
Lake*, The Porcupine's Quill, Erin, Ontario, 1988.

Lines from "Lake Superior" by the late Lorine Niedecker
are from *North Central*, Fulcrum Press, London, 1968.

Andrew Nikiforuk for a quote from *Pandemonium: Bird
Flu, Mad Cow Disease and Other Biological Plagues of the 21st
Century*, Viking Canada, Toronto, 2006.

The University of Minnesota Press for a quote from *Runes of
the North*, by Sigurd F. Olson, University of Minnesota Press,
Minneapolis, Minnesota, 1997.

The heirs of Rutherford Platt for permission to quote from
The Great American Forest, by Rutherford Platt, Prentice-Hall
Inc., Englewood Cliffs, N.J., 1965.

Copy edited by Barbara Czarnecki
Jacket and text design by Naomi MacDougall
Front jacket photograph © Willard Clay/Getty Images
Back jacket photographs: *left:* by Eleanor Kee Wellman;
middle and right: by Scot Stewart
Maps by Eric Leinberger
Printed and bound in Canada by Friesens
Printed on acid-free paper that is forest friendly
(100% post-consumer recycled paper)
and has been processed chlorine free

Distributed in the U.S. by Publishers Group West

We gratefully acknowledge the financial support of
the Canada Council for the Arts, the British Columbia
Arts Council, the Province of British Columbia through the
Book Publishing Tax Credit, and the Government of Canada
through the Book Publishing Industry Development

PAGE II: Evening paddle on Smoke Lake
in Ontario's Algonquin Provincial Park.

PAGE VI-VII: Precambrian rock and white
pine, Georgian Bay, Ontario.

CONTENTS

PREFACE

T HE GREAT LAKES ENDURE THE fate of all familiar features in nature: they are taken for granted equally by those who know them and by those who don't. Like mountain ranges or prairie skies, their size makes us forget they're there; we may cast a glance at them in the morning to make sure the universe is arranged more or less as it had been the previous night, but then we don't think of them for the rest of the day. When I lived in Toronto and visitors asked me how to get to the lakefront, I'd have to think before replying, "Oh yes, go south." When I moved to Kingston, Ontario, and was asked the same question, I'd be turned around: "It's south—no, east!" In Windsor, on the Detroit River, where I was born, it was: "Up that way, north." The simple truth is that, to me, the Great Lakes seem to be everywhere.

I have lived on them all my life, except for a brief period spent in northern Quebec, and even then I felt connected to the Lakes by the St. Lawrence River. Windsor is an upside-down Canadian city: we looked north to the United States. I remember skating on Lake St. Clair, on transparent ice that had frozen so quickly its surface held the shape of waves. I looked down giddily between my skates to see schools of minnows darting among fronds of bottom-anchored plants. I recall swimming in Lake Erie, off Point Pelee, and being

FACING PAGE: A bull moose enjoys a tranquil meal in a shallow northern lake.

1

taken to visit the bird sanctuary established in Kingsville by the legendary Jack Miner, who saved the threatened Canada goose from extinction. My father, too, had been born in Windsor, and although he spent World War II on the North Atlantic, when the war was over he brought his Newfoundland bride back to his hometown because, as he said, he missed the water.

My great-grandfather had moved to Windsor from Cass County, Michigan, at the end of the nineteenth century. Cass County and its seat, Cassopolis, was named for Michigan Territory's first governor, Lewis "Big Belly" Cass, who, with the geologist Thomas McKenney and Henry Rowe Schoolcraft, the future Indian agent, explored the country around Lake Superior in 1825. By the time my father's family moved to Michigan, shortly after the American Civil War, Cass County was a major stop on the Underground Railroad. Andrew Jackson Grady had a cup of coffee there, as they say in baseball, and then moved on to Windsor.

We later lived for a time north of Toronto, not far from Lake Simcoe, part of the ancient water route through which, 4,000 years ago, Lake Huron drained directly into Lake Ontario, bypassing Lake St. Clair and the Detroit River and Lake Erie. I fished for chub in the narrow creeks that cut through pastures and cedar bushes, watched ducks and turtles and frogs in the few remaining wetlands in the area, and tobogganed in valleys laden with snow in the lee of the Niagara Escarpment. My brother now lives in Sault Ste. Marie. The web of my family thus embraces all five Lakes and two of the three waterways between them.

Even so, I did not fully appreciate the Lakes until I boarded a freighter in Thunder Bay, at the western end of Lake Superior, and sailed through all five as the ship carried a load of wheat to the St. Lawrence. Standing on a throbbing deck, under the limitless expanse of sky, I lost sight of land in every direction. It took us all night to sail the length of Lake Superior, and I saw no other lights but the stars. The historian Arthur Lower, who had made the same journey three decades earlier, wrote that "Superior is impressive at all times, never more so than at midnight." Impressive, yes, but also somehow comforting, as though the knowledge of all that clear sky above us, and all that freshwater beneath us, and our ability to traverse both in safety, suggested to me that our survival as a species was both miraculous and assured.

Since then I have come to know the Lakes more intimately still. They have been studied, assessed, analyzed, sampled, probed, and researched by scientists from the fifteen universities and the governments of the seven states and one Canadian province that surround them, and the fruits of those endeavors are largely what inform this book. More data has come from the hundreds of nongovernmental agencies and citizens' groups that are working to preserve the natural beauty and quality of the Lakes and the Lakes basin. I am grateful to all who have published their findings in scholarly journals, in books, and on Web sites. The names of the individuals who agreed to form the panel of experts are listed elsewhere, and I am grateful that they made themselves available in the midst of their own busy schedules.

Many others have been generous with their time and expertise, some of whom I thank here by name: George Barron, soil biologist, University of Guelph; Peg Bostwick, Michigan Department of Environmental Quality; Paula Fedeski-Koundakjian, International Joint Commission; Graeme Gibson, Pelee Island Bird Observatory; Melissa Helwig, Library of the Canadian Centre for Inland Water; Judith Jones, biologist, Manitoulin Island; Jerome Keen, Great Lakes Fisheries Commission; Hugh MacIsaac, University of Windsor; Robert Montgomery, Queen's University; Geoff Peach, Lake Huron Centre for Coastal Conservation; Richard Ubbens, city forester, City of Toronto; and Paige Wilder, Biodiversity Project, Madison, Wisconsin.

This book would not exist in anything like its present form without the patience and persistence of Jan Walter, its editor. Barbara Czarnecki's diligence and exactitude have also been invaluable. Bruce Litteljohn is a brilliant photographer and a devoted environmentalist, and his assistance has contributed not only to the look but also to the integrity of this book. And I would also like to thank Bella Pomer, Rob Sanders, and, as always, Merilyn Simonds.

Athens, Ontario, June 2007

ONE

THE
FRESHWATER
SEAS

SEEN FROM ABOVE, FROM ONE of NASA's Radar Topographic Mapping satellites, for example, the Great Lakes appear to cinch North America's midsection like a belt, their cluster forming an aquamarine clasp set slightly off-center on the geographic waistline of the continent. From such a height their immensity is apparent, but we need to draw much closer to appreciate their true nature. Depending on our vantage point, we might find high cliffs towering over deep, brooding water, or rounded, rocky islands peppering the bays, or sandy spits and shoals forever shifting under wind and waves. There is also a good chance we'd see city skyscrapers, rolling farmland, or tidy fishing villages. Immensity, diversity, and beauty are qualities so breathtakingly apparent that the adjective *great* seems almost redundant, which may be why most people who live within their influence call them simply "the Lakes."

In elementary school, we remembered the names of the lakes with the acronym HOMES: Huron, Ontario, Michigan, Erie, and Superior. To identify their shapes, we devised other mnemonics: Lake Superior looked like a cartoon wolf's head, with Isle Royale its slitty eye. Lake Michigan and Lake Huron were a pair of blue woolen mittens (Michigan sopping wet and stretched), dangling on

FACING PAGE: Shining big-sea water: Pie Island in Lake Superior, near Thunder Bay, Ontario.

5

> And all things are ordered together somehow, but not all alike,
> both fishes and fowls and plants; and the world is not such that one thing
> has nothing to do with another, but they are all connected.
>
> ARISTOTLE, *Metaphysica*

a string from the cuffs of a green snowsuit. Lakes Erie and Ontario resembled organs, maybe a pair of kidneys, or a liver and a pancreas. As an adult, those childhood images still resonate: the wolf's head reminds me of the Great Lakes' wilderness heritage; the mittens represent the role the Lakes play in moderating the region's climate, especially in winter; and what are organs but filters that cleanse the body of toxic substances and regulate the flow of fluids through the system?

From whatever vantage point we view the Lakes, and no matter what yardsticks we use to measure and study them, our admiration for their grandeur and endurance never ceases. One recent February afternoon I stood on the north shore of Lake Ontario, looking south toward the invisible coast of New York State. We'd been having another mild winter, but it was beginning to turn cold; there was almost no snow on the ground, and no ice on the lake except for a few thin pans blown up by the bracing wind, which sifted through a stand of white cedars beside me. The water was the same battleship gray as the clouds, except that there were rows of white-capped ridges rushing toward shore like legions of soldiers storming a rampart. Gulls—ring-billed, greater black-backed, maybe a few herring gulls in their first-year plumage—struggled to remain stationary above the fray, their bulletlike heads tilted downward in search of small fish thrust to the foam-flecked surface by the waves.

It was a timeless vista, one a Paleo-Indian might have appreciated 10,000 years before me, or a coureur de bois three centuries

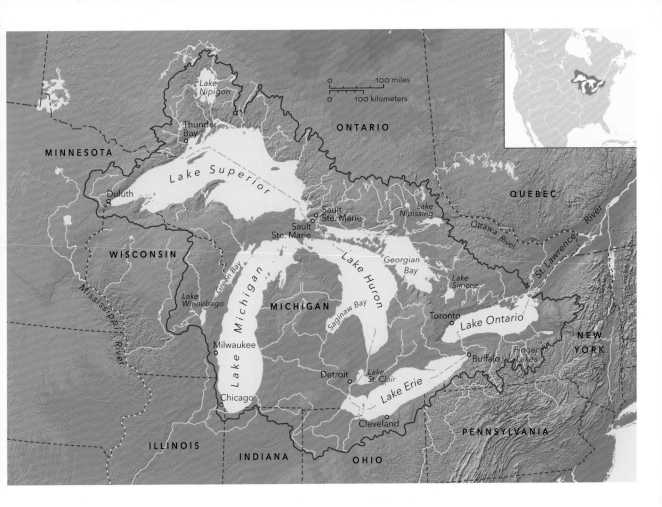

ago. Of course the intervening years have wrought many changes in and around and above the Lakes; they are no longer what they were. But this view was still magnificent. I felt part of the vortex of life being lived from top to bottom, from roiling storm cloud to churning lake bottom, as invigorating as a shot of adrenalin. They are still the Great Lakes, I thought; they still have the power to make the spirit soar.

THE FIRST EUROPEAN to record that sense of grandeur was the French geographer and explorer Samuel de Champlain. On his inaugural journey to the New World in 1603, he spoke with a group of Algonquins at the Lachine Rapids, near what is now Montreal. He asked them what lay farther up the St. Lawrence and was told that if his party carried on upriver, it would come to another set of rapids and pass the mouth of another large river (the Ottawa) leading north into Algonquin territory. Continuing on the St. Lawrence, he would encounter more rapids, then a lake 45 or 50 miles in length, then more rapids, and, still farther upstream, "a large lake 250 miles long." As Champlain reported in his *Brief discours,* published on his return to France later that year, the Algonquins told him that this immense body of water contained "a number of islands, and at the end of the lake the water is salty and the winters mild."

Although he did not attempt the trip that year, Champlain's imagination was fired. He could comprehend a lake 45 or 50 miles long (about 75 kilometers); France's largest lake—Lake Geneva, on the border between France and Switzerland—was of that order. But a body of water, especially saltwater, extending for 250 miles? He thought it must be the Pacific Ocean. He calculated that at Lachine (which he had earlier so named because he originally believed it to be China), he stood 400, maybe 450 miles (640 or 720 kilometers) from Cathay. And the riches of the Orient were, after all, what they had come so far from France to find.

The illusion that the Great Lakes were actually the Pacific Ocean lasted for decades. Throughout the early 1600s, as each lake was discovered in turn by French commercial adventurers or proselytizing missionaries, the first to dip his paddle in the new body of water believed that by crossing it he would arrive in China. As late as 1634, Jean Nicollet de Belleborne, sent by the Compagnie de Cent-Associés to live among the *gens du mer* (people of the sea) to learn their ways and secure their beaver pelts, stepped ashore at Green Bay on the west side of Lake Michigan, donned a robe of scarlet Chinese damask, and asked the astounded Winnebagoes who greeted him to conduct him to the court of the emperor.

When Champlain finally paddled down the French River into Lake Huron in August 1615, he was still expecting to taste saltwater. The only European to have made the trip before him was Étienne Brûlé, a French scout, whom Champlain had sent ahead to explore the country and learn the Algonquins' language. Brûlé had lived among the Huron for twenty years, but he left no record of his

sojourn among them. When Champlain dipped his hand into Georgian Bay, at the mouth of the French River, he must have been both surprised and disappointed to find that the water was fresh. He had not reached the Pacific, but he had paddled onto a lake that certainly looked as big as an ocean. He called it, in his journal, *la mer douce,* the freshwater sea. The French had a perfectly good word for lake—*lac*—and the fact that Champlain chose *mer* indicates that he knew he was entering a body of water closer in size to the Mediterranean Sea than to Lake Geneva, something large enough to divide continents.

The Lakes inevitably came to be known as the "inland seas." John MacTaggart, a Scottish engineer who arrived in Canada West (now Ontario) in 1826 to survey the route of the Rideau Canal that would link Kingston and Ottawa, later published a memoir, *Three Years in Canada,* in which he enthused that the natural wonders of Canada were "not to be matched in the world." He particularly recommended

Near the mouth of the French River at Georgian Bay: Champlain's first glimpse of the "inland sea."

Discovering how different organisms in an ecosystem relate to one another is a relatively new goal in biology, and unsuspected relationships come to light all the time. The mycorrhizal (fungus-root) relationship between fungi and trees, for example, is still something of a mystery. A fungus has no green chloroplasts, and so cannot manufacture its own food through photosynthesis; instead, it must steal food from other plants. Its root hairs will penetrate the cells of a vascular plant, a tree for example, and feed on sugars that the tree sends to its own roots for storage. Thus nourished, the fungus spreads to form a dense mat of tendrils, or hyphae, that can fill a vast amount of underground space, often several square kilometers or square miles. There it attaches itself to the roots of other trees and, in return for its sugar meals, pumps water and nutrients into the host trees.

The mushroom *Paxillus involutus*–"Poisonous Paxillus"–helps red pines fight off root rot.

Both plants and fungi benefit from the exchange. Sometimes a fungus will take nutrients from one tree and transfer them to a second tree that is low on food. Some fungi even produce poisons that protect their hosts from invading pathogens: the mycorrhizal fungus *Paxillus involutus,* for instance, has been found to produce a fungicide that increases a red pine's resistance to fusarium root rot. A lone *Paxillus* mushroom poking its reddish-brown cap through the needle-strewn floor of a pine forest in July is more than just a tasty morsel for deer mice, red squirrels, and porcupines; it is the fruiting body of a fungus that is helping to keep the entire forest healthy.

"the great inland seas," which, he thought, could be made to form part of an ambitious canal system connecting Quebec with the Pacific Ocean. It was Champlain's dream revived.

To think of such lakes, however great, as seas is not unreasonable. Once out of sight of land, with the tempestuous swell exhibiting many of the properties normally associated with oceans, it's easy to forget you are on a lake. In *Moby Dick,* Herman Melville wrote that the Great Lakes "possess an ocean-like expansiveness, with many of the ocean's noblest traits." Their expansiveness is most dramatically reflected in the size of their waves; all five lakes are large enough to create waves comparable to those experienced at sea. Four-and-a-half-meter (15-foot) waves have been reported on Lake Michigan, and waves of 7.5 meters (25 feet) are common on Lake Superior, especially in November, which prompted Rudyard Kipling to call that lake "a hideous thing to find in the heart of a continent."

After Champlain, it would be centuries before the Lakes were seen as something more than avenues of commerce, convenient if occasionally treacherous means of getting somewhere else. But they eventually became homes to colonists, farmers, fishermen, miners, industrialists, and entrepreneurs. Only recently, within the past few decades, has there been a wider understanding that the Lakes are homes in a deeper sense, a vast, complex, and interconnected ecological system that is the natural habitat of an unimaginably large array of organisms, each so delicately dependent upon the other that whatever affects one inevitably affects the whole. And the whole includes us.

AROUND THE LAKES

The nineteenth-century German zoologist Ernst Haeckel (1834–1919) coined the term *ecology* (from the Greek *oikos,* meaning "household") after an extensive study of marine organisms—in particular Portuguese man-of-wars, sponges, starfish, and sea urchins, filter-feeding creatures that lived in intense intimacy with water—and after reading Darwin's *Origin of Species* (1859), with its insistence that species were shaped by their environments. In his own monumental work, *The General Morphology of Organisms* (1886),

Haeckel proposed a revolutionary approach to the study of biology, a way of viewing nature that went beyond the endless cataloguing of organic forms and their affinities, as Linnaeus had advocated. He wanted instead an examination of the interrelationships and interdependencies among species, how they were affected by their proximity to one another and by their surroundings, including such inanimate influences as soil and climate. He opposed the then prevailing concept of "dualism," the separation of mind and matter, and promoted the idea of "monism," the integration of mind and matter, and therefore of human beings and nature.

The science of ecology led naturally to a consideration of ecological systems, or ecosystems, now broadly defined as communities of living organisms interacting with one another and with their physical environments. Ecologists look for patterns in the distribution of and relationships among plants and animals, and for ways to understand and therefore preserve those patterns. An ecosystem can be as small as a backyard, as large as a river valley, or as vast as a continent. In fact, James Lovelock, the British scientist who proposed that our planet should be regarded as a single organism, which he named Gaia, described the earth in precisely those terms: "a self-regulating system made up from the totality of organisms, the surface rocks, the ocean and the atmosphere tightly coupled as an evolving system." In every case—backyard, river system, or planet— every species in it, and every individual within that species, exists in a mutually beneficial relationship with all other plants, animals, and non-living elements with which it shares its habitat.

The complex ecosystem that is the Great Lakes basin rests in a bowl defined by the height of land that separates it from neighboring watersheds. The rivers above Lake Nipissing and Lake Superior, on the other side of that tipping point, flow into Hudson and James bays; south of it, the Pic, the White, the Magpie, the Montreal, and the rivers that form the Lake Nipigon watershed all drain south, into Superior. Similarly, almost immediately south of Lake Michigan, the rivers drift toward the Mississippi valley, but the St. Joseph drains into Lake Michigan and the Maumee and Sandusky rivers run north into Lake Erie. In the west, the basin captures the

St. Louis River, which flows through Duluth, Minnesota, and the Dog River, whose mouth is at the city of Thunder Bay, Ontario. The Wolf and Menominee Rivers, which flow southeast into Lake Winnebago and Lake Michigan, respectively, have their sources in the Menominee Highlands, south of Lake Superior. The Appalachian watershed to the southeast also cuts close to the Great Lakes, but several small rivers choose Lake Ontario: the Gennessee and the Black are both in the basin. The Great Lakes watershed is the sum of five separate watersheds—one for each of the Lakes—and claims tens of thousands of wetland bogs, verdant swamps, quickening streams, and robust rivers, named and unnamed, as its own.

Although the size of the watershed is small relative to the area of the lakes it feeds—a fact that has major ecological implications for the species it harbors—the land and water surfaces encompassed by it constitute an area the size of France and the United Kingdom combined, about 540,000 square kilometers (208,000 square miles). North to south, it stretches 965 kilometers (600 miles), over 10 degrees of latitude, from 51°N, above Lake Nipigon, down into central Ohio. East to west, it occupies 18 degrees of longitude, from the eastern mouth of Lake Ontario to eastern Minnesota, more than 1,200 kilometers (750 miles) across. To walk the circumference of the Great Lakes watershed is to travel nearly 6,000 kilometers (3,725 miles).

Such a tour passes through scores of distinct terrestrial and aquatic ecosystems. For research and conservation purposes, these ecosystems have been grouped into larger units called ecoregions, geographical zones that link ecosystems with their respective climate factors, plant and animal assemblages, and soil types. The World Wildlife Fund Canada (WWF) and its American counterpart (WWF-US), working with government environmental scientists in both countries, have devised one such classification system that divides North America into 116 land-based ecoregions and 60 freshwater ecoregions. Eight land-based and four freshwater ecoregions are found inside the boundaries of the Great Lakes basin. Given the size of the human population and the extent of urban development, a surprising percentage of it is still forested.

Central Canadian
Shield Forests

Eastern Forest-
Boreal Transition

Western Great Lakes Forests

Upper Midwest Forest-
Savanna Transition

Eastern Great Lakes
Lowland Forests

Southern Great Lakes Forests

Allegheny
Highlands
Forests

Central Forest-
Grasslands Transition

ECOREGIONS OF THE
GREAT LAKES BASIN

Lake Superior's drainage basin is 91 percent forested; that of Lake Huron, 68 percent; Lake Ontario's, 49 percent; Lake Michigan's, 41 percent; and even Lake Erie, with its heavily industrialized western end and denuded north shore, drains an area that is 21 percent forested. Many of these forests are, of course, second or third growth, or in some cases are composed of species different from those that grew here before European settlement. Even so, it is for the most part a forested ecological system, or rather a series of contiguous forested ecosystems.

Defining an ecosystem by any one element in it—trees, in this case—is merely a shorthand method of imposing order on the mind-boggling diversity of species and influences in the Lakes basin. We might have classified it by microclimate or chosen nematodes instead of trees, but trees are conveniently accessible identifiers: they stay in one place and require no complicated equipment for observation. They are also the products of specific climate and soil types. You can walk along a shaded hiking trail or paddle down a canopied river and recognize that you are in an eastern hemlock, red maple, and paper birch forest, and therefore in a cool, moist, temperate climatic zone with moderately well-drained, sandy soil. Trees are markers for entire assemblages of organisms, including reptiles, birds, mammals, and nematodes; in the words of the Harvard biologist Edward O. Wilson, "Who speaks for the trees, speaks for all of Nature."

A circumferential journey of the basin that starts in the northernmost region above Lake Superior passes through some of the most starkly beautiful terrain on the continent. This is the Central Canadian Shield Forests ecoregion, a large swath of territory with thin, acidic soil overlying gneiss and granite bedrock, shoulders of which often thrust up through the soil and tower over the region's myriad lakes and wetlands. In this southern boreal forest,

Wetlands like this one in New York's Adirondack Mountains provide vital resting and feeding stations for waterfowl migrating to breeding grounds farther north.

the dominant tree species are spruce, fir, pine, and paper birch, with quaking aspen growing along the stream banks and in the clearings. The climate is moist and humid, though cool and therefore drier than the climate farther east, with an annual mean temperature of only -2°C (28.5°F) and a yearly precipitation of less than 800 millimeters (31.5 inches), most of it falling in the form of winter snow.

The wildlife diversity is the lowest in the watershed, but moose, woodland caribou, black bears, and gray wolves make their livings here. One hears the drumming of ruffed grouse and sees American black ducks and common mergansers in the lakes.

Meandering south and east above Lake Huron, the basin rim moves into the Eastern Forest—Boreal Transition ecoregion, where the forest gradually shifts from boreal to temperate broadleaf with some mixed conifers. These woods are part of the Great Lakes—St. Lawrence forest, the multifaceted woodland that dominates the Lakes region. Here in its northern reaches the microclimate warms slightly above the boreal, with the annual mean temperature between 1.5°C and 3.5°C (34.7°F and 38°F) and annual rainfall approaching 1 meter (39 inches). The underlying bedrock is still Shield, but it's buried deeper beneath undulating gravel lowlands with only an occasional outcropping of granite. Spruce, fir, and aspen begin to mix with sugar maple, yellow birch, and, on the warmer, south-facing slopes, white pine and beech. The wolves are smaller, the species having changed from gray to red wolf, and coyotes and white-tailed deer are plentiful. Pileated woodpeckers, mourning doves, and cardinals brighten the dark forest.

Above Georgian Bay, in the Algonquin Highlands, the height of land marches north and east toward the Ottawa River. Just east of Lake Nipissing, the basin boundary cuts southeast toward the St. Lawrence River Lowlands at the mouth of Lake Ontario. Swinging around the lake, the basin rim runs through upstate New York's Adirondack Mountains and into the Finger Lakes district. This is the Eastern Great Lakes Lowland Forests ecoregion, and although it is still part of the extensive Great Lakes–St. Lawrence forest, the tree species in this zone change again, with sugar maples joined by red maples and red oaks. Elms, cottonwoods, eastern white cedar, and ashes occupy the moist bottomlands, while red oaks and red pines mix with white pine and sugar maples on higher, drier sites. Glacial features such as moraines, drumlins, and eskers create a rolling landscape of silt, clay, sand, and gravel soils interspersed with peat, muck, and marl. Moose and white-tailed deer share the forest with wolves and coyotes, and chipmunks, squirrels, foxes, raccoons, and porcupines enliven the woods. Flying squirrels and screech owls make their nests in hollows of the larger trees.

FACING PAGE: The brilliant crimson flash of a male northern cardinal brightens the boreal forest.

As it turns westward under Lake Ontario, the eastern extreme of the basin catches a northern section of the Allegheny Highlands Forests ecoregion. In this zone, the Great Lakes–St. Lawrence forest is heavily populated by eastern hemlock and beech, and black cherry joins stands of sugar maple, yellow and gray birch, white ash, and white pine. The basin's boundary then runs south and west, approaching the south shore of Lake Erie along the Appalachian Plateau, where the hardwood species belong primarily to the Carolinian forest, and where urbanization begins to blur the natural landscape under the highly industrial cities of Buffalo, New York; Erie, Pennsylvania; and Cleveland, Ohio.

Cradling the south shore of Lake Ontario and encircling Lake Erie is an extension of the Southern Great Lakes Forests ecoregion, a lowland dish that fills the gap between the western shores of Lakes Erie and Huron and the southeastern coast of Lake Michigan. This is also the industrial heartland of the basin. The mean annual temperature is the highest in the watershed—8°C (46.4°F)—with the mean summer temperature a warm 18°C (64.4°F) and the winter mean 2.5°C (36.5°F). Precipitation is under 900 millimeters (35.5 inches) a year, but the climate is still humid, with lots of snow in the winters and tornadoes occurring frequently during the summers. The forest—what there is of it—is mostly deciduous, 80 percent sugar maple and beech, but also with basswood, oaks, and hickories in the drier areas and elms, ashes, and red maples in the wetter zones. On the north shore of Lake Erie, at Point Pelee and Long Point, are extensive coastal wetlands and dune systems, all crucial stopover spots for migrating waterfowl and songbirds. The northern extension of the Carolinian forest is also a part of this multifaceted and ecologically threatened region.

Continuing southwest through northern Ohio and northwestern Indiana, the height of land turns up toward Fort Wayne, through reclaimed wetlands tilled flat and planted with endless expanses of corn, and past South Bend, until it comes close to the southern tip of Lake Michigan between Gary, Indiana, and Chicago, Illinois. Here the land is seldom more than 200 meters (656 feet) above sea level, the lowest point on the basin's circumference.

Lake Michigan dips its toes into the northern reaches of the Central Forest–Grasslands Transition, a large savanna-type ecoregion that separates the eastern deciduous forests from the tallgrass and mixed-grass prairies to the west. Its distinctive natural features are more pronounced outside the basin, however; inside, they have been all but obliterated by urbanization. Close to Lake Michigan less than 1 percent of the natural habitat is intact. Oaks and hickories are the predominant tree species, and before settlement this ecoregion marked the eastern extent of the prairie bison.

Once round Lake Michigan, the basin's edge heads north, past Milwaukee, Wisconsin, where it veers west again to round Lake Winnebago and up through Wisconsin's central lowlands. Just south of Milwaukee, the basin enters the Upper Midwest Forest–Savanna Transition, another complex ecoregion. This zone incorporates features of the Great Lakes–St. Lawrence forest with its oak, maple, walnut, and basswood assemblages, but it also contains the last remaining tallgrass prairie savanna in the United States as well as a rich, dynamic oak savanna, now one of the world's most endangered

FACING PAGE: A pileated woodpecker listens for insects before excavating for them. Holes left by these prehistoric-looking birds are used by owls and flying squirrels for nests and shelter.

Clouds gather over the Sleeping Giant in Nipigon Bay, Lake Superior.

ecosystems. These three systems coexist in a unique mosaic that acts as a transition between the grasslands to the west and the taller, fuller-canopied forests to the east.

Although there are wetlands in the central areas, where towns have telling names like Grand Marsh and Marshfield, the climate is generally drier here, as the prevailing easterly winds coming off the prairies have not yet picked up moisture from the Lakes. The exception is the pocket of this zone that crosses Lake Michigan and wraps around Grand Traverse Bay, where warm, moist air makes that region one of the basin's most productive soft-fruit belts. Throughout the ecoregion, prairie plant species abound, and in the fall and spring its lowlands provide a resting place for millions of migrating waterfowl.

Due west of Green Bay, near Timm's Hill, the highest point in Wisconsin, the basin boundary crosses into the Western Great

Lakes Forests ecoregion, which spreads east and west to include all of northern Michigan (east and west of the lake), northern Wisconsin, and northeastern Minnesota up to the Canadian border. Like the Eastern Forest–Boreal Transition ecoregion, this zone enjoys a warm, humid microclimate in the south and cooler boreal transition conditions farther north. Its mean temperature is low, 1°C to 2°C (around 33°F), and its mean annual precipitation under 800 millimeters (31.5 inches). It differs from its eastern counterpart in that its southern range is situated on thick glacial deposits, which make for less acidic soil and a more mixed forest cover, which includes northern pin oak, hazel, sugar maple, and American beech along with the paper birch, jack pine, white spruce, and balsam fir associated with the boreal transition. In the northern reaches of this ecoregion we are back among moose, black bears, wolves, lynx, and snowshoe hare, with terns and plovers nesting on the many offshore islands of Lake Superior.

The basin boundary rounds the snout of Lake Superior in a generous arc and from there follows the ridge of the Vermilion Range, keeping 701-meter (2,300-foot) Eagle Mountain to its right. The height of land leads well west and north of Lake Nipigon before dropping down again behind the wolf's head. The round trip has been the equivalent of a journey from New York to San Francisco.

THE INLAND SEAS

The Great Lakes are often referred to as North America's fourth coastline. If you walked the shores of each lake in turn you would cover more than 17,000 kilometers (10,500 miles), a distance equal to halfway around the earth at the equator. The surface area of all five lakes, 244,160 square kilometers (94,250 square miles), is nearly equal to that of the United Kingdom. They are the largest readily available source of freshwater in the world, about 20 percent of the earth's available supply. Russia's Lake Baikal has approximately the same volume of water as the Lakes: only the polar ice caps hold more.

The Lakes contain more than 95 percent of North America's freshwater: if all the water they held were to spill out and spread evenly across North America, it would cover the continent to a depth of 1.5 meters (5 feet). Even though nearly 2,150 cubic meters (75,000 cubic feet) of water flows out of Lake Superior every second, a single drop entering that lake would take three hundred years to make its way to the St. Lawrence River. In other words, the water flowing out of Lake Ontario today may have carried the canoes of French fur traders crossing Lake Superior in the late eighteenth century.

Only about 1 percent of the water in the Lakes is new water, added by rivers and the streams feeding them from the surface, by groundwater reservoirs around their peripheries, and by precipitation. This added water is offset by evaporation and outflow, so that water levels historically have remained fairly constant, give or take a meter or so over a six- or seven-year cycle.

HOMES may have helped schoolchildren remember the names of the Great Lakes, but to list them in altitudinal order, another mnemonic is called for: SHMEO: Six Hungry Monkeys Eating Oranges, or, more germane, Surface Heat Means Elevating Oceans. Descending from highest to lowest above sea level, their order is Superior, Huron and Michigan, Erie, and Ontario.

In *Paddle-to-the-Sea,* a popular children's book by Holling Clancy Holling published in 1941 and still in print, a carved wooden canoe makes the 1,900-kilometer (1,200-mile) journey from Lake Nipigon, high above Lake Superior, all the way to the Atlantic Ocean. Holling, an artist who worked at Chicago's Field Museum of Natural History, explained at the beginning that the trip was possible because the Great Lakes were "set like bowls on a gentle slope. The water . . . flows from the top one, drops into the next, and on to the others." The "top one," at 183.2 meters (601.1 feet) above sea level, is Lake Superior.

Superior is the largest of the Great Lakes in both area and volume; in fact it holds more water than the other four Lakes combined. It has the largest surface area of any freshwater lake in the world (82,100 square kilometers, or 31,700 square miles) and ranks fourth in volume (at 12,100 cubic kilometers, or 2,900 cubic miles). The Caspian Sea, between Iran and Central Asia, is larger in area and vol-

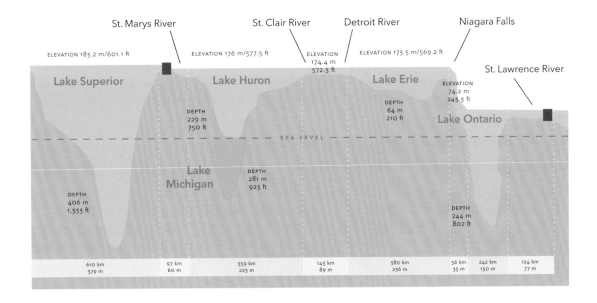

St. Marys River St. Clair River Detroit River Niagara Falls

ELEVATION 183.2 m/601.1 ft ELEVATION 176 m/577.5 ft ELEVATION 174.4 m 572.3 ft ELEVATION 173.5 m/569.2 ft St. Lawrence River

Lake Superior Lake Huron Lake Erie ELEVATION 74.2 m 243.3 ft

DEPTH 229 m 750 ft DEPTH 64 m 210 ft Lake Ontario

— — — — — — — SEA LEVEL — — — — — — —

Lake Michigan DEPTH 281 m 923 ft

DEPTH 406 m 1,333 ft DEPTH 244 m 802 ft

| 610 km 379 m | 97 km 60 m | 359 km 223 m | 143 km 89 m | 380 km 236 m | 56 km 35 m | 242 km 150 m | 124 km 77 m |

ume, but it is a saltwater lake and so, like the polar ice caps and Lake Baikal, adds nothing to the world's ready supply of potable water.

The average depth of Lake Superior is 149 meters (483 feet), with its greatest depth lying off Grand Island, on the southern shore not far from Munising, Michigan, where it plunges down 406 meters (1,333 feet). In many places, 240-meter (800-foot) cliffs overlook 275 meters (900 feet) of water. In the days of canoe travel, paddlers stuck close to land, even though the coastline is mostly sheer rock face and pounding waves, with few calm landing places. "Lake Superior," remarked Jonathan Carver, an American entrepreneur who explored this part of the continent in 1768, "is so called because it is superior in magnitude to any of the lakes on that vast continent." Not so. The French called it Superior because it was above the other lakes. But Carver was right to say its water was "as pure and transparent as air...My canoe seemed as if it hung suspended in that element."

Next in size and elevation are Lakes Huron and Michigan, the surfaces of which are, on average, 176 meters (577.5 feet) above sea level and 8.2 meters (27 feet) below Lake Superior. Hydrologists have taken to referring to them as a single body, Lakes Michigan-Huron, since they are connected not by a river but by a strait 90 meters (300 feet) deep—the Straits of Mackinac—and their water-movement patterns are closely integrated. Taken as one lake, they would be much bigger in area (117,400 square kilometers, or 55,300

square miles) than Lake Superior, but they are geographically distinct. Michigan, with an average depth of 85 meters (279 feet), is the only Great Lake that lies entirely within the borders of one country. It supports an extensive commercial fishery and is the most populated and industrialized of the five, although most of that activity is confined to its southern end. At one time, Chicago was the fourth-largest port in the world, and it is still the third-largest city in the United States, after New York and Los Angeles. The southern and southeastern shore of Lake Michigan also has the world's largest freshwater dune system, stretching for 160 kilometers (100 miles) east of Gary, Indiana, and reaching several miles inland in a succession of spectacular dune sequences.

Lake Huron, on the other hand, is shallower than Lake Michigan, with an average depth of 59 meters (195 feet), and reaches far up into the Algoma Highlands where, like Lake Superior, it is encased in solid Canadian Shield bedrock. Its shores are sparsely inhabited, and it is the only Great Lake with no major city bordering its waters. In the 1970s and '80s, when Lake Michigan was highly polluted, Lake Huron registered far lower pollution levels, reinforcing its separate status. The second-largest of the Lakes, it holds Manitoulin Island, the largest freshwater island in the world, and Georgian Bay, the huge expanse of crystal water that greeted Champlain in 1615. The bay holds a maze of 30,000 smaller islands, the largest freshwater archipelago in the world.

Somewhere on Lake Huron is the wreck of the first wooden ship that sailed the Great Lakes. It was built by Robert Cavelier de La Salle, one of the most prominent of the French explorers who shared Champlain's quest for a route to the Pacific Ocean. In 1677, La Salle portaged around Niagara Falls with a team of craftsmen and sailors, and near the entrance to the Niagara River he set about building a stockade and an 18-meter, 40-tonne (60-foot, 45-ton) barque, which he named the *Griffon*. (A griffon, a chimera with the head and wings of an eagle and the body of a lion, figured on the coat of arms of La Salle's commander, Count Frontenac.)

The following summer, with a crew of thirty-four, he sailed the *Griffon* the length of Lake Erie, then up the Detroit River into Lake St. Clair and the St. Clair River and through Lake Huron to the Jesuit mission at Michilimackinac, in the Strait of Mackinac. He reached the mission in early September and continued from there into Lake Michigan as far south as Green Bay, where he took on a load of beaver pelts from agents who had been sent ahead the previous year. He then dispatched the *Griffon* and twenty men back to Niagara, while he and the rest of his party continued south down the St. Joseph

FACING PAGE: The Thirty Thousand Islands in Georgian Bay, on Lake Huron, are the largest freshwater archipelago in the world.

We...reached Penetanguishene, where we obtained a fresh supply of provisions, after which we threaded a labyrinth of islands of every size and form, amounting, as is said, to upwards of 30,000; and both being strangers to the navigation, we continually lost ourselves in its picturesque mazes, enchanted with the beauty of the ever-varying scenery, as we glided along in our light canoe. We fished and hunted for 14 days, almost unconscious of the lapse of time so agreeably spent.

PAUL KANE, *Wanderings of an Artist,* 1859

River to the Mississippi. The *Griffon* was never seen again. At least not until a few years ago, when a cottage owner stumbled over what are thought to be pieces of it near Port Elgin, Ontario, on the eastern shore of Lake Huron.

Whatever the *Griffon*'s fate, its voyage marked the beginning of Great Lakes navigation. La Salle's vision reached beyond fur trading almost before that exploitative enterprise was properly under way. He imagined a series of permanent settlements around the lakes different from the Jesuit missions and the rough-hewn forts built by the fur trading companies. His would be outposts of French civilization, with well-built houses, churches, manufactories, and homesteads, populated by farmers, seamen, and craftspeople as well as commercial agents for locally produced goods and trappers who would send furs back to Montreal in sturdy longboats rather than in flimsy canoes. Although the loss of the *Griffon* set the enterprise back a hundred years, La Salle had looked into the future of the Great Lakes and seen exactly what would become of them.

The drop from Lake Huron to Lake Erie is only 3.5 meters (11.5 feet), and so gradual—comprising a linkage of two rivers, the St. Clair and the Detroit, connected by modest Lake St. Clair—that no lock is required. Early mariners referred to Lake St. Clair as the St. Clair Flats, so shallow that ships routinely ran aground trying

For thousands of years, Niagara Falls kept aquatic species such as alewives and Atlantic salmon from invading the upper Lakes.

to get to and from Sault Ste. Marie. Geologically an embayment of Lakes Michigan-Huron, Lake St. Clair is little more than a flooded wetland, once an important stopping point for migrating waterfowl, with only a narrow, central channel for navigation. In the 1860s, Thurlow Weed, the editor of the Albany *Evening Journal,* traveled this route to Chicago and noted wryly that a barrel of water added to Lake St. Clair would flood the surrounding fields, an understandable exaggeration. Certainly today a meter or a yard taken from it would reduce much of the lake to a thin trickle of muddy sludge. Below Lake St. Clair, the Detroit River was also a mere stream through a marsh that extended a kilometer and a half (almost a mile) inland on each side for its entire 51-kilometer (32-mile) length.

Lake Erie takes its name from the people who lived on its southern shore, the Erie, or, as the Iroquois called them, the Erieehronons, meaning "people of the cougar." It is the second-smallest of the Great Lakes and the shallowest, not much deeper than Lake St. Clair at its western end. Erie's average depth is 19 meters (62 feet), but in its western basin it is a mere 9 meters (30 feet) deep, with a volume one-thirtieth that of Lake Superior. It is, however, even more famous for its storms than that upper Lake, since shallow water whips up faster and more furiously than deep. Its 387-kilometer (241-mile) length makes for a significant fetch when sudden storms come up, as they often do. Wind blowing at 75 kilometers an hour (40 knots) over 160 kilometers (100 miles) of ocean can kick up 9-meter (30-foot) waves; over the same distance on a shallow lake, the big waves develop sooner and closer together. Seemingly mild-mannered, Lake Erie, which the Canadian poet Robert Finch calls "temperamental, unpredictable, vagrant but never brooding," is regarded by some mariners as the graveyard of the Great Lakes: a 6,500-square-kilometer (2,500-square-mile) section of it, between Long Point, Ontario, and Erie, Pennsylvania, has been called the Lake Erie Quadrangle, since it boasts a total of 429 wrecks; the Bermuda Triangle, which is five times larger, has only 112.

The water in Lake Erie is rich in nutrients thanks to the fertile, easily eroded soils that surround it and the roughly 86 centimeters (34 inches) of precipitation that falls annually in its drainage basin, washing soil and minerals into the lake in the spring and after each rainfall. As a result, Lake Erie has usually supported more fish and a greater diversity of aquatic life than any other of the Great Lakes: its fish population is about 46 million, compared with only 4.5 million in Lake Superior and 11 million in Lake Huron.

The surface of Lake Erie is 173.5 meters (569.2 feet) above sea level; that of the last Great Lake, Lake Ontario, is 74.2 meters (243.3

feet). Most of the roughly 100-meter (325.9-foot) difference is the height of Niagara Falls, the point at which the Niagara River tumbles over the Niagara Escarpment at the rate of about 5,700 cubic meters (200,000 cubic feet) per second. Father Louis Hennepin, the first European to record his impressions of the falls as he portaged past them with La Salle's troop, estimated their height at closer to 182 meters (600 feet), but the sight of such a powerful surge of water has been known to addle the brain. "He who sees them instantly forgets humanity," wrote Rupert Brooke after visiting them in 1913. Nathaniel Hawthorne, who traveled from Salem, Massachusetts, to view them in 1835, was so certain they would not live up to his expectations that he stayed in his hotel or dawdled in town for two days before summoning the resolve to confront them in person. When he finally beheld their thundering magnificence, he was far from let down: "I climbed the precipice, and threw myself on the earth—feeling that I was unworthy to look at the Great Falls." Fifty years later another visitor, Oscar Wilde, did register his disillusionment, but by then it was the fashion to disparage what other mortals found exhilarating. Since Niagara Falls had become the honeymoon capital of North America, Wilde famously declared them "one of the keenest, if not the keenest, disappointments in American married life."

For millennia, the Niagara Escarpment—geologically, a cuesta—formed a species barrier between Lake Ontario and the four other Great Lakes; aquatic species endemic to the former couldn't make it up the falls to colonize the upper Lakes. Alewives and Atlantic salmon, for instance, both saltwater species that had invaded Lake Ontario and become landlocked as the lake's outlet at the St. Lawrence rose above sea level about 6,000 years ago, remained solely in Lake Ontario until the opening of the Welland Canal in the early 1800s. Not only aquatic species were isolated by the falls; because hostile Iroquois nations inhabited the south shore of Lake Ontario and portaging around the falls was difficult, Lake Erie was the last of the Great Lakes to be seen by European explorers. The favored route to fur country was the one Brûlé and Champlain had taken to Lake Huron: up the Ottawa and Mattawa rivers to Lake Nipissing, then down the French River to Georgian Bay, remaining in friendly Algonquin territory the whole way.

According to Father Hennepin, *ontario* is an Iroquois word meaning "sparkling or beautiful water," and despite its position downstream from the others, Lake Ontario is still sparkling and beautiful. Except at its western end, where Toronto, Hamilton, and Buffalo are situated, its shoreline is sparsely populated: 49 percent of its watershed area is still forested, compared with 21 percent for Lake Erie. At 18,960 square kilometers (7,320 square miles), it is the smallest of the Great Lakes in area, but, as Wilfred Campbell noted in his somewhat boosterish *The Beauty, History, Romance and Mystery of the Canadian Lake Region,* just before World War I, Lake Ontario is big enough that "all the navies of the world could float within its confines."

With the shrinkage of the Aral Sea, Lake Ontario is now the thirteenth-largest lake in the world by volume and Lake Erie the eleventh, with Lake Winnipeg squeezing between. Since its average depth (86.25 meters, or 283 feet) is second only to that of Lake Superior, Lake Ontario is almost four times greater in volume than Lake Erie, which means its deep water provides habitat for more cold-tolerant fish species, such as the salmonids and lake whitefish. And it is no less tempestuous than its sister lakes. As David McFadden wrote in his offbeat travel book *A Trip around Lake Ontario,* "some people claim there are tidal waves on the Great Lakes," and there are, albeit small ones, even on Lake Ontario. What some people call tidal waves are in fact "wind setups," water pushed onto land by high winds. But wind setups can be tsunamilike in intensity. "During a summer storm [in the 1960s]," McFadden, citing a local legend, records, "a giant 'tidal wave'... came in at Salmon Point, with boats crashing through the roofs of barns half a mile from the shore."

THE HUMAN FACTOR

Writing in the early nineteenth century, Thomas Malthus posited that the earth's human population would increase to absolute unsustainability in very short order were it not for built-in checks and balances, such as diseases, epidemics, wars, and the other 997 natural shocks that flesh is heir to. In the Great Lakes basin, since

LAST COUNT

The *ss Edmund Fitzgerald,* the largest man-made object ever launched into freshwater when it was built in 1958, sailed out of Superior, Wisconsin, on November 9, 1975, with a load of taconite pellets; the next day it was hit by 154-kilometer-an-hour (96-mile-an-hour) winds and 10.7-meter (35-foot) waves off Whitefish Point, Michigan, and sank with all hands. During the Great Storm that blew over all five lakes for five days in November 1913, nineteen vessels sank—ten on Lake Huron, three on Michigan, one on Erie, and five on Superior—eight of them with all hands, and 248 lives were lost. As the British poet Rupert Brooke had noted in 1913, "These monstrous lakes, which ape the oceans, are not proper to fresh water or salt. They have souls, and they are wicked ones."

Waves like these in Old Woman Bay, Lake Superior, can build up in minutes, especially during the stormy months of October and November.

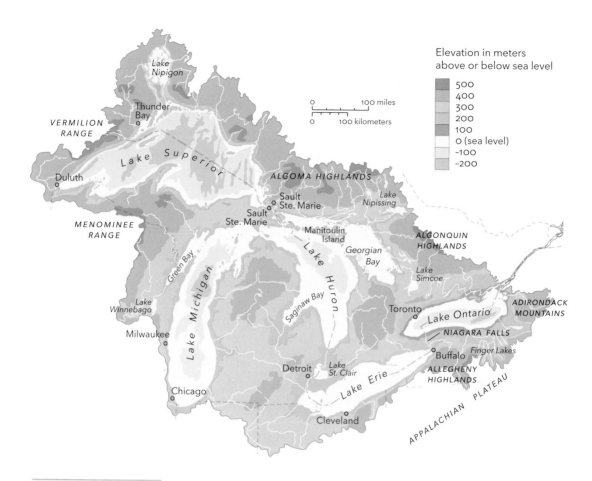

Elevation in meters
above or below sea level

500
400
300
200
100
0 (sea level)
−100
−200

0 ___ 100 miles
0 ___ 100 kilometers

Lake Nipigon

VERMILION RANGE

Thunder Bay

Lake Superior

ALGOMA HIGHLANDS

Duluth

Sault Ste. Marie

Sault Ste. Marie

Lake Nipissing

MENOMINEE RANGE

Manitoulin Island

Georgian Bay

ALGONQUIN HIGHLANDS

Green Bay

Lake Huron

Lake Simcoe

Lake Winnebago

Lake Michigan

Saginaw Bay

Toronto

Lake Ontario

ADIRONDACK MOUNTAINS

Milwaukee

NIAGARA FALLS

Buffalo

Finger Lakes

Detroit

Lake St. Clair

ALLEGHENY HIGHLANDS

Chicago

Lake Erie

APPALACHIAN PLATEAU

Cleveland

THE GREAT LAKES
BASIN IN RELIEF

the days of Jesuit missionaries and French and English fur traders, the human population has shot up at a rate that would have made Malthus's heart beat like the wings of a ruffed grouse in mating season: from a few thousand to 40 million people in fewer than four hundred years. Indeed, the basin's population has quadrupled in the past century. At about 78 people per square kilometer (202 per square mile), it's well above the North American average of 14.6 per square kilometer (38 per square mile).

Compared with the population of France, a similarly sized land-mass holding 60.6 million people, or the population density of the United Kingdom at 244 people per square kilometer (632 per square mile), the basin's statistics may not sound bad. However, the vast majority of the 40 million Great Lakes basin inhabitants live in the southern third of the basin, below a curved line from the southern tip of Georgian Bay through Saginaw and Green bays. Fewer than a million people live in the Lake Superior basin, for example, and only 4 percent of the land surrounding the lake itself is residential or agricultural, compared with 77 percent around Lake Erie. The actual population density for the southern basin is more like 230 people per square kilometer (596 per square mile), double what demographers consider to be "densely populated" and rapidly approaching the density of England or France. The twentieth century deftly managed to remove many of the checks and balances that so comforted Thomas Malthus.

The people of the Great Lakes drainage basin, representing a tenth of the population of the United States plus a third of the population of Canada, live in seven American states—Minnesota, Wisconsin, Illinois, Indiana, Ohio, Pennsylvania, and New York—and one Canadian province, Ontario. For these people the region provides transportation, occupation, and recreation, as well as food, wood, and mineral resources such as iron, copper, nickel, coal, and salt. And water, lots of water. Great Lakes water is used for drinking, cleaning, flushing, crop irrigation, creating electricity, refining, bleaching, distilling, and cooling. For the past four centuries, the Lakes have played a major role in the exploration, settlement and development of North America. In turn, these activities have significantly altered the natural history of the watershed.

As the population grows, so too do its demands on the lakes. One way to measure the escalating impact on the environment is to look at how much water is withdrawn from the lakes for human use, and for what purposes. In 1985, about 120 million cubic meters (4.24 billion cubic feet) of water was withdrawn every day to turn the turbines that create electricity; this was roughly half of all water withdrawn for municipal or industrial needs. By 2002, the most recent year for which figures are available, the amount of water withdrawn for electrical generation alone had soared to 3 billion cubic meters (106 billion cubic feet) per day and accounted for more than 95 percent of total water withdrawals. More people were using more water, and using more of it to produce electricity. In 2002, power plants in the Great Lakes basin withdrew more water for hydroelectricity generation in an hour than was withdrawn in a day in 1985.

Not surprisingly, so large a population inhabiting what biologists refer to as a "closed" ecological system has a huge and cumulative influence on its natural environment. To cite just one consequence, a water-level study conducted in 1982 by the International Joint Commission, the body created in 1909 to monitor and regulate the effect of humans on Great Lakes water, predicted that if withdrawals continued to increase at historical rates, the amount of water exiting the system through the St. Lawrence River would be reduced by 8 percent by the year 2030. Water withdrawals have continued to increase, as has evaporation caused by climate shifts, so significantly lowered lake levels by mid-century appear inevitable. The combined effects on the ecosystem are still being intensively studied, but they include the draining of lake-margin wetlands, increased shoreline erosion, and damage to nearshore-spawning fish populations as well as to coastal-dwelling reptiles, amphibians, shorebirds, and aquatic vegetation.

The human population has blossomed in inverse proportion to those of most other species. In the four centuries since Étienne Brûlé paddled his canoe down the French River, marveling (we imagine) at the gigantic white pines, the woodland caribou, and the abundant beavers, the Great Lakes ecosystem has suffered tremendous and, in some cases, irreversible losses. Since European settlement of the basin, thirteen wildlife species have become extinct. Let us name the dead: the eastern elk disappeared in 1880; by 1900 the eastern cougar was gone; the last passenger pigeon died in the Cincinnati Zoo in 1914; and the last Carolina parakeet, which ranged as far north as the Great Lakes basin, died in 1918. Five species of fish have disappeared forever from the Great Lakes: the blackfin, the longjaw and the shortnose cisco, the blue pike, and the harelip sucker. Two species of clam were declared extinct in 1988: the leafshell and the round combshell. Two vascular plants are now extinct: the bigleaf scurfpea and *Thismia americana*. And the list of species that were once common in the journals of the early field naturalists but are now rare, threatened, or endangered grows longer with each new

CRANE REVIVAL

The sandhill crane is the oldest living species of bird on earth: 10-million-year-old fossils found in Nebraska are identical in structure to the modern sandhill. There are 650,000 sandhill cranes in North America, about 80 percent of the world's entire population of all species of cranes. Of six subspecies, the greater sandhill is the one found in the Great Lakes basin; some birds stop over during migration to their Arctic breeding grounds, and an increasing number are expanding their breeding range south into the Great Lakes basin.

The greater sandhill crane formerly bred on the shores of Lake St. Clair but has not been seen there since the draining of that lake's surrounding wetlands. Although nearly extirpated as a breeding species from the whole basin in the 1800s, it has made a remarkable comeback: it is commonly found on Manitoulin Island in August, and every October and November, more than 30,000 sandhills can be seen gathering at the Jasper-Paluki Fish and Game Area in Indiana, just south of Lake Michigan, arriving from Minnesota, Wisconsin, Michigan, and Ontario to begin their fall migration to Georgia and Florida.

Sandhill crane beaks are short enough to forage for seeds in dry areas, yet long enough for wetland feeding.

study. This trend is not unique to the Great Lakes basin, of course. Of the 16,000 plant species in the United States, 4,640 are now endangered.

At the same time, there is encouraging news to report. Piping plovers, once down to fewer than a thousand mating pairs in all of North America, have been seen nesting on the shores of Lake Michigan; the bald eagle population has increased by 500 percent on some lakes; and in June 2006, a pair of whooping cranes successfully hatched two chicks in central Wisconsin, the first wild whoopers hatched in the Great Lakes basin in more than a century. Throughout the region great advances have been made in halting water and air pollution, restoring wetlands and fish habitat, identifying and protecting species at risk, and generally lightening the footprint that humankind has made upon the Great Lakes landscape and waterscape in past centuries. Scientists and community groups are working to identify threatened areas and halt the degradation of dozens of ecosystems. If they succeed, we may be able to preserve the many thousands of species that remain, and learn how to live with them in harmony and health.

ABOUT THIS BOOK

There are about 170 species of fish living in the Great Lakes, and 71 species of mammals inhabiting the surrounding basin. Some 300 species of birds have been recorded nesting or resting in the region. Thousands of plant and insect species grace the hillsides and stream banks—in the fruit belts of Michigan and southwestern Ontario, there are more than 100 insect pests of apple trees alone. No single book can include every species and their interactions within a region as large as the Great Lakes watershed, or even within one of its component ecoregions.

I have, however, tried to cover the three major forest types—the boreal, the Great Lakes–St. Lawrence, and the Carolinian—and the animals and plants that define them, thoroughly enough that the reader will derive an appreciation of the splendor and complexity of these living ecological entities. Chapters 3 through 5 deal with each in turn. Chapter 6 looks at specific habitats, such as wetlands, urban forests, and alvars, some of which are unique to North America. Chapters 7 and 8 concern the Lakes and examine the many aspects of life in and on the water, including fish, amphibians, plants, insects, shorebirds, and water itself. They also provide an overview of the two most urgent problems facing the Great Lakes today: pollution and invasive species. Finally, in Chapter 9, we peer into the future to discern what the Great Lakes might be like a century from now, if all the mistakes of the past—including pollution and invasions, as well as water diversions and global warming—are at least halted, if not corrected, and all the hopes for the future are realized.

We begin with a chapter on the early geology and the subsequent formation of the Lakes following the retreat of the glaciers. The Great Lakes is a distinctive and definitive region, but just as each of its ecoregions interacts with the others to form a vaster system, so the basin is itself part of a continent, and holding a magnifying glass to the Great Lakes is a way of arriving at a better understanding of all life on the planet Gaia.

FACING PAGE: The whooping crane population sank to a low of only 23 birds in 1941, but intense conservation efforts have aided its comeback to nearly 300 individuals today.

TWO

FOUNDATION STONES

N 1880, WHEN MOST SCIENTISTS believed the earth was no more than 40 million years old, the eminent Canadian geologist John William Dawson wrote in *Fossil Men and Their Modern Representatives* that "no subject of geological investigation is perhaps in a more unsatisfactory state than that which relates to the connection of the modern or human period with preceding epochs."

Our sense of the earth's timeline has changed exponentially since Dawson's day, and our appreciation of how present environments and landscapes are a direct consequence of past events has also sharpened. Lines of descent have been drawn from then to now, from nonhuman to human, and our connection to major events in the distant past is felt more strongly with each new discovery. We now know, for instance, that our planet was formed more than 4.5 billion years ago, that life appeared about a billion years later, that continents drift about on the earth's surface like ice floes in a windbound bay, and that entire families of animals and plants, not just species but whole kingdoms, have evolved, dominated their environments, and vanished. If the earth's history were compressed into a single day, life would first stir at about 6 AM and "fossil men and their modern representatives" would show up only a few seconds before midnight.

FACING PAGE: A lone red pine flourishes in a solid quartzite outcrop in Killarney Provincial Park in central Ontario.

. . .

In every part of every living thing

is stuff that once was rock

LORINE NIEDECKER, "Lake Superior," 1968

But there is still much we don't know—for example, the spark that transformed a solution of inorganic chemicals into living, single-celled organisms capable of reproducing themselves has yet to be identified—and what we do know probably wouldn't astound Professor Dawson. A hundred years before him, James Hutton, the father of geology, had gazed over his shoulder at what he knew of the earth's origins and had found "no vestige of a beginning"; he had peered into the future and discerned "no prospect of an end." That is as true today as it was in Hutton's and Dawson's times.

COMING TO LIFE

The earth is a slightly lopsided conglomeration of minerals, chemicals, and gases—space debris left over from the formation of the universe—that were separated by centrifugal force and gravity into distinct layers as the planet cooled. Think of the earth as an egg. The yolk at the center, which begins 5,150 kilometers (3,200 miles) below the earth's surface, is thought to be a solid mass of iron roughly 2,400 kilometers (1,500 miles) in diameter. (No one knows for certain, because no one has been able to drill more than 12 kilometers, or 7.5 miles, into the earth's crust—which, if the earth were an egg, wouldn't even pierce the shell.) Although the temperature at the core is at least 7,000°C (12,500°F)—hotter than the surface of the sun—it is solid because pressure at that depth is 3.5 million times greater than at the surface. This inner core is thought by some to be one enormous, hexagonal crystal of iron, spinning in the same direction as the earth but at a slightly faster pace.

FACING PAGE: The layered dolostone of the Niagara Escarpment on the Bruce Peninsula, overlooking Georgian Bay.

This solid inner core is encased in an outer core, probably composed of iron and nickel, that begins 2,900 kilometers (1,800 miles) below the surface and is 2,250 kilometers (1,400 miles) thick. Cooler than the inner core—about 4,500°C to 6,000°C (8,000°F to 11,000°F)—it is also under less pressure, and is therefore liquid. This outer core is itself surrounded by a 2,400-kilometer (1,500-mile) semisolid mantle composed of the elements silicon, magnesium, and more iron. The mantle's temperature is 870°C, or 1,600°F.

Both cores and mantle are covered, as a shell covers an egg, by a multilayered outer band consisting of the asthenosphere, the lithosphere, and the crust. The asthenosphere (from the Greek *asthenia*, meaning "weakened") is about 300 kilometers (186 miles) of hot, molten rock, semiliquid but very sluggish—molasses in January is a metaphor that comes to mind. The lithosphere (*lithikós* is Greek for "stone") is solid rock, up to 100 kilometers (62 miles) in thickness. The crust is the upper part of the lithosphere, varying in thickness from 8 to 75 kilometers (5 to 45 miles), depending on where it is measured: it is thin and dense at the bottom of the oceans, thickest but less dense in the continents' mountainous regions.

If you place a raw egg horizontally on a table and try to spin it like a bottle, you will find that it wobbles around a few turns, then comes to a stop. It won't spin because inside the shell the yolk and the white are of different densities and so are pulled by centrifugal force at different speeds. The earth, too, is made up of layers of varying densities, from solid to liquid to semisolid and back to solid, and it, like the egg, wobbles as it spins on its axis. It doesn't wobble much—the inner core makes one rotation more than the crust every four hundred years—but enough that the contrary forces set up by its off-kilter spin, combined with thermal convection from its superheated mantle and asthenosphere, have caused the brittle lithosphere and the crust attached to it to break up into large, irregular chunks that drift erratically over the surface of the planet.

These chunks, called tectonic plates, float on the sludgelike asthenosphere and are constantly on the move. As they drift and collide they either slide under one another (a process called subduction) or rub against one another, causing their edges to crumple and thicken at the points of contact. These collisions are barely measurable—the plates move a few centimeters, an inch or so, per century—but they are inexorable. The plates are continuously shifting, melding together, and tearing apart, crumbling and eroding at the edges.

Although parts of the Great Lakes basin were formed earlier, the landmass that became the future continent of North America came together 2 billion years ago, when two tectonic plates jostled together and fused. The seam between them remained a fault line, and when, a billion years later, the continent split apart along that seam, the gap filled with molten rock, or magma, from deep within the earth's mantle. Now called the Midcontinent Rift, it is a permanent scar beneath Lake Superior and the state of Michigan. When North America divided again, 570 million years ago, a second fault line formed; it's thought that the St. Lawrence Rift now underlies Lakes Ontario and Erie and has determined the course of the St. Lawrence River. The Great Lakes and their basins are thus the remainders and reminders of tremendous tectonic forces that have shaped, and are still shaping, our planet.

At the center of every continent is a large, stable landmass, called a craton, to which smaller masses, or terranes, are added over time. North America's core, the Canadian Shield craton, is the largest on earth and has experienced a great many changes since its creation. It has drifted below the equator and back again. It has been repeatedly submerged by ancient saltwater seas and reemerged with fresh deposits when those seas receded or evaporated. It has been thrust upward to form mountains when continents collided, and buried under volcanic ash and sediment when those collisions caused volcanoes to erupt and the mountains eroded away. And, most recently in geological time, it has been compressed by glaciers, then scraped clean as those glaciers flowed outward from high, Antarctic-like domes of ice. The early story of these changes is told by the region's rocks and fossils, pieced together by geologists and paleontologists who have sought to tie the Great Lakes into the larger picture of how life on earth began and evolved, and how the contours of the land on which that life took hold were shaped over billions of years of geological history.

In the Great Lakes region, the Canadian Shield craton is made up of three smaller geologic units, or provinces as geologists call them, each formed at a different time. The oldest is the Superior Province, which came slowly into being between 4.5 billion and 2.5 billion years ago and consists of metamorphosed rocks and granite. Metamorphic rocks are created when plates and terranes collide. Granite is silica-rich volcanic magma that has been allowed to cool over a long period of time.

FACING PAGE: Palisade Head, in Tettegouche State Park, Minnesota, is solidified lava extruded into the Midcontinent Rift approximately 1.1 billion years ago.

ERA	PERIOD	EPOCH	YEARS AGO		EVENT
CENOZOIC	Quaternary	Holocene	present–10,000		
		Pleistocene	10,000–1,800,000		glaciations, megafauna, humans in Great Lakes region
	Tertiary	Pliocene	1,800,000–5,000,000		
		Miocene	5,000,000–25,000,000		
		Oligocene	25,000,000–35,000,000		
		Eocene	35,000,000–60,000,000	T	
		Paleocene	60,000,000–65,000,000	H E B I G G A P	mammals
MESOZOIC	Cretaceous		65,000,000–145,000,000		flowering plants
	Jurassic		145,000,000–210,000,000		birds
	Triassic		210,000,000–245,000,000		protomammals, dinosaurs
PALEOZOIC	Permian		245,000,000–285,000,000		early reptiles
	Carboniferous		285,000,000–360,000,000		conifers, amphibians
	Devonian		360,000,000–410,000,000		complex vertebrates, animal life on land, gymnosperms, first insects; Acadian Orogeny
	Silurian		410,000,000–440,000,000		land plants
			440,000,000		Taconic Orogeny
	Ordovician		440,000,000–505,000,000		early fish
	Cambrian		505,000,000–570,000,000		complex marine creatures
PRECAMBRIAN			1,800,000,000		Grenville Orogeny
			3,500,000,000		bacteria and algae
			4,500,000,000		formation of Earth

GEOLOGICAL TIME

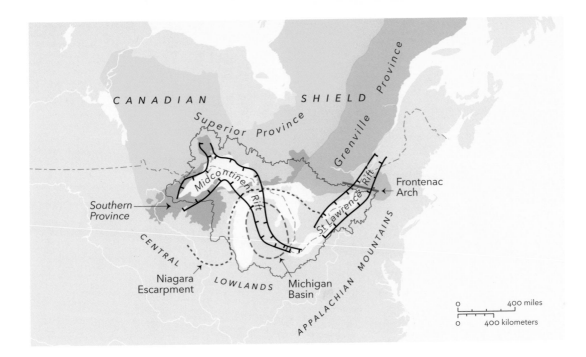

The Southern Province joined the Superior Province 2.5 billion years ago and now underlies southern Ontario, parts of Michigan, and most of Minnesota and Wisconsin. Its sedimentary rocks, along with some volcanic material, are also exposed north of Lake Huron. Sedimentary rock forms from sand or mud or the calcium-rich shells of marine animals deposited at the bottom of the sea. In the enormous heat and pressure generated by the collision of plates and terranes, sedimentary rock is stretched, squeezed, folded, and pummeled to such an extent that a boulder could end up looking like a log.

The third and youngest province dates from about 1.8 billion years ago, when the Canadian Shield collided with South America and West Africa to become the supercontinent Rodinia (from the Russian word for "motherland"). The impact, known as the Grenville Orogeny (an orogeny is a mountain-building event), created a range of high, jagged, Himalaya-like peaks that stretched from Labrador to Texas along North America's eastern coastline and extended well into present-day southern Ontario and northern New York. This area, named the Grenville Province, became the third segment of the Shield craton. Where it lies under the Great Lakes

GEOLOGICAL PROVINCES
AND FEATURES

A cliff of Shield granite rises above a lake along the Frontenac Arch, which links the Algoma Highlands with the Adirondack Mountains.

basin, the Grenville Province is made up of two different rock assemblages or belts. The Central Gneiss Belt underlies the Algoma Highlands from Sudbury to Pembroke, Ontario, between Georgian Bay and the Ottawa River, and is composed of ancient gneisses shot through by large granular bodies of granite, called plutons. The Central Metasedimentary Belt continues from Pembroke down to the St. Lawrence River and is made up mostly of marbles, volcanic rock, and other forms of metamorphosed sediments. The two belts are separated by the Central Metasedimentary Belt Boundary Zone, which runs from Pembroke southwest toward Lake Simcoe, under Lakes Ontario and Erie, and down into Pennsylvania.

In the period when the Grenville Province was joining the craton, life existed in the oceans surrounding the continents in the form of single-celled bacteria and blue-green algae, but there was nothing resembling life on the continents themselves, which were bare, metamorphic gneiss mixed with granite. Gneiss forms from rock that has been pushed deep into the earth by previous tectonic collisions, where it is heated to 750°C (nearly 1,400°F), melted, and then is slowly exposed on the surface as overlying layers of sediments are eroded away. In the Canadian Shield, Grenville gneiss was exposed after as much as 20 kilometers (12.4 miles) of rock were stripped away by the inexorable action of rain, rivers, and wind. The gneiss beds are often underlain by layers of granite, called sills, and punctuated with plutons of granite pushed up through cracks by intense pressure.

These are the rocks that make up Layer I, remnants of the Superior, Southern, and Grenville provinces that form the deep basement of the entire Great Lakes basin. They are the smooth, gray to pinkish, undulating surfaces that poke up throughout the boreal forest, creating the soaring cliff faces that surround northern lakes and channel rivers from the high watershed. The Adirondack Mountains of New York are part of the Grenville Province, as is a narrow ridge known as the Frontenac Arch, a band of Layer I rock that has been exposed by the wearing away of more recent limestone in eastern Ontario, creating a granitic connection between the Adirondacks and the Algoma Highlands.

About 800 million years ago, during the Precambrian era, Rodinia began to rise and continued to do so for the next 200 million years. It then split apart, with what is now North America separating from South America and West Africa to form a new, if smaller, continent called Laurentia. The breakup of Rodinia was a pivotal geological moment; it brought massive changes to the earth's marine life and marked the boundary between the Precambrian era and the Cambrian period. Where there had been relatively simple life, complex animals now began to evolve rapidly. This burgeoning of bizarre, soft-bodied marine creatures in the warm Iapetus Ocean, which rushed in to fill the gap between the retreating continental plates, is known as the Cambrian Explosion; fossil reminders of it have been found in the Burgess Shale deposits in western Canada and on Newfoundland's Avalon Peninsula.

RIM SHOT

Charity Shoal, in the eastern end of Lake Ontario about 19 kilometers (12 miles) southwest of Wolfe Island, is a circular rim of rock, 1 kilometer (0.6 miles) in diameter, that rises to within 2 to 5 meters (6 to 16 feet) of the surface. In places, the rim lurks barely 30 centimeters (1 foot) beneath the surface, especially when the lake's water level is low, and for centuries sailors in the area have had to keep careful watch on their charts and depth meters. Inside the rim, a central, bowl-shaped depression goes down to a depth of 19 meters (62 feet).

In 2001, geologists with the U.S. National Oceanic and Atmospheric Administration and the Canadian Hydrographic Service suggested that the feature may be an impact crater from a meteorite that struck the earth either during Precambrian time, more than 500 million years ago, or during the more recent Pleistocene epoch, possibly during the period of interglaciation just before the last, Wisconsinan ice age.

There are about 160 known meteorite impact craters on the planet. If Charity Shoal is one of them, it would have been made by a meteorite less than 2000 meters (6,600 feet) in diameter penetrating to a depth of 280 meters (920 feet) through the overlying layer of sedimentary rock and 150 meters (490 feet) of Precambrian Canadian Shield granite. This hole would have filled immediately with 150 meters (490 feet) of impact breccia and later with glacial gravels and lake sediment.

The rim of a similar impact site in Arizona, the Barringer Meteorite Crater, rises 43 meters (141 feet) above the surrounding land; scientists speculate that the Charity Shoal's rim was also significantly higher than it is today, but that it has been eroded by the action of glaciers. If a meteorite did strike the spot some 60,000 years ago, it would have had a significant effect on the area's flora and fauna, similar in a more localized and less dramatic way to the impact that struck the Yucatan Peninsula 65 million years ago and ended the age of the dinosaurs.

A three-dimensional perspective of Charity Shoal, exaggerated approximately twenty-five times, shows its distinct bowl-shaped depression and rim.

Four hundred and fifty million years ago, what are now the St. Lawrence River and Great Lakes basin were Laurentia's southern coastline. The marine environment was tropical, much like that of the present-day Bahamas Banks, with corals, trilobites, shelled pelecypods, and brachiopods living and dying in a hypersaline sea, and contributing their calcareous bodies to the ocean sediments. As the level of the Iapetus Ocean rose and fell, eroding the shoreline, great layers of sand accumulated and eventually slid into the ocean, where they were covered by vast offshore reefs. In the northern United States, these sandstone deposits cover the Grenville formations, providing the bedrock of much of New York, Ohio, and Indiana.

During the Ordovician period, Cambrian life mysteriously died out and was replaced by new, more recognizable (to us) creatures with hard parts that have evolved into present-day marine communities. It was also during this period that animal life began its tentative transition from sea to terra firma. Evidence of the oldest known animal activity on land exists as a set of trackways preserved in sandstone and estimated to be about 500 million years old, discovered in 1983 in a quarry near Kingston, close to the northern shore of Lake Ontario. The marine creatures that made the tracks appear to have sculled out of the ocean on eight pairs of legs, wandered about on dry land for a while, and then scurried back into the ocean to breathe and feed. They were euthycarcinoids, early arthropods that are the ancestors of today's centipedes and millipedes and possibly the forerunners of modern insects. At that time, there was virtually no land vegetation and hence no sheltering swamps to act as transition zones for intrepid land explorers. The landscape was all rock and

Evidence of the oldest known animal life on earth, these trackways in southern Ontario sandstone were left 500 million years ago by euthycarcinoids, estimated to have been 20 centimeters (8 inches) from head to tail tip.

CAMBRIAN EUTHYCARCINOID

DEVONIAN TRILOBITE

ORDOVICIAN BRACHIOPOD

sand, with perhaps some coastal algae and fungi, but hardly hospitable. The area later occupied by the Great Lakes was then as far south of the equator as it is north of it today.

About 440 million years ago, toward the end of the Ordovician period, western Europe and North America (or Laurentia) began drifting together again. In the subduction zone—the area where the North American plate slid beneath the European—a new surge of mountain-building called the Taconic Orogeny occurred on what is now North America's east coast. Over the next 100 million years, volcanoes among these enormous mountains spewed vast amounts of ash across Ontario and the northeastern states and eventually contributed the mud that completely buried the middle Ordovician limestone deposits. The mud became shale, which was itself eventually covered by sand deposited by rivers rushing down the slopes during the Silurian and Devonian periods. The tectonic collision also reheated and folded the strata of Grenville rocks. The Silurian limestone sediments became dolomite, a harder type of limestone composed of calcium magnesium carbonate. The Niagara Escarpment, which arches from northern Michigan across Manitoulin Island, down through the Bruce Peninsula, and under Lake Ontario and the Niagara River, is made of dolomite-capped limestones formed at this time, hard enough to resist erosion by waves of water and ice for the past 430 million years.

Between 400 and 350 million years ago, during the Devonian period, the continents Laurentia and Gondwana (essentially Africa and South America) collided, giving rise to the Acadian Orogeny and eventually forming the supercontinent Pangaea. The collision caused the Canadian Shield to crumple, creating the Appalachian Mountains and the Michigan basin, which filled with sedimentary limestones, sandstones, and shales. These overlying limestones and sandstones form the upper parts of Layer II of the region's basement and hold the geological narrative from the Grenville Orogeny to modern soils, more than a billion years of deposition and erosion. Thanks to glaciation, we have been left with only a fragment of the story: geologically speaking, there is virtually nothing in the Great Lakes basin between the Devonian and the recent past.

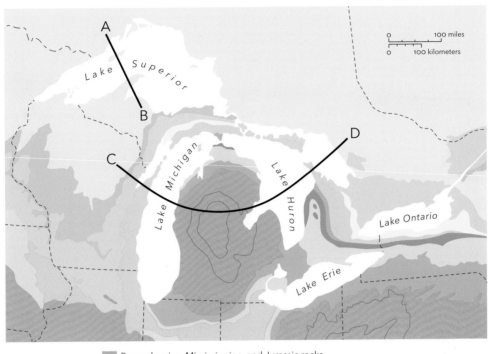

- Pennsylvanian, Mississippian, and Jurassic rocks
- Upper Devonian rocks, mainly shales; Antrim shale in Michigan
- Lower Devonian limestone
- Upper Silurian rocks; in Ontario and New York, mainly dolomite
- Silurian Salina group rocks in northern Michigan and Ontario (includes salt beds)
- Middle Silurian Niagaran rocks in northern Michigan, Ontario, and New York
- Lower Silurian rocks in northern Michigan, Ontario, and New York
- Ordovician sedimentary rocks, mostly shales and limestones
- Cambrian sandstones and conglomerates
- Precambrian rocks, mainly metamorphic and igneous

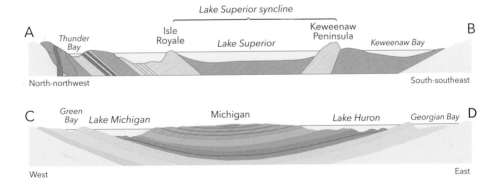

An outcropping of quartzite, or metamorphosed sandstone, on Lake Superior's north shore.

During the brief Devonian period, marine organisms evolved into the precursors of every vertebrate animal that now inhabits the Great Lakes watershed: the ancestors of all fish, amphibians, and reptiles, and therefore all birds and mammals, including humans, first appear in the fossil record in that remarkable period. The only organisms still with us from the time of the Iapetus Ocean are corals, shrimps, lobsters, mollusks, worms, and the arthropod descendants of creatures that crawled out and colonized the land before that ancient ocean disappeared. Everything else, from salamanders to *Homo sapiens,* can be traced back to the Devonian. Most modern fish, all 25,000 species of them, are descended from a major Devonian class known as the Osteichthyes, which are characterized by skeletons on the inside of their bodies. Earlier fish had exterior armored plates and sharp spikes supporting their fins; these new creatures developed endoskeletons as well as regular tooth replacement and swim bladders. Osteichthyes were originally saltwater fish, but some species moved gradually into brackish estuaries and from there eventually into freshwater rivers and lakes.

Within the Osteichthyes were two subdivisions: actinopterygians, or "ray-finned fish," and sarcopterygians, or "lobe-finned fish." As their names imply, they differed chiefly in the construction of their fins: actinopterygians controlled the movement of their fins by means of muscles that were inside their bodies, while sarcopterygians had muscles inside their fins. This may seem a small distinction, but it would have some startling consequences.

DEVONIAN HORN CORAL

One small group of actinopterygian fishes retained some of their ancestral traits. The chondrosteans were holdovers from the early Paleozoic era, probably the Silurian period (410 million to 440 million years ago), but achieved their greatest diversity during the Devonian. They were small—the largest was *Cheirolepis,* which grew to half a meter (1.6 feet) and had small, overlapping, rhomboid-shaped scales. It looked like a young shark, especially with its vertical, asymmetric tail (the top fork extending well beyond the bottom fork), except that it was bony, not cartilaginous, as modern sharks are. The chondrosteans' success was due to the evolution of a truly effective feeding apparatus: their jaw muscles were attached to the back of the jaw, rather than to the front, giving them an extremely wide gape and a quick, snapping bite. Living descendants include the sturgeons, two species of which are found today in the Great Lakes, and the gars, another Lakes family. Both are more cartilaginous than bony, but that doesn't link them to sharks. Sharks never were bony; sturgeons and gars once had bones but gave them up in favor of hard, exterior scutes. Their cartilaginousness is therefore a specialization, not a throwback to some sharklike stage.

DEVONIAN GASTROPOD

All actinopterygians that are not chondrosteans are neopterygians, and they almost certainly appeared during the Devonian although they don't show up in the fossil record until the Upper Permian, around 250 million years ago, and not at all in the area that became the Great Lakes basin, although they must have been here. Neopterygians evolved an even more efficient feeding

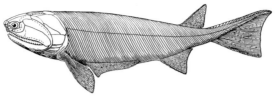

CHEIROLEPIS CANADENSIS

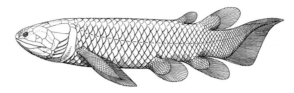

DEVONIAN RHIPIDISTIAN

and breathing mechanism: while more primitive fish fed by simply opening their gaping mouths and engulfing their prey, the neopterygians developed the ability to suck; in other words, they could become selective rather than passive predators, and therefore more prey specific. They were also more agile, their lighter scales and musculature allowing them greater flexibility. Whereas earlier fish swam by undulating, in the manner of eels, neopterygians developed the stronger muscles and backbones and greater fin manipulation that allowed them to swim, turn, and even reverse. They soon became the dominant fish in the ancient Atlantic Ocean, and they are the ancestors of all modern bony fish.

Meanwhile, the second major group of Osteichthyes, the sarcopterygians or lobe-finned fish, were evolving along different lines. This group produced three subgroups: the lungfish, the coelacanths, and the rhipidistians, all of which appeared during the Devonian. The two living subgroups, the lungfish and coelacanths, don't concern us in the Great Lakes basin except that they once swam—or perhaps crawled—over this region when it was inundated by saltwater. Lungfish flourished during the Permian and have since trailed off to three modern families found only in Africa and South America. Small fish but with a very strong bite that allows them to feed off bottom-dwelling shelled organisms, they inhabit areas of seasonal drought and have the ability to "estivate," or burrow into the mud of dried-up lake bottoms and live at a reduced metabolic rate for up to a year, until the next rainy season. They have openings in their palates that connect to their nasal capsules, which allow them to breathe atmospheric air.

Coelacanths were thought to have been extinct until one turned up in a fisherman's net off Madagascar in 1938 (about two hundred have been caught since then): a large, armored, tuna-sized fish, it too has external nares or nostrils that place it in close relationship to lungfish. Most remarkably, it also had bones and muscles extending from its body into four of its fins: as with lungfish, it is thought that muscled fins were adaptations to living on or in the bottom mud in warm, shallow water. Muscled fins—in effect, primitive legs—would have enabled them to push against the bottom mud, and perhaps even to burrow into it. Coelacanths must have swum above our region, feeding off the numerous shelled creatures that eventually contributed to the thick limestone and dolostone deposits of Layer II.

Which brings us to the rhipidistians. Although definitely fish, they exhibited so many elements later associated with amphibians that they are the acknowledged ancestors of that class. Rhipidistians had bones in their skulls not formerly found in fishes but now seen in amphibians—parietals, for example, which are small bones above and between the eyes. They also had internal air passages more highly developed than those of lungfish and coelacanths, allowing them to breathe both in and out of water, plus pectoral and pelvic girdles supporting limbs that extended into paired fins, with bones that included the radius, ulna, and humerus, as well as the fibula and tibia, all of which are elements of modern arms and legs. If lungfish and coelacanths could push themselves along the bottom with their muscled fins, it's possible that rhipidistians could walk, possibly even on dry land. Although their fish lines died out about 230 million years ago, at least one line evolved during the Devonian into primitive amphibians, the direct ancestors of modern terrestrial vertebrates, including all amphibians, reptiles, mammals, and birds. When, as humans, we acknowledge our common ancestry with fish, Devonian rhipidistians are the fish we mean.

THE BIG GAP

Around the time the dinosaurs began appearing on the earth, about 245 million years ago, Pangaea started to uplift, rising over the next 100 million years until it started to rupture and split apart. By the Oligocene epoch, this process was complete and North America was left much as it is today. Once again, saltwater flowed between the drifting land masses, this time from the Atlantic Ocean (named after Atlas, in Greek mythology the son of Iapetus). At first, Atlantic water poured over eastern and central North America, areas still deeply depressed by the weight of the Iapetus deposits. Barrier and pinnacle sponge reefs grew in the shallow, saline sea, producing more limestone.

There is, however, no fossil record of life in the Great Lakes basin from the end of the Devonian, about 360 million years ago, to the recent ice ages, the first of which began about 1.8 million years ago, marking the beginning of the Pleistocene epoch. Fossils are preserved in sedimentary rock, and all the sediments laid down since the Devonian have disappeared, either worn gradually away during the 65 million years of the Cretaceous period or, more recently, scraped or pulverized by the succession of glaciations that covered the region during the Pleistocene. This is a huge hiatus—geologists refer to it as the Big Gap—encompassing the rise and fall of dinosaurs, the evolution of birds and mammals, and the appearance of vascular plants. All of those events took place in the Great Lakes region—dinosaurs walked the earth here as they did elsewhere, and huge fern forests covered the land—but the fossil evidence of them no longer exists. The land was like a gigantic chalkboard, once displaying the formula for the evolution of life, then wiped clean by a powerful but careless hand.

The term "ice age" was first used by the German poet and botanist Johann Wolfgang von Goethe in the 1840s, although the existence of extended periods in the dim past when much of the earth had been covered with ice had been theorized earlier by Louis

Agassiz, a Swiss geologist and paleontologist who studied striations and gravel deposits in the Alps. John William Dawson was
one of many scientists at the time who thought Agassiz wrong: he
held that striations on the earth's surface had been caused by huge
icebergs floating in the waters of Noah's flood, which had scraped
the ground as the floodwaters subsided. Agassiz's theory prevailed,
but the cause of ice ages is still much debated. Modern science has
shown that they coincided with variations in the planet's orbit that
occur at intervals of 20,000, 40,000, and 100,000 years, the first
two intervals possibly resulting from the out-of-sync spinning of
the earth's inner core. The variations affect the amount of sunlight
striking the planet's surface and the size of the seasonal difference
of the sun's intensity, and so may account in part for periods of
global cooling, but ice ages also coincide with the periodic buildup
and collapse of carbon dioxide and other greenhouse gases in the
earth's atmosphere.

It takes only a small fluctuation in surface temperature to set off a period of glaciation, and glaciations can end "overnight" in geological time, going from maximum to no ice coverage in as few as 10,000 years. Glaciers formed on land in the polar region during periods of global cooling, expanded into the temperate regions when it was really cold, and shrank back into the polar zones when the climate warmed. At their mightiest, they were kilometers thick, multitongued caps of ice that spread toward the equator, covering most of the northern half of the landmasses that are now North America and Europe.

Although there is evidence that several major glaciations have occurred since the Precambrian, those that affected the formation of the Great Lakes took place during the Pleistocene. In that time there were four major glaciations, each named after its most southerly extent: the Nebraskan (1 million to 900,000 years ago), the Kansan (700,000 to 600,000 years ago), the Illinoian (300,000 to 200,000 years ago), and the Wisconsinan (90,000 to 10,000 years ago). Long periods of glaciation are called glacials, and the extended warmer periods between them are interglacials. Glacials are divided into stadials, which are intensely cold, and interstadials, which are warmer than stadials but not as warm as interglacials. Some climatologists believe that these recent Pleistocene ice ages have not yet ended, and that we are simply in the midst of an interglacial that has, so far, lasted a mere 10,000 years.

During each of the Pleistocene interglacials, the region that is now the Great Lakes basin was populated by descendants of the mammals, birds, and reptiles that had survived mass extinction at the end of the Cretaceous period, 65 million years ago. Protomammals were small, rodentlike multituberculates (the term refers to the internal structure of their teeth) that, following the disappearance of the dinosaurs, suddenly found they had the terrestrial environment more or less to themselves. Over the next several million years they grew in size and diversified in species until, by the Pleistocene, they had evolved into the large animals known as the Pleistocene megafauna. There were at least six species of proboscideans in North America during the Pleistocene, including the two northern species, the woolly mammoth and mastodon; a North American variety of giant ground sloth called nothrotheres; giant beavers; several species of saber-toothed tiger; the short-faced bear, which, at 700 kilograms (1,500 pounds), was one and a half times bigger than a modern grizzly; and the dire wolf, similarly, much larger than modern wolves. There were smaller animals as well; Pleistocene horses and llamas were tiny compared with their current counterparts.

Some North American animals migrated off the continent, possibly in search of warmer climates. Llamas and sloths, for example, traveled south and eventually ended up in South America. Opossums, on the other hand, migrated north from South America to become North America's only marsupial. Camels, horses, and cheetahs crossed over into Asia, whereas bison and bears used the same land bridge to reach North America. (Although horses originated in North America, they evolved in Asia and weren't known again on this continent until brought here by European soldiers and settlers after Columbus.)

Early representatives of many species of modern birds were present in the region during the Pleistocene: eagles, quail, vultures, turkeys, doves, crows, owls, and a large number of shorebirds and songbirds. Some birds were common here that are no longer found this far east: the bones of California condors, for example, have been found in upstate New York. An even larger vulture, *Teratornis incredibilis,* which had a wingspan of 4.8 meters (16 feet), is now extinct, as are the large, flightless, ostrichlike birds known as phororhachids, which throughout the Pleistocene were the dominant land carnivores of South America and whose fossil bones have recently been unearthed in North America. A similar but much older North American family, the Diatrymidae, resembled the ostrich but was more closely allied to modern cranes.

SHORT-FACED BEAR

The alternating periods of cooling and warming that characterized the global climate up to and including the Pleistocene were responsible for the widespread dispersal of species throughout North America and may help explain the enduring mystery of bird migration. In 1888, the British ornithologist Henry Seebohm proposed a theory of adaptive radiation for shorebirds that is still the most probable interpretation. Seebohm suggested that before the Pleistocene the ancestral species of all shorebirds evolved in the polar regions during a period of warm climate. This species was subsequently driven south by global cooling, with different flocks or colonies ending up in different parts of the globe. At the North Pole, a variance of a few degrees of longitude at the start could mean the difference between one destination in southern North America and another in tropical Asia. The separated populations gradually evolved into different species. When the climate warmed again, these species followed the ice edge north, met at the pole, and during the next cooling phase once more spread out into southern latitudes, where they diversified into yet more species. Repeated episodes of this warming-cooling, north-south migration and speciation, with each phase lasting 100,000 years, led to the present plethora of shorebird genera, which are now divided into two great families—the Charadriidae (plovers and related species) and the Scolopacidae (sandpipers)—comprising fifty species in North America.

It was also during the Pleistocene that humans first inhabited North America, although exactly when they migrated to this continent is a matter of some debate. The traditional view is that the first human inhabitants arrived about 13,000 years ago, a migration that coincided with the beginning of the retreat of the Wisconsinan ice sheet. These early North Americans, called the Clovis culture people, are thought to have traveled over a land bridge, exposed by lowered sea levels, from Siberia to Alaska, migrated down an ice-free corridor between the two North American ice sheets—the Cordilleran in the west and the Laurentide in the east—approximately where the Mackenzie Valley is today, and to have fanned out below the glaciers, living off the large herbivores they found thriving in the subglacial habitats. Named for the town in New Mexico where evidence of their existence first came to light, the Clovis people spread across the entire continent south of the glaciers.

Challenges to this "Clovis first" hypothesis began to appear in the 1980s, not from archaeologists but from linguists, who argued that North America's 1,200 native languages must have required more than 13,000 years to evolve. In 1990, two geneticists study-

ing mitochondrial DNA in two Central American Indian groups determined that their ancestors had arrived in North America from Asia at least 22,400 years ago, perhaps as long ago as 29,500 years. This was followed in 1993 by genetic evidence from Brazil that placed the earliest migrations across the Bering Strait at 33,000 to 43,000 years ago: the Brazilian scientists Sandro Bonatto and Francisco Bolzano proposed that although there was only one major migration, half the migrants headed directly south while the other half stayed in the north, in present-day Alaska, until glacial conditions allowed them to move south, following the retreating ice edge, about 13,000 years ago. This theory was given archaeological support in 1997 with the publication of data from Monte Verde, in Chile, where the anthropologist Tom Dillehay and his Chilean colleague Mario Pino found artifacts that they dated from between 32,000 and 12,800 years ago. If this recent genetic and archaeological evidence prevails, the "Clovis first" theory is

Retreating glaciers scraped striations, shown here parallel to the geologist's hammer handle, in this granite outcrop from the Grenville Province on Georgian Bay.

overturned. However, it still means that the first humans to inhabit the Great Lakes basin may have been part of the delayed southerly migration hypothesized by Bonatto and Bolzano, whether we call them Clovis people or not.

Whoever these Paleo-Indians were, the land they found in this region was high and dry, covered predominantly by sparse spruce forests and large, grassy meadows growing on the flat, dry beds of former glacial lakes. Archaeological sites in the Great Lakes region—at Cardoc, Ontario; Gainey, Michigan; and Nobles Pond and Sandusky, Ohio—show that they hunted woolly mammoths and mastodons, long-horned bison and possibly musk oxen, as well as horses, camels, bears, and rabbits. They also ate foraged vegetation in the wetlands and used stone implements to grind wild grain.

Although they seem to have been primarily nomadic hunter-gatherers, they also lived in established settlements. One remarkable excavation, the Paleo Crossing site near Akron, Ohio, has yielded numerous artifacts, including spear points and stone scrapers, as well as post holes and fire pits, indicating long-term habitations at least. Charcoal from the pits has been carbon-dated to 12,125 years ago, making Paleo Crossing the oldest known Paleo-Indian habitation in North America.

It is generally held that these early peoples hunted the Pleistocene megafauna, especially mammoths, to extinction, and there is much evidence to support this conclusion. Woolly mammoths had been around for 4 million years, but within a few generations of the arrival of the Clovis people they had vanished. The archaeologist Tim Flannery, in *The Eternal Frontier: An Ecological History of North America and Its Peoples,* notes that "the last mammoth, woolly rhino and Irish elk in the northern mainland of Eurasia," where the Clovis people came from, "date to about 14,400 [years before the present]," suggesting that after the Clovis people wiped out the megafauna in their native land, they crossed the Bering land bridge looking for more big game.

They were efficient hunters with technologically sophisticated weapons, and once here their population increased rapidly. They fashioned superb spear points, developed tools for shaping and straightening spear shafts, and launched their spears by means of atlatls, wooden throwing sticks that greatly increased the velocity and force of the spear. The megafauna, moreover, were unafraid of humans. Wherever Paleo-Indian sites have been excavated, large mounds of mammoth and bison bones have also been found, 7,000 or more bones in a pile, some still containing up to eight chert or flint spear points and displaying evidence of knowledgeable butchering.

The Paleo-Indians died out around 11,000 years ago, slightly more recently than the megafauna, which means they had had more than two millennia of hunting, surely enough time to deliver the coup de grace to species that may have already been in decline. Alternative theories of megafauna extinction include global

FACING PAGE: A few of the 117 pictographs painted in red ocher at Agawa Canyon, on the north shore of Lake Superior, by Ojibwa shamen between 3,000 and 500 years ago. The pictographs depict animals and spirits, including fish, cranes, eagles, turtles, and beavers. Shown here is the "Great Cat," Michipeshu, on the right; two giant serpents, Chingnebikoog, below; and, to the left, a canoe carrying six warriors.

warming, which altered vegetation patterns and water tables, causing mass starvation and, in the case of the mastodons, some kind of viral epidemic. (Woolly mammoths carried a herpeslike disease that is deadly to the modern African elephant.) Those factors may have played a part in the mammoth's disappearance, but there is tangible evidence that Paleo-Indian hunters killed a lot of mammoths. And when the game was gone, they themselves disappeared.

THE GREAT PLOW

Since the end of the last ice age, the earth's average surface temperature has hovered at around 14°C (57°F). When the glaciers were at their peak, the average was about 9°C (48°F). A difference of 5°C (9°F) may not seem significant, but it's an average; it reflects almost no change in daily temperatures at the equator and as much as a 20°C (36°F) drop in the average temperature at the poles. As a result, polar ice expanded to cover the northern hemisphere to more than 45 degrees of latitude, half the distance to the equator. During the Wisconsinan glaciations, the Laurentide ice sheet alone, centered over Hudson Bay, covered 16 million square kilometers (6 million square miles) and consisted of nearly 30 million cubic kilometers (7.2 million cubic miles), or 35 percent of the world's ice volume. Since the amount of water on the planet is more or less constant, a great deal of the earth's water at that time existed in the form of ice, and sea levels were extraordinarily low—up to 120 meters (nearly 400 feet) lower than they are today. Land bridges connecting North America, Asia, and South America were exposed, allowing frequent exchanges of plants and animals between continents. Almost everything familiar about the northern half of North America today, including the shape and arrangement of the Great Lakes, was determined by what ice did to the land during the final years of the Big Gap.

Glaciers are vast juggernauts of ice that spread across the landscape in perpetual stages of advance and retreat: Louis Agassiz referred to them as "God's great plough." They form when snow and freezing rain accumulate faster than they can melt, in other words when summers are too brief to carry off the winter snows, year after year, millennia after millennia. Ice cores taken from the center of

FACING PAGE: Aerial view of the glacially formed Oak Ridges Moraine, rising above the landscape in southwestern Ontario. Hardwoods cover the higher kames, and conifers darken the shores of kettle lakes.

THE OAK RIDGES MORAINE

The Oak Ridges Moraine, north of Toronto, is one of the region's best examples of a glacial moraine. A ridge rising above the surrounding landscape, it was created between the tongues of two glacial lobes 12,000 years ago. Now it is a swath of south-central Ontario running east-west for 160 kilometers (100 miles) and up to 15 kilometers (9 miles) wide, a roller-coaster ride of steep, closely packed hills above 50 to 200 meters (165 to 655 feet) of glacial till, sand, and gravel. Beneath the farmland and the wildlife corridors, the Oak Ridges Moraine also contains two large pockets of pure sand and gravel separated by a layer of sandy silt. The pockets are enormous aquifers, vast natural reservoirs of pure, drinkable, groundwater, much of it (especially in the larger, lower aquifer) meltwater left behind by the Laurentian glacier that formed the moraine. The aquifers are so immense that 40,000 rural wells and several large towns have been drawing water from the smaller, upper aquifer for 300 years without making a significant dent in the volume of water it contains.

Greenland have yielded unmelted glacial snow, or firn, that is more than 250,000 years old. During the Wisconsinan ice age, the Great Lakes region looked very much as central Greenland does today: a monumental central ice cap with a few trees and grass, animals, and, toward the end of the glaciation, humans eking out a meager existence at the edges of the ice.

Agassiz's ice ages theory sought to explain such geographical oddities as erratics, those large boulders marooned on flat terrain, as well as sudden gravel ridges, kettle lakes in sandy plains,

and polished and striated rocks. Observing the movement of glaciers in the Swiss Alps, Agassiz saw their potential for altering the surface of the earth; glaciers could level mountains, carve out river and lake beds, grind stone, and change landscapes over enormous areas. More than that, by changing the features and even the climate of specific areas, they affected the distribution and evolution of plants and animals. Unfortunately for scientific investigators, glaciers also erase most of the evidence of such changes.

Glaciers expand when the temperature drops. As they advance, they distribute huge piles of till composed of silt, clay, sand, and gravel in grains ranging in size from dust to bowling-ball dimensions. They also scratch deep grooves in bedrock with debris caught under their weight. As the Laurentide ice sheet repeatedly advanced and retreated over the area north of the present-day Great Lakes, it crushed the soft sandstones, shales, and limestones that had accumulated over the Canadian Shield, right down to the hard granite and gneiss bedrock of the Grenville Province, and spread the resultant gravel south to cover the accumulated limestones and sandstones of Layer II. Only a few harder rock formations remained poking above the glacial debris. The material left behind by the glaciers is now known as Layer III; when the milled rock became mixed with decayed vegetable matter, it turned into soil.

Most of the landforms visible in the Great Lakes region today were sculpted by glaciers. Outwash—sediments carried and deposited by glacial meltwater—spread in thick, irregular layers to become undulating hills and valleys called moraines. Huge rivers of meltwater cut through the undersurface of the ice and the resulting boreholes gradually filled with outwash, to be left behind as ridges of sand and gravel known as eskers when the ice disappeared. The

Jack pines, trembling aspens, and white birches surround remote Devil's Crater, 150 kilometers (95 miles) north of Thunder Bay, Ontario, formed 9,000 years ago by water rushing from Glacial Lake Agassiz.

meltwater also filled the lake basins and riverbeds between. Where meltwater entered a basin, it left larger materials, coarse deposits called kames, near its point of entry; the finer sediments settled out farther into the lake, and when the lake drained they made extremely fertile soils, which turned into lush meadowlands and, eventually, ideal farmland.

Where a glacier blocked the flow of its own meltwater, the run-off swelled into glacial lakes. Some of them were vast: Glacial Lake Agassiz, west of Lake Superior, contained more water than all the Great Lakes combined. When the ice dams melted or broke up, sudden deluges of floodwater—known by the Icelandic word *jokulhlaup*—carved new river valleys and deepened existing ones. When larger chunks of buried ice melted, the round holes they created in the till and outwash filled with water and became kettle lakes. All of this surface sculpting took place over thousands of years. Evidence from the Greenland ice cores suggests that it took a mere ten years for the earth's average surface temperature to rise the 5°C (9°F) necessary to trigger the end of the Wisconsinan ice age, but it was another 10,000 years before the ice had retreated and the present landscape was formed.

With the glaciers gone from the Great Lakes region by 9,000 years ago, the long process of soil formation began. Soil is to land what water is to the lakes: almost all life on land (with the exception of mosses, lichens, ferns, and epiphytic plants such as orchids) begins and ends in soil. The ice left behind crushed limestone and the crystalline rock of the Canadian Shield; exposed to the freeze-thaw cycles that cause physical weathering and to subsequent chemical weathering, these stones and rocks broke down into minerals. But minerals alone do not support plant life. Fine-grained minerals retain water, but they are easily washed into rivers and lakes. In order for minerals to be changed into soil, something has to come along that will grow on bare rock and eventually add its organic remains to the matrix.

Glacial erratics—large rocks moved to distant locations by glacial action—are used by geologists to determine the direction of glaciers' advances and retreats.

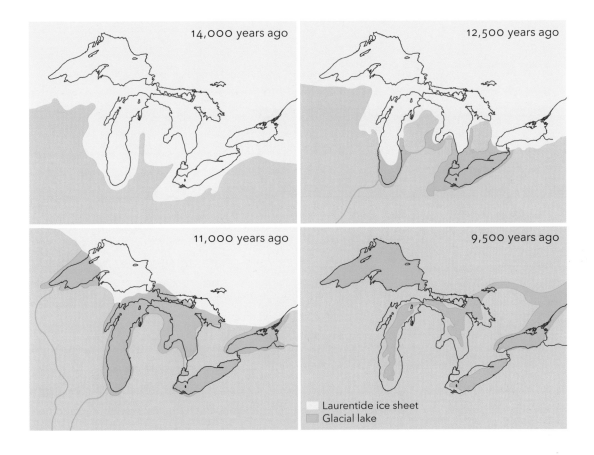

14,000 years ago

12,500 years ago

11,000 years ago

9,500 years ago

Laurentide ice sheet
Glacial lake

RETREAT OF THE
WISCONSINAN GLACIER

The first to do that were lichens, organisms that grow on virtually any substrate, from rocks to the backs of beetles and snapping turtles. After lichens, mosses and club ferns moved in—plants whose root systems do not require soil—followed by the higher, flowering plants, whose seeds blew in or were carried north by birds or animals from the more verdant south. Plants need soil, but soil also depends on plants for replenishment and growth.

As plants grew and died, their decomposition was aided by a teeming army of soil microbes, microscopic creatures that exist in the billions in every handful of soil. A single gram of soil, about a third of a teaspoon, contains an estimated 3 billion bacteria, and under favorable conditions they can double their population every hour. Other legions in the invisible army include the herbivorous fungal mycelia and actinomycetes, which feed on microscopic

A spray of speckled alder, which grows along the edges of streams and swamps, showing new, unopened cones (left) and the previous year's empty female cones (right).

Nitrogen is an abundant and vital element in the earth's atmosphere, almost as important to life on earth as oxygen. More than 78 percent of the air we breathe is nitrogen. Living organisms need nitrogen to make proteins, nucleic acids, and other parts of cells, but they cannot take it directly from air. Animals get their nitrogen from the leaves of plants—which contain up to 17 percent nitrogen—and plants get nitrogen from the soil.

To become available to plants, however, nitrogen must be "fixed," which means it must be combined with hydrogen or oxygen to form either ammonium or nitrate, which plants are then able to take up through their roots. Lightning converts small amounts of nitrogen into ammonium, but most ammonium is produced by the earth's oldest living organisms, the single-celled prokaryotes, also known as bacteria.

Some prokaryotes, such as cyanobacteria, are free-living and self-sustaining in soil; others form symbiotic relationships with certain plant species. Bacteria of the genus *Frankia,* for example, adhere to the roots of the alder family. In the Great Lakes basin, the family is represented by the speckled alder, a low shrub with smooth, reddish-brown bark and ovate leaves that grows in boreal and mixed forests on moist, poorly drained sites and along stream banks and the margins of swamps. By fixing nitrogen and making it available to other plants, alders perform a vital role in the forest ecosystem. They help to create the rich, organic soil that is the natural habitat of such larger species as black spruce and eastern hemlock.

organic matter and break it down into soil nutrients. Moving up into the visible range, detritivores such as nematodes, rotifers, and protozoa feed on the microflora and on plant roots, and insects such as mites, springtails, spiders, sowbugs, ants, and centipedes feed on the detritivores. Earthworms digest raw organic material and aerate the soil, and small rodents—moles, mice, voles—come to prey on the earthworms and insects. All these organisms are part of soil, a living ecosystem that produces, consumes, and recycles organic matter. Fertile soil is 40 percent minerals, 10 percent humus, and 50 percent pore space, which retains the air and water needed to produce and sustain life.

NEMATODE

The process of soil accumulation is extremely slow; from 2 to about 10 centimeters of soil is produced every hundred years, depending on the amount of vegetation it supports and factors such as rainfall and drought. But over time, as the climate continued to warm and vegetation zones migrated north, a land that was once covered by ice overlying barren rock was converted to rolling, grass- and tree-covered hills and burgeoning vegetation in the form of plants, shrubs, and trees—from tundra to boreal to deciduous forest—that fed and sheltered an increasingly diverse range of animal life.

Soil scientists divide the world's soils into ten basic types, depending on the climatic and geologic conditions that formed them. Broadly speaking, the soils of the Great Lakes basin are of two types. In the upper Lakes region, covered by mostly coniferous trees and a dark, wet forest floor, podzols predominate. These are somewhat acidic soils from the composted evergreen needles that make an organic humus high in aluminum and iron. They are light-colored and silica-rich at the surface, with a darker underlayer ranging from black to reddish-brown. Podzols exist in many consistencies, from coarse-grained sands and gravels to silts and clays; they are not particularly fertile, and so make poor farmland, but they can be improved with the addition of lime as one moves south out of the influence of the Canadian Shield.

ROTIFER

SPRINGTAIL

In the lower Lakes area, where the vegetation is primarily deciduous and glacial deposits cover the bedrock, alfisols are more common. Fine-loamed but still well-drained, with clays in the subsurface because they were formed on lake beds, alfisols belong to temperate, humid climates. The finer particles of alfisols may have originated as wind-borne dust, or loess, that was deposited near the ice margin as the glaciers retreated. The state soil of Minnesota—Lester loam, which covers 243,000 hectares (600,000 acres) of the state between Lakes Superior and Michigan—is an alfisol, as is the deeply porous Honeoye, the state soil of New York, containing pulverized limestone and calcareous shale. Both Lester loam and Honeoye lie in a thin layer above deep deposits of glacial outwash.

EBB AND FLOW

Before the Wisconsinan, the basin now embracing the Great Lakes was drained by means of a huge river that to a large extent followed the zigzag course of the current Lakes, except that it bypassed Lakes Michigan and Erie. Tracing the Midcontinent Rift through Lake Superior, it began at the head of the lake, near the present-day mouth of the St. Louis River, followed the lake (along what's known as the Lake Superior syncline) to the St. Mary's River, near present-day Sault Ste. Marie, then flowed south through a gap in the Niagara Escarpment that now lies on the floor of the northern part of Lake Huron (called the Main Channel). From there it poured into Georgian Bay and across the Huron Peninsula to empty into Lake Ontario near the site of present-day Toronto. It then encountered the Niagara Escarpment again and took a sharp easterly turn, flowing into the St. Lawrence Estuary, a deep arm of the Atlantic that penetrated inland almost to the Ontario border.

During the four periods of advance and retreat of the Laurentide ice sheet during the Wisconsinan, which at its peak about 18,000 years ago covered all of what are now the Great Lakes, meltwater and ice dams at the glacier's edge formed glacial lakes that drained directly south into the present-day Mississippi Valley. Estimates of the thickness of the ice vary, but it was probably more than 4 kilometers (2.5 miles) thick at its center, over Hudson Bay, and 2.5 kilometers (1.5 miles) thick above the Lakes. The weight of so much ice was enormous: it pushed the earth's crust deep into the viscous asthenosphere, so that in some places the surface was as much as

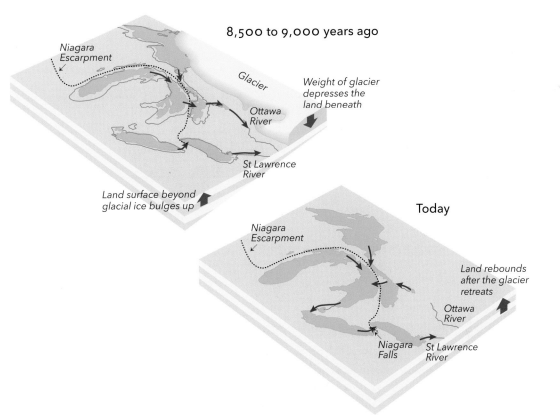

8,500 to 9,000 years ago

Niagara Escarpment

Glacier

Weight of glacier depresses the land beneath

Ottawa River

St Lawrence River

Land surface beyond glacial ice bulges up

Today

Niagara Escarpment

Land rebounds after the glacier retreats

Ottawa River

Niagara Falls

St Lawrence River

600 meters (2,000 feet) lower than it is today. The greatest depression was to the north, where the ice was heaviest.

By 14,000 years ago, gradually rising temperatures had caused the ice sheet to begin withdrawing northward. It was a slow retreat: after 3,000 years it had reached only as far as the top of Lake Huron, but by then the present-day forms of the Great Lakes were discernible. Lake Superior was assuming its present shape, but the weight of the glaciers had forced down the area around Lake Nipissing nearly to sea level, well below the level of the upper Great Lakes. What is now Lake Huron and Georgian Bay was swollen into a vast, glacial lake called Glacial Lake Algonquin, which drained to the Ottawa River. Roughly 2,000 years later, Lakes Superior, Michigan, and Huron, though much diminished in size, continued to drain north, flowing above Manitoulin Island, combining with

A storm is brewing over Stockton Island, off the coast of Wisconsin.

water flowing out of Glacial Lake Agassiz, into Lake Nipissing and thence into the Ottawa Valley through what is known as the North Bay Outlet, where it eventually joined with water draining into the St. Lawrence Estuary from Lakes Erie and Ontario.

As the glacier withdrew further, the land it had depressed began to rise, a process known as isostatic uplift, allowing Lake Nipissing to rebound to more than 120 meters (nearly 400 feet) above sea level. This diverted water from the upper Lakes down through Lake St. Clair and the Detroit River into Lakes Erie and Ontario. By about 4,000 years ago, most Great Lakes water drained much as it does today, although a considerable amount still flowed eastward through the North Bay Outlet into the Ottawa Valley along the

WHITE-WATER SQUALLS

Widespread windstorms that bring severe thunderstorms and incredibly high winds across the Great Lakes basin are called derechoes. Unlike a tornado (from the Spanish *tornar*, meaning "to turn"), a derecho wind (from the Spanish word for "straight") advances along a line rather than in a cyclone, stretching across a bow-shaped front that could be up to 400 kilometers (250 miles) long. Derecho winds have been clocked at 160 kilometers per hour (100 miles per hour), are usually associated with summer heat waves, and are most common in the Ohio and Mississippi valleys and in the Great Lakes basin.

A severe derecho can do as much damage on land as on the inland seas. One swept through the Great Lakes region in May 1998, raging in a squall line that advanced from southern Minnesota to New York State in only 15 hours. It became the most destructive natural disaster to hit the area in nearly a century. Coming in off the Great Plains, in Minnesota it leveled tens of thousands of trees and cut off power to 500,000 homes. In Wisconsin the wind picked up speed to 203 kilometers per hour (126 miles per hour), damaged 5,000 homes, and caused a seiche—a wind-driven rise in lake level at the downwind end of a lake—on Lake Michigan that raised the water in Muskegon County, Michigan, by 3 meters (10 feet) in two hours.

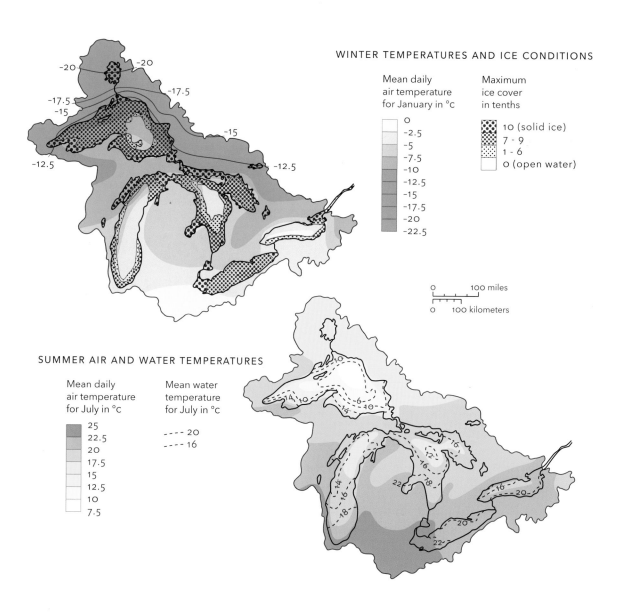

WINTER TEMPERATURES AND ICE CONDITIONS

Mean daily
air temperature
for January in °C

0
-2.5
-5
-7.5
-10
-12.5
-15
-17.5
-20
-22.5

Maximum
ice cover
in tenths

10 (solid ice)
7 - 9
1 - 6
0 (open water)

0   100 miles
0   100 kilometers

SUMMER AIR AND WATER TEMPERATURES

Mean daily
air temperature
for July in °C

25
22.5
20
17.5
15
12.5
10
7.5

Mean water
temperature
for July in °C

--- 20
--- 16

routes of the Matawa and Petawawa rivers. As the land continued to uplift, however, water from Lake Nipissing ceased flowing east, draining instead southwestward down the French River into Lake Huron. Lakes Michigan and Huron filled to their present volumes and began to flow south, through Lakes Erie and Ontario. In fact, they overfilled, so that the remnant of the great glacial river that once flowed south from the southern tip of Lake Michigan, from about where Chicago is today and following the route of the current Illinois River, resumed the Lakes' previous drainage into the Mississippi Valley for a short period. Water levels dropped eventually, until even that vestigial outlet lost its connection with the Great Lakes: the Illinois River now begins well inland, at the junction of the Des Plaines and Kankakee rivers, neither of which drains into or flows out of Lake Michigan.

In short, the history of the formation of the Great Lakes is the most recent chapter in the story of the retreat of the Laurentide ice sheet. At the outset, each lake was considerably larger than it is today because the basin it occupied had been depressed by the weight of the ice, and because present-day outlets were blocked by ice. As the ice sheet retreated, formerly blocked northern outlets opened up, in some cases causing catastrophic drainage that dropped lake levels well below what they are today. Then, as the outlets slowly rose because of continuing isostatic rebound, the lakes filled up to their present levels.

OVERLEAF: The Ouimet Canyon, near Black Bay, Lake Superior, was scoured by glaciers out of a billion-year-old magma sill. Diabase pinnacles, far right, form the lookout area known as Indian Head.

LOCATION, LOCATION, LOCATION

The physical landscape is determined by only two factors: tectonics and climate. The movement of continental plates forms the rough contours of a landscape, and then climate proceeds to refine those features as an artist uses knives and scrapers to create the likeness of a face in wet clay. Climate's tools—water, wind, sedimentation, plant species, glaciers—shape and alter river valleys, bluffs, hills, and soil.

Tectonics accounts for the primary elements of the Great Lakes climate. The region lies almost precisely at the center of the continent, about halfway between the equator and the North Pole.

Apart from the air masses moving up, down, and across the central continental corridor, the greatest influence on the climate of the Great Lakes is the lakes themselves. The Lakes act as huge heat sinks; in the fall, they remain warm after the land begins to cool. The opposite takes place in the spring: the lake water remains cold even after the land begins to heat, so it's not uncommon to see grass growing on the land while there is still ice on the lakes. This variation in temperature between the land and the water keeps shoreline areas cooler longer in the spring and summer, decreasing precipitation, and warmer longer in the fall, which is why the Niagara Peninsula, for example, is such a prolific area for soft fruit such as peaches and grapes. In winter, the warm lake water provides heat and moisture to air passing over it, causing lake-effect snowstorms that may dump 65 centimeters (25.6 inches) of snow close to shore while a short distance inland the sky is calm and clear.

As this NASA satellite image shows, prevailing westerly winds pick up moisture over the Lakes and deposit huge snowfalls in the snowbelts around their eastern ends.

In some cases, the Lakes make storms worse. A recent study conducted by researchers at the University of Illinois and the Illinois State Water Survey found that cyclones in the basin actually increase in speed and intensity as they pass over the Lakes. This phenomenon is most pronounced from September to December, when the water is warmer than the surrounding land and cyclones are energized by the addition of heat and moisture. But it is also significant in May and June, when the water is cooler; warm air passing over cool water causes condensation, which abruptly drops the air temperature while increasing its moisture content.

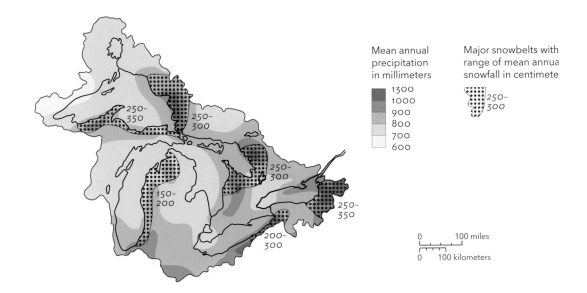

Mean annual precipitation in millimeters

1300
1000
900
800
700
600

Major snowbelts with range of mean annua snowfall in centimete

250–300

0   100 miles

0   100 kilometers

It rests in a lowland corridor midway between two mountain rang-es, the Rocky Mountains to the west and the Appalachians to the east, and therefore directly beneath the head-on collision of warm, humid air masses from the south, flowing north along the corridor, and cold, dry air masses funneling down from the Arctic. They are joined by prevailing winds from the west, warm Pacific air that has cascaded down the Rocky Mountains and dried out while crossing the prairies. The result is a roiling melee of rising, falling, and spinning air producing some of the most changeable weather pat-terns on the continent.

The size of the basin means that there is much variability from region to region, especially as we move from north to south, where the number of daylight hours in a year changes dramatically. The southern ecoregions in the basin receive 25 percent more solar en-ergy than the northern regions. This means that the mean tempera-ture for January on the north shore of Lake Superior, for example, is more than 17°C (30.6°F) colder than that on the south shore of Lake Erie: -20°C (-5°F) as compared with -2.5°C (27.5°F). The summer spread is much less, only about 8°C (14.5°F): a mean of 17.5°C (63.5°F) in Thunder Bay, Ontario, in July, and 25°C (77°F) in Toledo, Ohio.

PRECIPITATION AND

SNOWBELT AREAS

Because warm air masses pick up moisture from the Lakes and then rise into the cooler Arctic air, dropping water as they cool, the Lakes basin receives a lot of rain, sleet, and snow. Up to 1300 millimeters (51.2 inches) of precipitation per year falls in some areas, including the Grey and Algoma highlands, the Muskoka–Parry Sound area, and the eastern ends of Lakes Ontario and Erie. On average, about 6,000 cubic meters (200,000 cubic feet) of precipitation fall on the Lakes every second, 85 percent of it on the upper Lakes. Because the prevailing winds are from the west, the great snowbelts are wrapped around the eastern ends of the Lakes, with up to 3.5 meters (nearly 12 feet) of snow blanketing the land east of Georgian Bay and Lake Ontario every year.

A lot of rain comes as thunderstorms: about forty storms per year south of Lake Michigan and twenty-five per year in the more northerly regions, with June being the month when the most softball games are called because of lightning, and October and November the windy months when sailors on Lake Superior keep their life jackets on during meals. Spring and early summer are tornado months: Illinois and Indiana receive an average of six tornadoes per year per 160 square kilometers (60 square miles) of land, although the average drops to one tornado every two years over the same area north of the forty-fourth parallel. The region north of Lake Superior and western Michigan receives up to twelve freezing-rain storms a year, but ice storms are familiar calamities throughout the basin. Eastern Ontario and western Quebec experienced one in 1998 that flattened forests, knocked down 1,000 transmission towers and 30,000 power poles, and killed twenty-eight people.

YOUNG AND RESTLESS

Though the foundation stones of the Great Lakes are unimaginably old, in geological terms the Lakes themselves are quite young, having assumed their present shape only about 4,000 years ago, around the time that the great pyramids were being built in Egypt. This was long after the disappearance of the Pleistocene megafauna and the Paleo-Indians, the last truly nomadic hunter-gatherers in North America. They were followed by a native culture from the south, whose hunting camps are found on the ancient shorelines of the now-vanished Glacial Lake Agassiz, which covered most of southern Manitoba, western Ontario, northern Minnesota, and North Dakota. When it experienced its own cataclysmic *jokulhlaup* 8,500 years ago and vanished in a raging exodus of water, much of it drained south to carve out the Mississippi River valley. Some of it flowed into Lake Superior and thence to the St. Lawrence Estuary, and, according to recent conjecture, a great deal of it may have emptied via the Mackenzie River basin into the Arctic Ocean. In any event, its draining left only a remnant of its former self as Lake Winnipeg.

Such an event would be long remembered by anyone who witnessed it, and the memory would be handed down from generation to generation, possibly even across cultures. When the French Jesuit explorers penetrated to the western shores of Lake Michigan in the seventeenth century, they encountered a Dakota-speaking people who described an ancient culture living on the shore of a much greater body of water to the west. Like Champlain before them, the Jesuits thought they were hearing stories of the Pacific Ocean, but in fact what they received was an oral epic of the demise of Glacial Lake Agassiz, the sixth and mightiest of the Great Lakes.

Nothing in nature is static; everything is in perpetual motion. In the past 10,000 years, isostatic uplift has raised Hudson Bay 285 meters (935 feet); Lake Nipissing 122 meters (400 feet) and the state of Wisconsin 45 meters (150 feet). Isostatic rebound is still taking place, although at different rates in different parts of the region: the Lake Superior basin is currently rising at the rate of 53 centimeters (20.5 inches) every century, while the Niagara Peninsula has risen about 0.3 meters (about 1 foot) in the past 100 years. Rebound is expected to continue for the next 10,000 years. Meanwhile, the European and North America continents are moving away from each other at the rate of 3 centimeters (1.25 inches) every century. If we are, indeed, living in a fourth interglacial since the beginning of the Pleistocene, then the Great Lakes are far from having assumed their final shapes; everything about them is young and constantly changing.

THE BOREAL FOREST

THERE IS A SENSE, WHEN traveling along the highway that hugs the north shore of Lake Superior, of floating between two limitless universes. On one side you have the lake, an expanse of shining, deep-sea water that stretches to the distant horizon. You catch glimpses of its surface, rippling in the clear, northern sunlight like the skin of some huge reptile, between soaring cliffs of granite. On the other side, crowding down to the lakeshore from somewhere far to the north, is the silent, indifferent forest, obviously the near fringe of a verdant realm that both invites and defies attention. Depending on your frame of mind, you want to either press your foot to the accelerator to escape its omnipresence or else stop, get out of the car, and start walking into it. If you do the latter, the saying goes in the north, the next person you meet will probably be speaking Russian.

This jumble of dense vegetation is part of the largest forest regime, or type, in the world, the circumpolar boreal forest. The Siberian you would eventually encounter would call it the *taiga,* the Russian word for "conifer"; our word *boreal* comes from Boreas, in Greek mythology the god of the north wind. The boreal forest covers all the forested northern regions, below the tundra, of Canada, Siberia, Scandinavia, and Japan, occupying the territory between

In a coniferous forest, after a long spell of trapping or cruising, I begin to
think I hate trees. Any swamp or lake or mountain slope, any open place at all becomes
a haven of light and space, freedom from the overpowering density of evergreen
and the enclosing trunks of the forest's infinity. Many of the pioneers felt this
and fought timber with as much intensity and determination as they fought Indians
and wild beasts and climate. In any country that was once forest, a contempt for
trees carries over far beyond its purpose into years of wanton and brutal destruction.

RODERICK HAIG-BROWN, *Measure of the Year*, 1950

the southern grasslands and the northern barrens. It comprises one-
third of earth's forested land while accounting for only 14 percent
of its forest biomass; the equatorial rain forests are smaller in area,
but their trees are bigger. Closer to the tree line, taiga grows in such
austere climatic conditions that a 200-year-old trunk may be only
5 centimeters (2 inches) in diameter.

The Great Lakes basin portion of the boreal forest represents its
southernmost range, an area that coincides with the Central Canadian Shield Forests ecoregion—a vast, U-shaped swath that swoops
down from the Ontario-Manitoba border, sits atop Lake Superior
like a voyageur's tuque, and swings east into northern Quebec and
Labrador. It is a close-canopied forest in which the predominant
tree species are black and white spruce, jack pine, and, to a lesser
extent, red and white pine, balsam fir, and tamarack, with a few deciduous species—quaking and big-toothed aspen, paper birch, and
balsam poplar—crowding in the sunlight along riverbanks, around
bogs, and in burned-over areas. There are many of the latter, fire
being the principal way in which this wild tangle cleanses and re-
news itself.

Boreal soils in the basin are mostly thin, acidic podzols over outcrops of the Canadian Shield's signature gneiss and granite. It is damp under the continuous evergreen canopy, tinder dry in the clearings. Small pockets of wetlands abound—on average, about 25 percent of the land is bog. The cold, rushing rivers are the favored spawning grounds of salmon and trout, and moose stand knee-deep in the wetlands, grazing on the buds and shoots of the aquatic plants and young deciduous bushes that grow there. American black ducks and common goldeneyes swim serenely in the lakes and ponds, as unperturbed as the forest itself by quiet human intrusions, and move calmly out of the way of a silent canoe.

That, at least, is what Jonathan Carver discovered when he circumnavigated Lake Superior in 1768: extremely harsh conditions supporting an amazing variety of tenacious life. "The country on the north and east parts of Lake Superior," he wrote, "is very mountainous and barren. The weather being intensely cold in the

Rainbow Falls tumbles over granite bedrock through the boreal forest into Lake Superior between Schreiber and Rossport, in northern Ontario.

winter, and the sun having but little power in the summer, vegetation there is very slow; and consequently but little fruit is to be found on the shore. It however produces some few species in great abundance." Beaching his canoe on a rare stretch of white sand, he walked a short distance inland and found black currants, gooseberries, and "whirtleberries of an uncommon size and fine flavour." Whirtleberry, or red whortleberry, is another name for the mountain cranberry, which grows in the clearings and around sphagnum bogs, and even on moss-covered rocks. Like all the plants and animals found in this starkly beautiful and forbidding forest, it needs very little to survive.

STAYING GREEN

To survive at all, let alone flourish, in such a region, plants have had to evolve coping strategies, and the key to the conifers' success is their reliance on needles, rather than leaves, for photosynthesis. Photosynthesis is the means by which trees turn sunlight into food (and, coincidentally, carbon dioxide into oxygen), a transformation that takes place in the chlorophyll contained in their leaves. The leaves inhale carbon dioxide through millions of tiny stomata, or valved breathing holes, and with water from the soil and energy from sunlight, the chlorophyll converts the carbon dioxide into carbohydrates (sugars), then at night exhales the waste oxygen and water vapor through the stomata.

While it's true that broad leaves are more efficient solar collectors and offer more room for stomata, after they drop off in the fall no photosynthesis can take place until spring. Deciduous trees must store nutrients in their large, deep root systems in order to get through the winter, and then produce new leaves when the warm weather arrives, a process that consumes a great deal of energy in itself. In the boreal forest, however, with bedrock lurking just beneath the soil, large root systems are not often possible and yet the winters are long. The remedy is to generate energy by photosynthesizing right through all four seasons, as conifers do with their needles. Studies have shown that, despite the fact that needle-leaf trees have a smaller total leaf surface area than deciduous trees, by

In the boreal forest, animals have developed different ways to cope with the long, cold winters. Birds migrate to warmer climates; lynx grow thicker coats; bears hibernate. The most drastic coping mechanism, however, belongs to three species of boreal amphibians: spring peepers, wood frogs, and boreal chorus frogs. They allow themselves to freeze almost solid.

Boreal-zone frogs spend their summers on the damp forest floor, eating ants, beetles, leafhoppers, and spiders, and scurrying under wet leaves or logs when a predator approaches. They also hibernate in such places in winter, when snow cover adds to the insulation. Their metabolism slows down so dramatically that their hearts stop beating, their breathing stops, and their brains cease to function. Two-thirds of the water in their bodies freezes, and their body temperatures drop to -6°C (21°F). They are able to do this by freezing very slowly, and by secreting a natural antifreeze—glucose—that prevents their cells from dehydrating during freeze-up. When they thaw in the spring, they thaw from the interior out: first the heart, then the brain and the liver, and finally the limbs, over a period of two to three hours.

The "quack" of the wood frog is a common May evening chorus throughout the basin.

Medical scientists have been studying boreal frogs to see if there is a way of applying the amphibians' freeze tolerance to human organ transplants. Organs now must be transplanted five to six hours after being harvested. Attempts to freeze mammal organs using artificial "cryptoprotectants" have so far not worked: rats implanted with frozen livers die after a few days. Biologists at Carleton University in Ottawa, and at Miami University in Oxford, Ohio, have determined that the frogs' secret is in the slow pace at which they freeze, the amount of natural glucose they secrete—up to 100 times their normal levels—and the fact that they remain at temperatures just a few degrees below freezing in winters that often get as cold as -40°C (-40°F).

retaining most of their needles year-round they produce nearly 60 percent more sugars and other nutrients than deciduous trees.

Conifers and deciduous trees also differ in their seed designs. All plants are divided into two distinct groups: gymnosperms and angiosperms. Gymnosperms, from the Greek meaning "naked seeds," include most coniferous trees—yews, pines, firs, hemlocks, spruces, cypresses, and cedars (and junipers), the seeds of which are not enclosed within the carpel, the female ovary. They lie open and exposed on cone scales waiting for an opportune wind or a surge of water to disperse them. Angiosperms—"enclosed seeds"—include grasses, herbs, and deciduous trees, all of which are flowering plants, flowers being simply ovaries in attractive party dresses.

Conifers are a much older form of plant life than deciduous trees, descendants of the ancient ferns and treelike horsetails and club mosses that covered the planet's landmasses 400 million years ago. Gradually, coniferous trees evolved from ferns by developing stiffer trunks, strengthening the outer rings of their stems with lignin, an organic polymer that is tougher than the silica-based stems of ferns, and filling the hollow centers with the previous years' deadwood. This greater structural integrity allowed them to stand taller, above the neighboring ferns and mosses, and so capture more sunlight. But conifers retained the fern's open-seeded reproductive strategy. Angiosperms did not appear for another 250 million years, during the Cretaceous period. By the time the Cretaceous ended 65 million years ago, there were enough insects around to ensure pollination by means other than wind and water. In the boreal forest, however, wind still moves more pollen from plant to plant than insects do.

Although ferns were originally plants of the tropics or subtropics, the Great Lakes basin harbors about 45 species of them, several unique to the boreal zone. Ferns, like the coelacanth and other lobe-finned fish, are "living fossils," as unchanged in appearance (except in size) as they are in their reproductive habits. The fern's reproductive cycle consists of two phases. In the first year, the mature fern disperses thousands of brown, dustlike spores; those that fall on favorable ground—moist, cool, and dark—begin to grow into low, flat plants called gametophytes. These produce leaves, and on

The most widely distributed defoliating insect in North America, the spruce budworm chomps its way through a number of conifer species. It prefers balsam fir but also attacks white, red, and black spruce, eastern hemlock, and white pine—all of which are found in the Great Lakes basin boreal forest.

The caterpillar, or larval, stage of the spruce budworm.

The budworm is the larva of a moth that lays its eggs on conifer needles in July; the larvae hatch and overwinter in silk hibernaculae spun at the tips of the trees' boughs. The following spring the budworms or caterpillars feed on needles, buds, flowers, and shoots, completely defoliating up to half or more of the affected areas. Many trees die—budworms destroy about 500,000 hectares (1.2 million acres) of forest each year—and those that eventually return to health are susceptible to attack by other stresses, such as drought or fungal diseases.

North of Lake Superior, major infestations occur about every thirty years; during the most recent, in the 1970s, the Canadian Forest Service sprayed a bacterial insecticide, *Bacillus thuringiensis,* known as Bt, to protect a percentage of the foliage. The infestation caused major irruptions of several species of boreal songbirds, including evening and pine grosbeaks, purple finches, red and white-winged crossbills, and black-capped and boreal chickadees, which had to range farther south in order to find food and nesting sites.

But the news isn't all bad. Defoliated stands of conifers allow sunlight and rain to penetrate to the forest floor, allowing the generation of herbaceous plants that benefit wildlife, and the insects' frass, or droppings, supply valuable nutrients to the soil.

the leaves' undersides are found the typical fern's sex organs—the male antherides and the female archegonia. These organs produce the seeds and pollen that, when combined during the second year, grow into ferns.

Some, such as bracken and polypody ferns, which are the most widely distributed in the Great Lakes basin and, indeed, in the world, also reproduce by means of underground tendrils, like strawberry plants—again without reliance upon insects or animals to disperse pollen or seeds—and thrive in acidic northern soils or, in the case of the epiphytic polypodia, sometimes on solid rock. Other ferns that grow along Lake Superior's north shore include the fragrant cliff fern, the leaves of which give off a spicy odor when dried and crumbled, and the alpine woodsia, a rare and unusual fern in that it is a hybrid of two other woodsias. It grows on rocky ledges and cliffs, and its fronds are only 10 centimeters (4 inches) long and remain green year-round, even under deep snow.

Conifers likewise rely on wind and water for pollen and seed dispersal, and fortunately for them the Great Lakes boreal regime contains one of the world's most extensive systems of rivers and lakes. So much groundwater makes for an extremely damp climate; where there is soil shaded by close-growing evergreens, the boreal forest creates a cool, moist understory microclimate. Typical observations in the region give a mean annual temperature of 1°C (33°F) and a mean annual precipitation of only 700 millimeters (27.5 inches). But the boreal's myriad streams, lakes, and bogs make it the perfect habitat for conifers. A balsam fir seed falling onto a river will be carried far from its natal tree, where there is less risk of growing into a tree that might be pollinated by its own parent. Genetic diversity keeps a species healthy.

Balsam fir is a shade-tolerant conifer, one of nine species of North American firs but the only one found in the Northeast. Constituting a little less than 5 percent of the boreal canopy in the Great Lakes basin, it is well adapted for northern life. Balsam fir saplings can persist on the forest floor for decades, waiting for their taller neighbors to succumb to old age, severe winds, or infestations of spruce budworms. (Despite its name, the spruce budworm prefers

BALSAM FIR

mature balsam fir to all other species.) When sunlight finally reaches the forest floor, the saplings shoot up to their majestic 21-meter (70-foot) height.

Perfectly symmetrical in outline, the balsam fir is wide at the base and tapers to a spirelike crown, with branches that lift slightly upward rather than droop down. The needles are short, about a centimeter or less than a half-inch long, dark green on top and with two white stripes underneath, and blunt, not prickly to the touch. They also have a delightful scent: Donald Culross Peattie, in his *A Natural History of Trees*, remarks that "to anyone whose childhood summers were luckily spent [in the great north woods], the delicious spicy fragrance of Balsam needles is the dearest odor in all of Nature." Cottagers would fill pillowcases with balsam fir needles and, sleeping on them back in the cities, dream of gurgling brooks and flashing rainbow trout.

For years, balsam fir was the most popular species of Christmas tree, not only for its woodsy smell but also because it holds onto its needles even when watered only sporadically. In its natural habitat, it keeps its needles for three years, replacing about a third of them annually. Balsam fir is highly susceptible to fire, possibly because its bark is covered with blisters filled with oleoresin, a highly flammable, turpentinelike substance. Extracted oleoresin is called Canada balsam, used to fix biological specimens to glass slides; it has exactly the same refractive index as glass.

Sphagnum moss floats on a bog in Slate Island Provincial Park, in Lake Superior. Dead sphagnum becomes peat, which eventually petrifies into coal.

Another characteristic conifer of the boreal forest is the white spruce, also known as skunk spruce thanks to a faint skunklike or garlicky odor given off by its small, sharp, blue-green needles when crushed. The white spruce/balsam fir association occupies the middle ground between the bog-bound species (black spruce and tamarack) and trees found in the higher, drier, sandier ridges (jack pine, quaking aspen, and white birch). Occasionally a pure white spruce

WHITE SPRUCE

BLACK SPRUCE

stand will claim the terrain, trees growing so thickly that virtually no light penetrates to the ground. The trees produce even more seeds than balsam firs—up to a million tiny winged seeds per hectare (2.5 acres) of spruce—and the seeds from an individual tree are released every two to six years. A white spruce can live up to two hundred years, although it won't begin to reproduce until it reaches twenty to forty years of age. Balsam fir also reproduces in its twenties and lives to be a hundred and fifty. Thus in a mixed stand of white spruce and balsam fir, there is usually a thick understory of young, opportunistic balsam firs, ready to take over the forest when the tall spruces succumb to windthrow or insect damage.

By far the most common boreal conifer is the black spruce, which accounts for more than 50 percent of the forest biomass. The black spruce is a narrow, dark tree with almost no taper from its lower to upper branches; the lower boughs droop dramatically, then curl up at their tips. At the top of the tree the branches form a dense ball that imitates the shape of its cones, which are ovoid and pointed when closed. The crown is where all of the cones appear, often above a stretch of bare trunk that has been nipped clean of cone-bearing branches by red squirrels. Unless opened prematurely by the heat of a forest fire, the cones remain closed for thirty years before spreading and releasing their seeds to the wind. Black spruce needles are about 2 centimeters (0.8 inches) long, four-sided, like a wooden matchstick, and grow around the twig in a spiral pattern. It is an extremely shallow-rooted tree, with roots spreading out widely but never penetrating more than about 20 centimeters (8 inches) into the soil, even where greater soil depth is available. In open, well-drained areas it can grow to 35 meters (115 feet) in height. Farther north, in the muskeg regions beyond the Hudson Bay watershed, black spruces have been found growing on floating islands of sphagnum moss in the middle of bogs, where there is no soil whatsoever. Although such specimens rarely grow more than a meter or a yard in height, they are impressive evidence of an endlessly adaptive species.

Eastern tamarack loves wet areas; in the Far North, around Hudson Bay, tamaracks are the true taiga. Closer to the Lakes, where they grow profusely in bogs and drained beaver ponds, they can reach 25 meters (80 feet) in height and half a meter (1.5 feet) in diameter. The tamarack is a natural curiosity: a deciduous conifer. It reproduces by means of cones like a conifer and has light lime-green needles like a conifer—each about 2.5 centimeters (1 inch) long, soft and delicate, clustered in sprays of twenty on mature twigs or singly in a spiral pattern on leader twigs. But every autumn its needles turn bright yellow and fall off, contradicting the general rule that holding onto needles is a necessary adaptation to northern climates. In fact, the tamarack is the northernmost-growing tree in the world, and yet it sheds its needles. In the west it is sometimes called juniper, to which it is entirely unrelated, or referred to by its formal name, larch. The common name tamarack and its alternative, hackmatack, are corruptions of the Algonquin word *akemantak,* which means "wood for making snowshoes." Tamarack wood is dense and resinous, making it pliable and as resistant to water and rot as cedar.

TAMARACK

Balsam poplar, also known as tacamahac or balm of Gilead, is North America's northernmost hardwood. (The true balm of Gilead is an introduced species, acknowledged since biblical times in its native Middle East for its curative properties: the word *balm* is a corruption of *balsam.*) Found from Newfoundland to Alaska, including the southern tip of Lake Michigan (with isolated stands in West Virginia), it has its true home in the northern boreal forest. A tall, slender, fast-growing tree with light brown, furrowed bark and an open crown of upright limbs, it thrives in moist soils along stream banks and on floodplains, where its shiny, dark green, serrated leaves (silvery-white underneath) flash in the cool, northern sunlight. Closely related to quaking aspen, it behaves in much the same way, hurrying in to colonize burned-out, windfallen, or logged areas and preventing soil erosion during heavy rains and spring runoff. Whereas conifers release their seeds in late fall, poplar seeds take flight during the summer, primed and ready to germinate (which they do in a matter of days) for a head start on other species. As their dark green leaves indicate, they require a lot of sunlight to photosynthesize, which keeps their seedlings out in the clearings, free of the shaded forest floor.

BALSAM POPLAR

WATER INTO WOODS

Although most of the boreal forest is a landscape of bedrock out-croppings and dense forest, there are numerous clearings that mark the footprints of former lakes and beaver ponds that have since drained or evaporated. These open areas are the forest's nurser-ies, meadows on their way to becoming new forest. Each stage of the process has its own plant regime: aquatic plants in the ponds; grasses, sedges, and low shrubs in the meadows; and larger trees crowding in from the edges to eventually obliterate the clearings altogether.

In saturated boreal bogs and ponds, the aquatic plants include the aquatic buckbean, a member of the gentian family, and the bullhead-lily, a yellow water lily related to the more southerly spat-terdock, with flowers less than 5 centimeters (2 inches) across. Tus-sock sedges grow in large, rooted clumps, like half-submerged por-cupines, heavy enough to provide stepping-stones across a wetland.

Around the edges of bogs, trees that thrive with wet feet—wil-lows, northern white cedars, and tamaracks—tower over forest shrubs such as Labrador tea and low-bush cranberry, also known as mooseberry, a smaller relative of the mountain, or high-bush, cranberry. Labrador tea has narrow, leathery leaves resembling those of rosemary, except they curl inward and their undersides are coated with rusty hairs. In late May and June, its white flowers ap-pear in umbel-like clusters at the tips of the sprays. Early settlers and woodsmen made tea from its dried leaves when China tea was unavailable, as it usually was. Catharine Parr Traill, a self-taught botanist who emigrated to Ontario in 1832, praised it in her *Stud-ies of Plant Life in Canada* for its health-promoting qualities "as a strengthener and purifier of the blood, and as being good for the system in various inward complaints." But she didn't recommend its astringent taste.

Two species of blueberry are found in the region. The low sweet blueberry bush, which grows to about 60 centimetres (23.5 inches) in height, is found in dry sandy areas, and the velvet-leaf blueberry, which prefers the more acidic environment of sphagnum bogs. The two blueberries also differ in their leaves: low sweet blueberry

Fire is the most significant disturbance factor in the boreal forest. In Canada, an average of 9,000 forest fires are started every year, 85 percent of them by lightning and most of them in the boreal forest. They consume nearly 3 million hectares (7.4 million acres) of forested area. By comparison, spruce budworm infestations destroy an average of 500,000 hectares (1.2 million acres) per year, and logging accounts for about 800,000 hectares (2 million acres).

But fire has been around far longer than budworms or buzz saws, and the boreal forest has adapted to it. Fire is now recognized as the primary force that determines the physical and biological attributes of the forest; in fact, the forest ecosystem has come to depend on fire for its well-being. It thrives on fire.

The cones of jack pine, for example, are sealed by resins and do not release their seeds until they are heated to more than 60°C (140°F), a temperature that can be achieved only by fire—which occurs in pine stands about every 50 to 100 years, the average life span of a pine tree.

Forest fires, like this one in Superior National Forest, Minnesota, are essential to the boreal forest for insect control and renewal.

The moose is also a fire-dependent species that does its part in the regeneration of the conifer forest. After a fire has cleared an area of conifers, often the first plants to move in are the deciduous aspens, willows, and birches. As moose browse on the abundant leaves and twigs, the deciduous plants are reduced, allowing the conifers to reclaim the burnover.

Foresters once suppressed fires in the boreal forest, but since the early 1990s the philosophy has changed to allow outbreaks to burn unless they threaten towns or villages. Research shows that active suppression does not reduce the extent of the area burned annually; when fires are not controlled they are larger, but they occur less frequently.

LICHEN AND REINDEER
MOSS ON GRANITE

This is a tiny language,
smaller than Gallic;
when you have your boots on
you scarcely see it.

A scorched brown dialect
or a grey one, brittle
and with many branches
like an old tree's, bleached and leafless.

In the rain they go leathery,
then sly, like rubber.
They send up their little mouths
on stems, red-lipped and round,

each one pronouncing a syllable,
o,o,o, like the dumbfounded
eyes of minnows.
Thousand of spores, of rumours

Infiltrating the fissures,
moving unnoticed into
the ponderous *is* on the boulder,
breaking down rock.

MARGARET ATWOOD

leaves are bright green and shiny on both upper and lower surfaces, whereas velvet-leaf blueberry leaves are darker on top, with pale, short hairs beneath. Both attract birds and bears, which eat the berries and scatter the seeds in their droppings. Also present is the closely related oval-leaved bilberry, which has sweet, blue-black berries covered with a dusty bloom and grows only near water.

Sphagnum moss, actually the name for a half-dozen or more peat mosses that are common in the boreal region, is the chief engine in the slow process of transforming bogs into woods. It is an ancient plant family: fossil sphagnum has been found in rocks of the Devonian period, 350 million years ago, indicating that the earth has been in wetland-to-woodland transition for as long as there have been plants on the planet. A bog is acidic water collected on either bedrock or hardpan clay with very poor to no drainage: the hollow fills with rainwater or meltwater, which is low in nutrients and remains there until it evaporates. If the hollow is deep enough, a bog can last for thousands of years.

New sphagnum moss builds up slowly, like coral, from moss growing on the bog bottom at the rate of about 1 meter (39 inches) every 1,000 years. Finally, it floats on the surface by means of its large, balloonlike cells, the walls of which are porous and readily absorb water. Sphagnum can hold up to twenty times its weight in water, making it a natural sponge that was highly useful to native people and settlers. The top, above-water layer of sphagnum is air-filled and produces a blanket of moss on the water that not only prevents sunlight from penetrating to the bog bottom but also inhibits surface water from evaporating. The result is a stagnant, oxygen-depleted, acidic soup that attracts acid-tolerant plant species such as cranberry and Labrador tea.

The sphagnum itself is host to entire colonies of microorganisms, including desmids, diatoms (types of algae), rotifers, nematodes, and rhizopods (amoebas). Biologists have counted up to 32,000 individual organisms in a cubic meter (1.3 cubic yards) of sphagnum. These feed larger creatures—dragonflies, damselflies, caddis flies, mosquitoes, midges, bloodworms, water lice—which in turn feed frogs, fish, and birds. Like a coral reef in an ocean, sphagnum

FACING PAGE: British soldiers lichen, from the Porcupine Mountain Wilderness Area in Michigan, tolerates pollution and therefore also grows well where there are people.

moss acts as a living substrate for hundreds of complex and interdependent organisms. Even dead sphagnum has a purpose: it sinks to the bottom of the bog, where it forms peat. A century ago peat was mined for use as a fuel; today it is bagged and sold to gardeners as a mulch. If left to compress and metamorphose for 200 million years, however, peat would become coal.

Eventually, cranberry bushes, ferns, and shrubs such as winterberry, a non-evergreen member of the holly family, will establish themselves on the bog's periphery and create nutrient-rich soil pockets around the bog and encroach on it. The bog will become a meadow over buried peat, ready to be invaded by trees. Grasses and common boreal plants move in first, including one-flowered wintergreen, so called to distinguish it from the more southerly spotted wintergreen, which bears two flowers. The northern white violet; twinflower, a member of the honeysuckle family; and starflower, which is a primrose, also adorn the cool woods.

LICHEN AND CARIBOU

If you look down on an expanse of boreal forest from a height of land, perhaps from the peak of a cliff overlooking a jagged river valley, the conifers' dark green mass appears shot through with the grays and blacks of gneiss and granite, and the whole is muted by a kind of bluish-green haze, as though an artist has set aside his palette knife and taken up a can of spray paint. The hazy effect is provided by lichens.

The northern woods are home to more than seven hundred species of lichens, a peculiar life-form that grows on trees, rocks, and fallen branches. Not all are blue-green; they vary in hue from gray and green to yellow and red. For centuries, botanists considered lichens to be a single plant form, but closer inspection has revealed a symbiotic relationship between two separate organisms: fungi and algae.

The fungus, lacking chlorophyll of its own, sinks its hyphillae—rootlike tendrils—into the alga's cells and takes advantage of the latter's ability to photosynthesize and produce sugar and other carbohydrates. It is less clear what the algae get out of the partnership. Although some 15,000 species of fungi have been identified as partners in the lichen dance, only 2 or 3 percent of all species

of algae are known to take part. There may be more, but most are too altered by their symbiotic associations to be identified individually. Some fungal-algal partnerships are mild cases of parasitism, with the fungi stealing food from the algae without actually killing them; others are more blatantly deadly, amounting to the algae contracting a life-sucking disease called fungi. But most lichens are successful, mutually profitable unions, in which the algae benefit from the fungi's superior ability to retain water and their structural support, which lifts the algae into sunlight part of the time and provides shade at others. Algae, after all, evolved in the ocean, where the problems of water retention and direct exposure to sunlight did not arise. Without their fungal partners, the algae found in lichen would not survive on land.

Lichen species found in the boreal forest enjoy a rich diversity of habitat. Each tree species is host to its own species of lichen, as is each type of rock, each mixture of gravel, and each kind of soil. Spruce and fir trees support a number of hair lichens, the kind that hang down in great, stringy masses. These include brittle horsehair lichen and pale-footed horsehair lichen on the spruces, as well as gray hair lichen on most conifers in the darker and moist regions of the forest and burred horsehair lichen on conifers in more open habitats. Common horsehair lichen is often found on birches. Two species of *Hypogymnia* lichens—large, greenish-gray lobed lichens that look like coral—most often grow on tree bark but are also found on rock or soil. Monk's-hood lichen and powder-headed tube lichen are usually found growing together on conifer twigs, or on birch or alder bark.

Several lichens are the principal food of the threatened woodland caribou. Various kinds of reindeer moss, which is actually lichen, cover the ground in the boreal regions. These include gray reindeer lichen, which is the true reindeer moss, and star-tipped reindeer lichen and black-footed reindeer lichen. The yellowish-green usnea—from which usnic acid, an important antibiotic, is extracted commercially—is eaten by caribou, as are pitted beard lichen and powdered beard lichen, which hang from spruce branches and, in the summer, are also used as nesting material by warblers and other birds.

Lichens grow extremely slowly. Some map lichens—the flat, splotchy lichens that spread on flat rocks and look like ancient sea charts—increase in size by less than 1 millimeter (about 1/25 of an inch) each year, advancing at a pace that makes large patches useful in dating glacier retreats: measure the radius of the patch, and its length in millimeters, expressed in years, tells you the age of the lichen. In the lower boreal forest, this slow growth has had severe consequences for the woodland caribou. Only in old-growth forests—that is, in forests aged 150 years or older—is monk's-hood gray horsehair lichen found in sufficient quantities to sustain caribou; the loss of old-growth boreal forest to lumberyards and paper mills, with the accompanying construction of access roads that also give access to hunters, has been a serious blow to the woodland caribou population.

FACING PAGE: Old man's beard, a hair lichen, drapes a spruce bough on one of Superior's Slate Islands.

Caribou are the most primitive of the deer family (Cervidae) and the only deer species in which both males and females always have antlers (only about one female white-tailed deer in a thousand has small, non-branching antlers). Woodland caribou are smaller than their northern tundra cousins but slightly bigger than white-tailed deer: adult males stand 1.1 to 1.2 meters (3.5 to 4 feet) high at the shoulder, and although they can weigh up to 270 kilograms (nearly 600 pounds), the average is closer to 180 (400 pounds); females average 115 to 125 kilograms (250 to 275 pounds). They once ranged over much of northeastern North America: in 1866, Major Ross King, author of *The Sportsman and Naturalist in Canada,* wrote that they were "common from Hudson Bay to the frontiers of Maine." But they were easily hunted. King related that "if one of the herd be shot dead, the sportsman being concealed from view, the remainder get quite bewildered and sometimes the whole herd falls to the rifle." In 1888 the season for woodland caribou was limited to three months, October to December, but by then the decline was already unstoppable. Now their range is limited exclusively to the northern boreal forest, and even there their numbers continue to decline.

FACING PAGE: A Slate Islands male woodland caribou takes a stand.

The caribou's living habits seem to dispose them to population instability. Unlike their northern counterparts, woodland caribou do not migrate from summer breeding to winter feeding grounds. When food in their home range is scarce, their only recourse is to reduce numbers by having fewer offspring. Nor do they congregate in large herds, which means that individuals are more vulnerable to predators. They move about their restricted ranges in small, family groups. The females take two and a half years to reach reproductive maturity (compared with 16 months for northern reindeer) and have only one calf per year.

Overhunting exacerbated a decline that had begun with the logging of the old-growth boreal forest in the early 1870s, when tamaracks and black spruces were cut to make railway ties, trestles, and bridges for the new Canadian Pacific Railway. Along the north shore of Lake Superior, 55 million railway ties were produced between 1875 and 1930. Even though a major infestation of the larch sawfly in the 1890s wiped out many of the boreal forest's tamaracks, by

1915 the Austin Nicholson Company of Chapleau, Ontario, was still producing 4,000 tamarack ties a day. The use of creosote, introduced in 1920, eased the pressure on tamarack by extending the ties' useful lives to twenty years instead of only seven.

By then, the pulp and paper industry had discovered the benefits of long-fibered spruce. In 1894 the Sault Ste. Marie Pulp and Paper Company received a license to cut spruce, tamarack, jack pine, and poplar anywhere within 5.6 kilometers (3.5 miles) inland from the shore of any lake or river from Sault Ste. Marie west. By the 1920s, American newspapers had bought and were harvesting huge tracts of Ontario's boreal forest, and more newsprint was being exported from Canada than from any other country in the world. While such commercial activity may have been good for the North Shore economy, it was not good for woodland caribou.

With the woodland caribou pushed out of its southern range, new species of large ungulates, more tolerant of cleared landscapes (and less dependent upon 150-year-old lichens), moved north. Farther south, white-tailed deer began to appear in the woodlands just below the boreal forest, while moose, which had always been in the boreal zone, were able to expand their territory beyond the wetlands. Today there are only about 12,000 woodland caribou left in the Great Lakes basin, mostly confined to offshore islands, such as the Slate Islands, and to Pukaskwa National Park, where the rocky terrain helps them to evade wolves.

THE BOREAL COMMUNITY

Despite its thin canopy and low productivity, the boreal zone is home to a range of smaller animals. The northern flying squirrel (*Glaucomys sabrinus*—*sabrinus* means "river nymph," a reference to the Severn River, which flows into Hudson Bay, where the species was first described by the zoologist George Shaw in 1801) is one of only two nocturnal members of the squirrel family (the other being the southern flying squirrel, which is not found north of Lake Huron) and so is rarely seen. Bigger than the southern flying squirrel, it is about 30 centimeters (1 foot) long and weighs up to 160 grams (4.9 ounces). Gray above with light buff-colored underparts, it has loose flight membranes that join the wrists of its forearms to the ankles of its hind feet. S.E. Woods Jr., in his *Squirrels of Canada*, called it "a red squirrel in a floppy grey overcoat." Flying squirrels nest in tree cavities created by northern flickers and three-toed woodpeckers, and they fill hollow trees with their droppings, which can be considerable since up to twenty flying squirrels will den together over the winter as a means of retaining body heat. They don't

FACING PAGE: The snowshoe hare's ten-year cycle drives the boom and bust of lynx and great horned owl populations, often forcing predators to forage farther south.

actually fly, of course: they soar from tree to tree, spreading their bodies like parasails and landing on their hind feet. They can glide up to 80 meters (260 feet) and make graceful, swooping turns; like bats, however, with loose skin encumbering their fore and hind legs, they are clumsy and slow on the ground. Because of their nocturnal habits, their natural predators are the nocturnal hunters, such as the great horned owl and the Canada lynx.

The great horned owl is a silent, efficient predator, the most powerful of all New World owls, including the larger great gray owl, which is also a boreal breeder. The great horned, sometimes called the cat owl because the feathery tufts on the top of its head resemble furry ears, preys on other birds as well as on most small mammals, including flying squirrels and skunks. (Except for turkey vultures and black vultures, birds have no sense of smell.) But its life cycle is geared to that of its most common prey, the snowshoe hare, the population of which collapses every ten years. Hudson Bay Company records of trade in hare show a remarkable ten-year consistency, with peak years falling on the half decade: 1875, 1885, 1895, and so on. In winters of abundance they can achieve astonishing numbers, up to 4,000 per square kilometer (10,000 per square mile). Five years after it peaks, the population crashes to equally astonishing lows—fewer than 1 per square kilometer—as the hares eat themselves into an empty pantry, and the remaining individuals are hunted by lynx and great horned and other owls.

Great horned owls have excellent day vision; their eyeballs are larger than ours. Musicians have noted that their eerie, nighttime calls—deep, muffled *hoo-hoodoo-hooo-hoos*—are delivered in the key of B-flat. They are not numerous, possibly because, as the explorer Samuel Hearne recorded in 1772, they are "easily shot" in the daytime, and "their flesh is delicately white, and nearly as good as a barn-door fowl; of course, it is much esteemed by the English and Indians." Perhaps the English came from Yorkshire, where owl soup was consumed as a cure for whooping cough.

Of the two smaller owls that frequent the boreal forest—the northern saw-whet owl and the boreal owl—only the boreal owl lives exclusively in the boreal forest. The boreal owl is tiny, about the size of a robin, and small enough to nest in tree cavities abandoned by three-toed woodpeckers. The call is a rather un-owl-like, high-pitched bell—Roger Tory Peterson notes that it sounds like the endless dripping of water: *ting-ting-ting-ting.* The female lays four to six eggs, and while she is incubating them, the male brings her food—rodents and sometimes, though rarely, other birds—which he catches at night with the aid of his incredibly sensitive ears. As in many owls, the ears, located on either side of the head, are not symmetrical; the right ear is much larger than the left, and the location of the tympanum, or eardrum, is higher on one side than on the other. In the boreal owl (and the closely related saw-whet owl), the difference is so pronounced as to render the skull slightly lopsided, but it allows the owls to hear in three dimensions and thus home in more accurately on the sounds of prey scurrying beneath snow.

When the snowshoe hare population collapses, predators such as the great grey owl and the Canada lynx range farther south in search of food, a phenomenon known as irruption. Overhunting by lynx was once thought to be the cause of hare fluctuations, but we now know that it's the other way around: crashes in the hare population lead to a delayed decline in the number of lynx. The name lynx, from the Greek word for *lamp*, refers to the feline's extraordinarily sharp night vision. Like all cats (and dogs, deer, and bottle-nose dolphins), lynx have a membrane in the eye, called a *tapetum lucidum,* which allows them to see in the dark. Inside the eyeball there are rods and cones, rods for black-and-white night vision and cones that distinguish color in daylight. Cats, being nocturnal hunters, have more rods than cones, and so can see more subtleties in the gray tones. In addition, the *tapetum lucidum* picks up light after it has passed through the rods and reflects it back, doubling the amount of light that reaches the retina.

A lynx resembles a large, fawn-colored, spotted cat with a stubby, black-tipped tail. Unlike domestic cats, however, it has a prominent facial ruff, black ear tips and two pointed fur tips on its chin, like a forked beard. An adult male can weigh up to 14 kilograms (30 pounds), females about 11 kilos (24 pounds), and both can live for

more than twenty years. A descendant of the slightly larger Eurasian lynx, which migrated to North America during the Pleistocene, it has adapted well to its present boreal environment. While the Eurasian lynx preyed on large ungulates, such as roe deer, the Canada lynx lives almost exclusively on snowshoe hare, although it has been known to take down white-tailed deer and even moose. Following the hare, lynx are generally found along riverbanks and in new-growth clearings. They have developed wide, furry paws that act as snowshoes, and they are more successful hunters in winter than in summer. Even so, the lynx population has declined drastically since colonial times: seventeenth-century records show that during peak years in the lynx's ten-year cycle (which follows that of snowshoe hare), lynx were seventy times more abundant than during the low years. Recent studies find the peak years only six times greater. For a year or two following snowshoe-hare troughs, lynx will irrupt into Minnesota, Wisconsin, and Michigan in search of food, but they are not resident in those states, and when the hare population in the north rebounds, lynx are no longer to be seen south of the boreal zone.

The bobcat, though closely related to the Canada lynx, is somewhat further removed from the Eurasian lynx line. It is smaller than the Canada lynx and more striped than spotted, and it lacks the lynx's long legs, wide paws, and flared facial ruff. It prefers more open and less snowy habitat and so is found much farther south, where it preys on cottontail rabbits rather than snowshoe hare. The bobcat also hunts birds—migrating sandhill cranes, among others—and small mammals. While it is still a distinctive boreal animal, the boreal forest is at the northern limit of its natural range.

Reduction of the boreal forest by logging has had far-reaching consequences for wildlife. According to a recent report published by Bird Studies Canada, the boreal forest provides breeding habitat for more than three hundred species of North American birds, including 80 percent of the waterfowl species that inhabit the Great Lakes basin, 63 percent of all finch species, and 53 percent of warblers. Many of these species either breed in the southern boreal zone or pass through it on their way north or south during spring and fall migrations. Altogether, the forest supports an estimated breeding population of up to 3 billion birds, more than 90 percent of which are migratory. The report expresses concern over the status of several species that have been declining in recent years because of habitat loss in their breeding areas: olive-sided flycatchers, rusty blackbirds, purple finches, nighthawks, and lesser scaup are all boreal species in decline, although there is some indication that the greater scaup and the lesser scaup are in trouble more because of high levels of selenium (a metalloid produced by the burning of fossil fuels) in the Great Lakes than because of habitat loss in the boreal forest.

Perhaps the most familiar denizen of the boreal forest is the irrepressible gray jay, one of the few North American jays that are not blue. It is mostly gray and, with its black cap and white neck ring, has been described as "an exaggerated chickadee." Because of its insolence and tendency to hang around human habitations pilfering food, especially meat, it is known variously as the moose bird, the camp robber, the butcher bird, the gut bird, and the venison heron. It is also called the whiskey jack or the whiskey john, a corruption of

FACING PAGE: The boreal owl, barely the size of a robin, can hear rodents scurrying for cover under deep snow.

its Cree name, *wis-ka-tjon*. Among the most graceful birds of the northern forest, gray jays will be observed swooping from tree to tree in family groups—the juveniles are almost as dark as crows, to which jays are closely related—sometimes following the hiker like silent woodland spirits. John James Audubon painted his pair of gray jays against a spray of white-oak leaves, but in the north they are most commonly found in conifers. There they build large, intricately woven nests of horsehair lichen and moss, which they bind with spider silk and insulate with fur and feathers—necessarily, perhaps, because they lay their clutch of three or four grayish-white, speckled eggs in February or March, when the snow is still deep. Like most jays and other nonmigrants, they are excellent food cachers, storing hundreds of mountain ash berries and insects under tree bark and on the undersides of branches, using their sticky saliva as an adhesive, and unerringly retrieving each one when it is wanted.

The range of the northern three-toed woodpecker just touches the north shore of Lake Superior. A medium-sized woodpecker, it sports black and white bars across its back and sides, much like a hairy woodpecker but without the white back, and the male has a yellow rather than red crown patch on its forehead. It shares much of its range with the black-backed woodpecker, which also has only three toes, although the two species are rarely seen together. As its name implies, the black-backed has no white on its back. Both birds nest in hollowed tree cavities, usually in coniferous trees, seldom more than 6 meters (20 feet) from the ground. Again, logging has seriously affected woodpecker habitat, as the birds depend on standing deadwood, which is most often found in old-growth stands, for their food and nesting sites.

Logging and mining have brought about drastic changes to the natural flora and fauna of Lake Superior's north shore. What was once a large-conifer-dominated forest has now shifted, with more deciduous species and smaller conifers filling the gaps, and the area's wildlife has adapted to reflect the altered habitat. Although it is one of the least populated regions of the Great Lakes basin, human activity has taken its toll here as elsewhere. Naturalist Percy Knauth has written that the southern reaches of the original, old-growth

FACING PAGE: With its large hind legs, thick coat, and ear tufts that amplify sound, the Canada lynx is perfectly adapted to life in the boreal forest.

boreal forest, a "vast and marvelous land of forest, lake and stream...exists as much in men's minds as it does on the North American continent." His words, once poetically true, unfortunately can be taken literally as well.

FOUR

THE GREAT LAKES– ST. LAWRENCE FOREST

IN *NATURE'S METROPOLIS,* A HISTORY of Chicago and its relationship to the natural landscape, William Cronon remarks that if, a century and a half ago, one had hiked up the west coast of Lake Michigan from Chicago to the Straits of Mackinac, a distance of 480 kilometers (300 miles), one would have cut through four radically different forest areas. The first would have been a long stretch of tall prairie grasses, virtually treeless but for a few isolated oaks. Then, somewhere around Milwaukee, the oak savanna would have given way to "a wetter and richer forest dominated by elms, basswoods and sugar maples." Near Sheboygan the forest would change again, this time to maples, hemlocks, and yellow birches, "the classic mixed-hardwood forest of northern Michigan, Wisconsin and Minnesota." Finally, at the top of the lake, approaching the heart of the north woods, would be "the enormous conifers, some well over a hundred feet tall, pushing airy crowns high above their deciduous neighbors."

These distinct growth areas have resulted from variations in soil types and weather patterns, but though they represent different ecoregions, they all belong to one forest regime: the Great Lakes–St. Lawrence forest, the most extensive forest in the Great Lakes basin. It is the western extension of the vast Northern Forest, which

FACING PAGE: This mix of hardwoods and conifers is typical of the transitional hardwood-boreal forest of the Haliburton Highlands of Ontario.

117

There is every variety of timber common to that zone, and an
ever-changing panorama unfolds itself along the River's course; the poplar
woods, with their bright trunks, restless fluttering leaves and lightly
shifting shadows; the tangled brakes of willows, ash or alders; the hard metallic
green of birch and maple; rich, grassy meadows and purple fen-lands;
the cloistered, brooding calm of towering pines.

GREY OWL, *Tales of an Empty Cabin,* 1936

stretches from Maine on the Atlantic coast, over the Adirondacks in Vermont and New Hampshire, across New York, Ohio, Michigan, and Minnesota in the west, and Quebec and Ontario in the north. The original forest was the mighty engine that drove New World colonization and commerce, that gave New England and the Great Plains pioneers their houses, buggies, barns, and churches, provided European ships with their masts and spars, and allowed English, Scottish, and Irish settlers their log houses and rail fences. Where it is intact, it remains one of the last major North American forests, home to more than 250 species of land vertebrates, 150 kinds of fish, 55 species of waterfowl, and more than 300 species of songbirds. Where it passes through the Great Lakes watershed, it is also the home of more than 40 million human beings.

So large is the Great Lakes–St. Lawrence forest that it encompasses six of the eight ecoregions that fall within the Great Lakes basin. Two transition zones between the boreal and Great Lakes–St. Lawrence forests, where balsam firs and white birches share habitat with sugar maples and yellow birches, divide the northern basin: the Western Great Lakes Forests ecoregion west and south of Lake Superior, and the Eastern Forest–Boreal Transition ecoregion above Lake Huron and down into the Algonquin Highlands. It also includes the transitional areas between the limestone-based forests of southern Ontario and the Shield-based Algonquin Highlands, sometimes known as "the Land Between." The Eastern Great Lakes Lowlands Forests ecoregion, with its warmer annual temperatures and higher rainfall, wraps red maples and eastern hemlock stands around the eastern end of Lake Ontario and up the Niagara Escarpment to Manitoulin Island. The Allegheny Highlands Forests ecoregion, south of Lake Ontario, is another transition zone, this time with the Carolinian forest. The Carolinian reaches north into southwestern Ontario, part of the Southern Great Lakes Forests ecoregion. Here the forest is almost all deciduous, except for stands of red and white cedars along the stream banks and in the swamplands. And lastly there is the Upper Midwest Forest—Savanna Transition ecoregion, the low, dry land of prairie grasses with oak, maple, and basswood clusters west of Lake Michigan where less than 5 percent of the forest remains intact. All six habitats share tree and animal species, although each makes up its own assemblages, according to its distinctive soil type and climate.

White pines, once "the lords of the north country," were all but extirpated by nineteenth-century logging.

The Great Lakes—St. Lawrence forest is a diverse and delicately balanced biological realm. In the central Great Lakes—St. Lawrence forest there are four major hardwoods and three conifers: sugar maple, American beech, yellow birch, and American basswood are the common deciduous species. The softwoods are eastern hemlock, eastern white cedar, and, especially in the regions near the top of the Lakes, eastern white pine. Most of these species are still present in great numbers, but the white pine has been so thoroughly harvested that it requires considerable detective work to find significant stands of it older than second or third growth. A century ago, however, as Cronon reminds us, they were "the lords of the north country."

THE AGE OF PINE

When Newfoundlanders say "fish" they mean cod; when settlers in the Lakes basin said "tree" they meant eastern white pine. White pines moved into the Great Lakes region about 12,500 years ago, during a brief period of global cooling known as the Younger Dryas, one of several periodic cooling events brought on by the melting glaciers but too localized and mild to be called true ice ages.

EASTERN WHITE PINE

Lasting a thousand years, the Younger Dryas saw sudden, immense gushes of fresh, cold water alter the direction of natural drainage in eastern North America. Instead of flowing south into the Mississippi Valley, meltwater was redirected along the St. Lawrence into the North Atlantic, blunting the warming influence of the Gulf Stream and allowing coastal cold air from the east to move inland. Temperate southern hardwoods such as maples, oaks, and ashes made room for the more cold-tolerant spruces, firs, larches, and pines that edged down from the north, thereby creating a mixed deciduous-conifer forest. When the planet warmed again and the glaciers retreated, the deciduous species had no need to move back south and the conifers stayed, too. Indeed, eastern white pines thrived in their new setting. Beneath their dense canopies, the environment remained cool and damp even when temperatures rose elsewhere. A forest, like a city, creates its own microclimate.

White pine is eastern North America's answer to the towering redwoods and Douglas-firs of the West Coast. Soaring 60 meters (200 feet) into the air, with a circumference at chest height of nearly 4 meters (13 feet) in mature specimens, in closed stands its trunk rises two-thirds of its height before spreading its first branches.

Above that, the crown is columnar rather than tapered, and the cones form at the top. An easy way to identify white pine is to look at the long needles; they are arranged in sprays of five, one for each letter of the word *white*.

When settlers first came to the Great Lakes, huge stands of white pine dominated major parts of the landscape in Michigan, Minnesota, Wisconsin, and Ontario. Their interlaced canopies formed a thick, continuous ceiling broken only where wind had leveled one of the shallow-rooted giants. Otherwise, the trees lived up to five hundred years and created a ground terrain so dark and dense that entering it was like being ushered into a hushed, many-columned cathedral. Traveling through it was not difficult since the trees grew some distance apart, there was almost no understory, and the lowest branches were high overhead. In an old-growth forest, however, windfalls, fallen branches, and exposed roots were common and all meant arduous cutting. The trees were so immense that individual settlers couldn't log them commercially. Although some were felled and hand-hewn for local construction, many at first were simply chopped down and burned to make way for farmland, even though the ground beneath the pines was often too sandy and acidic for agriculture. It was thought, erroneously, that ash from the burning forest would enrich the soil.

Commercial logging of the great pines began in the American colonies before the revolution. The first mill in the New World was built at York, Maine, in 1623. There had been some limited logging in Canada, particularly in Quebec, before 1700, to supply masts and spars to France and the West Indies. But after the British conquest of New France in 1759, business picked up sharply as the British navy became more avid for timber than the French had been. In 1763, General James Murray, Canada's first governor general under British rule, was instructed to set aside forest reserves in all townships, with the best "Quebec yellow-pines" (eastern white pines) stamped with "the King's Broad Arrow" for the specific use of the British navy. Similar measures were imposed upon the American colonies. Crown land reserves in New England infuriated the lumbermen as much as the tax on tea outraged the citizens of Boston

OVERLEAF: A black spruce stands out among white birch on Pictured Rocks National Lakeshore, Michigan.

and have been cited as an equal spark igniting the revolution. The Continental Congress stopped the export of pine masts to England in 1774, and it was not for nothing that the emblem on the first flag of the revolutionary forces was an eastern white pine.

The United Empire Loyalists, who remained loyal to the British Crown and moved to Canada after the revolution, brought commercial logging with them. The first timber raft sent to Quebec from Lake Ontario left the Bay of Quinte in 1790, having been put together by a Loyalist, Samuel Sherwood. This was the start of a huge enterprise that received added impetus from the Napoleonic Wars in Europe, which cut off Britain's supply of Scotch pine from the Baltic. By 1810, British North America was supplying the mother country with 50,000 shiploads of square-cut timber a year, for a total value of $400,000, a trade that continued to increase annually even after the defeat of Napoleon. Here's one way to comprehend how much white pine was being logged in Canada: lumber companies paid an annual ground rent of $1 per square mile (39 cents per square kilometer) of timberland, and in 1861 the Crown recorded revenues from ground rents of $327,503. Here's another: in that same year, 1861, 3-inch (7.5-centimeter) sawn lumber shipped to the United States sold for $5 per thousand board feet (a measure whose value has changed over time); revenues that year totaled $8,693,638. Two-thirds of all the timber sold was white pine, the rest being either red pine or oak. In 1866, sawmills in southern Ontario's Peterborough County alone produced 50 million board feet of lumber for export to the United States.

J.W. Bond, in *Minnesota and Its Resources* (1854), a book written to entice settlers to the grasslands of the Midwest, predicted that "centuries will hardly exhaust the pineries above us." Barely fifty years later, white pines of marketable size were gone from most of the Great Lakes basin. So thoroughly had they been logged that in most areas not enough mature trees remained to propagate. Large stands were found only in Minnesota and northwestern Ontario, west of Duluth and Fort William (now Thunder Bay), outside of the basin. Since most of the rivers in that region were unsuitable for floating logs to Lake Superior, logging railroads were built into the interior, where the last pure stands of red and white pine were hold-

RED PINE

ing out. The first railroad in Minnesota was built in 1886 to get at the tall pines; by 1900 there were thousands of kilometers of track, and pine logs were hauled to lakeshore towns such as Knife River, Two Harbors, Beaver Bay, and Grand Marais, where they were boomed and towed down the lake by tugboat to sawmills in Duluth; Ashland, Wisconsin; and Baraga, Michigan. Railroads greatly increased the lumber companies' output because, unlike rivers, they ran year-round and could carry hardwood logs that didn't float. In 1900, trains hauled 3 million board feet of pine to Duluth every day. By 1910, the trees were all but gone from the Northwest as well, the railways were abandoned and their rails sold for scrap metal.

From a natural history point of view, nearly extirpating pine from the basin was an ecological disaster. Henry David Thoreau noticed that oak seedlings grew much better in ground under pine trees than they did under oak trees. "Notwithstanding that the acorns are produced by oaks and not by pines, the fact is that there are comparatively few seedling oaks (one foot or less in height) under the oaks but thousands under the pines (pitch and white)." Removing the pines threatened to wipe out the oaks as well, and oaks are now much less common than they once were. Cutting the tall pines also had consequences for the ecosystem. Sunlight suddenly reached the ground and warmed the rivers, encouraging the growth of deciduous trees and altering the habitat of spawning fish. Wind blowing over cleared land dried and eroded the sandy soil, while spring runoff leached nutrients from earth no longer held firm by tree roots. Farmers drained their wetlands and hauled the rich, black earth onto their fields in an effort to restore the soil, but still it dried up and blew or washed away.

By the second decade of the twentieth century the age of pine, with the prosperity it had brought to the young Great Lakes economy, was at an end.

YELLOW BIRCH

OTHERS IN THE MIX

The deciduous trees that mingled with the conifers at the end of the Younger Dryas include the yellow birch, now one of the keystone trees of the Great Lakes–St. Lawrence forest and its transition zone with the boreal. The naturalist John Burroughs remarked that the Catskills range of New York ought to have been called the Birch Mountains, "as on their summits birch is the prevailing tree." Also called silver birch, it was once the largest hardwood in the forest; early settlers reported individual trees 30 meters (100 feet) high and 1.2 meters (4 feet) in diameter at chest height, although the average height today is closer to 20 meters (65 feet). In the transition zone, along the Algoma Highlands, the yellow birch is even smaller, rarely reaching higher than 12 meters (40 feet). Its favored location is in rich, moist soil on south-facing valley slopes. In the south it grows with other hardwoods such as beeches, maples, and basswoods; in the north, or in cooler, wetter, southern lowlands, it is found with such conifers as eastern hemlock and white and red spruce.

Yellow birch is easily distinguished from white birch by its bark: young yellow birches are more yellowish and, when mature, have dark reddish or brownish bark. Although it may appear to be peeling (defoliating) from the trunk, yellow birch bark cannot be stripped off in large swatches, as the bark of white birch famously can. The toothed leaves are oval, about 10 centimeters (4 inches) long and 5 centimeters (2 inches) wide, heart-shaped at the stem and tapering to a point at the distal end, with twelve or more pairs of veins extending from a central rib out to the edges. They are yellowish-green above and paler green and downy below.

Height notwithstanding, yellow birch has never been a great eye-catcher compared with the more majestic oaks, elms, and maples. Donald Culross Peattie notes that "tall as it may grow, it somehow manages to melt inconspicuously into the great forest mass; it does not shine forth like its relative the Paper Birch, save in autumn when it shows its rich, clear foliage." Yellow birch wood was prized for boat building and furniture making; it is hard, clear, and water resistant, and in its southern range is still cut in great quantities for interior trim and veneer. Writing in the 1960s, Peattie reported that 145 million board feet a year was being cut, mainly in the threatened Vermont and New Hampshire forests.

The white birch, also called paper or canoe birch, belongs to all three forest regimes in the Great Lakes basin; indeed, it grows right

WHITE BIRCH

across the continent in virtually every climate and habitat. It resembles the yellow birch in size and leaf design, but its bark is much lighter in color and is easily peeled from the trunk. Native people from Newfoundland to British Columbia used this bark for myriad purposes: as sheathing for their lodges and canoes, and as clothing, the pieces sewn together with peeled tamarack roots. The Algonquins made moose calls and even cooking vessels from it; they used shredded bark to light their fires, then boiled water by dropping heated stones into birch bark pots.

White birch grows wherever there is moisture and cool soil, and since it likes a lot of light when young, it is one of the few trees that have become more numerous since colonial times, having replaced the white pines and spruces in much of the Great Lakes area. Its brilliant white trunk stands out sharply against the dark green cedars and hemlocks surrounding the smaller satellite lakes. It is a short-lived tree, however, rarely lasting longer than forty to sixty years, and though technically a hardwood, it rots quickly on the forest floor, donating its nutrients to the soil.

The eastern white cedar is a cousin of the gigantic western red cedar. Neither is a true cedar—no North American cedar is; true cedars, such as cedar of Lebanon, are Asiatic species. Nor should eastern white cedar be confused with eastern red cedar, a member of the juniper branch of the cypress family. Suffice to say that all North American cedars, including the junipers, are members of the cypress family.

The strippable bark of the white birch has been put to many uses, from lodge and canoe coverings to material for moose calls and cooking pots.

White cedar grows to a considerable height in moist areas as well as in those of dry, limestone bedrock—the average is 14 meters (45 feet), but it can reach 24 meters (80 feet) in wet ground. It is the cedar that sprouts out of impossibly tiny cracks on the rocky islands of Georgian Bay and clings to the side of the Niagara Escarpment, where it grows so slowly that a trunk the size of a person's forearm can be eight hundred years old. It is also the cedar that grew in a swamp behind my childhood home near Barrie, Ontario, standing in water most of the year. White cedars were cut and split by the earliest settlers for fence rails. The trees can live for two hundred years, and the rails, which are still in use in zigzag fences along country roads, have lasted almost as long.

The only other cedar that grows naturally in the Great Lakes region is the related juniper, eastern red cedar, which is a transitional tree with the more southerly Carolinian forest. White and red cedars can be distinguished by their needles: red cedar needles are rounded, while those of the white cedar are flat, as though pressed by an iron. Also, red cedar berries are blue, reminiscent of juniper; white cedars do not have berries at all, but small, brown cones. Red cedar is one of the most widely distributed conifers in eastern North America; in the Deep South it is called *bâton rouge* in French and inspired the name for the capital of Louisiana. The cedar waxwing, one of the most beautiful birds of the eastern forest, with its black eye mask and backswept crest, was named for its fondness for the fruit and even the sap of the red cedar; *waxwing* refers to the bright red, waxlike

The red squirrel, a small but bellicose citizen of the conifer forest, noisily defends its territory against potential seed thieves.

secretions from its secondary wing feather shafts which reminded some observers of sealing wax.

The low, bushlike common juniper also grows in open rocky areas. Seldom more than 1.5 meters (4.5 feet) high, it has short, spiked needles with a bluish-white stripe down the middle and branches that ascend stiffly, usually without a leader. Juniper "berries"—the round, blue buds of juniper plants that are used to flavor gin and in fact give gin its name (*genièvre* in French)—are not berries but rather the female cones in their third season. Catharine Parr Traill and her sister, Susanna Moodie, picked them to add to venison and other game dishes, and many cooks still do.

EASTERN RED CEDAR

The eastern hemlock is a dominant conifer in the Great Lakes–St. Lawrence forest and is also found in the Carolinian zone, although it is becoming rare that far south. A tall conifer that grows well on rocky outcrops, especially on north-facing slopes, it has reddish-brown bark that was once used as a source of tannin in the leather trade. Pioneers in the basin made tea from its flat needles and brooms from its branches. The needles are eaten by white-tailed deer, and porcupines climb out to its branch tips and spend all night munching on young spring growth. A stand of healthy looking hemlock stunted at the tops is a sign that a family of porcupines has moved into the area.

Since the beginning of urban development and commercial forestry in the early nineteenth century, the area of land in the basin covered by the Great Lakes–St. Lawrence forest has been reduced by 40 percent and been altered dramatically in composition. When the pine-maple-oak forests disappeared, they were replaced by fast-growing aspens and birches (where they were not replaced by farms and shopping malls). Since presettlement days, the pine forest has declined by 78 percent; in the same period, the aspen-birch forest has increased by nearly 85 percent.

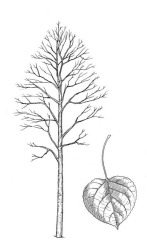

TREMBLING ASPEN

Aspens are members of the poplar family, and two are native to the Great Lakes region. Trembling or quaking aspen is the most widely distributed tree on the continent, which means it can grow in almost any soil type or location. It prefers sandy or gravelly, well-drained sunny slopes and fine-textured soils derived from either igneous rock, in its more northerly reaches, or limestones. It can grow to 15 meters (50 feet), with a rounded crown composed of toothed leaves that are shiny green on top and dull green underneath; because of the flattened profile of the leaf stem, when the wind shakes the tree, the leaves whisper and flash in the sun.

The bigtooth aspen grows in the Great Lakes–St. Lawrence forest and southward; it is slightly taller than trembling aspen (18 meters, or about 60 feet) but with a narrower crown. Its leaves are duller and more elongated, and the teeth are larger and rounder. Both aspens have smooth, greenish-gray bark and narrow trunks. Aspens propagate readily by cloning, with whole, single-sex stands sprouting from a single rootstock. (One male colony of trembling aspens in Utah covers 9 hectares, or 17 acres; its root is estimated to be more than a million years old, which would make it the world's largest and oldest living organism.) In the east, colonies can consist of thousands of trees connected by a network of roots underlying up to 80 hectares (200 acres). The trees can also reproduce in early spring by means of seeds that grow on mouse-colored, 6-centimeter (2.5-inch) catkins, males and females on separate trees. The fruit matures in late summer. Beavers cut aspens primarily for food (aspen is their favorite food tree) and for dam-making material. When Europeans first arrived in the Great Lakes basin, one of the first features they noticed was the extent of the area's wetlands that had been "artificially" created by beavers. They thus had two motives for ridding the area of these fur-bearing, industrious rodents.

DENS AND DENIZENS

The beaver is the mammal most associated with the central forested area of the Great Lakes basin. Large, semiaquatic rodents that feed on tree bark, they prefer aspens, but they will also eat apple and cherry bark and that of birches, willows, balsams, and cottonwoods. Beavers are well engineered for life in water: they have three separate eyelids, one of which is transparent so they can see underwater. Their nostrils are valved, and their lips close behind their large front teeth, enabling them to swim while transporting cut branches to their lodges. Unique among mammals, they have

FACING PAGE: White cedar twists through sedimentary rock on Flowerpot Island, near Tobermory, Ontario.

a birdlike cloaca—one vent for reproduction, excretion, and scent marking—that can be closed tightly in water to prevent heat loss. They are also the only mammal whose growth is indeterminate: beavers never stop growing. The heaviest beaver on record was trapped in Wisconsin, weighing 50 kilograms (110 pounds); the average for an adult male is about half that.

To maintain insulation and waterproofing, beavers clean and re-oil their fur with a double nail on each of their hind feet.

In spring, beavers eat the roots of aquatic plants, primarily water lilies and bulrushes. In the fall, they stockpile woody branches underwater to provide a cache of winter food. They feed and build their lodges in water for safety reasons, and in order to maintain water levels they build dams on creeks, causing wide-scale flooding

The "stately elm" is more than a poetic figure of speech; quiet lanes lined with first-class white or American elms were once the symbol of the American small town, and individual elms were famous. George Washington is said to have taken command of the Continental Army beneath the Elm of Cambridge Common, Massachusetts, and the Markham Elm in Avon, New York, was over 15 meters (nearly 50 feet) in girth and 654 years old when it died in 1950. One giant specimen in Pennsylvania measured 43 meters (140 feet) high when cut and yielded nearly 9,000 board feet of lumber.

The popularity of elm wood was as high as the desire for elm-lined streets, and European elms were imported to meet the demand. Unfortunately, a load of English elms shipped to Ohio in 1930 contained the beetle-borne fungus *Ophiostoma ulmi,* the cause of Dutch elm disease (DED), an affliction that clogs the trees' xylem, or woody tissue, and interferes with its water delivery system. Although some native elms showed resistance to DED, millions died and fears of elm extinction were widespread.

The American elm was once synonymous with main-street North America.

In the 1970s, Henry Kock, an arborist at the University of Guelph, Ontario, began collecting cuttings from isolated DED-resistant elms in that province and cultivating them at the university's renowned arboretum. The university now has more than 600 DED-resistant saplings in cold storage, and a field in the arboretum with dozens of more mature trees. Each year, the saplings are injected with DED fungus, and those that prove to be immune are transplanted to the field. When field trees are five to seven years old, they are moved again, this time to a grove in which the trees are able to cross-pollinate, a process that Kock called "the Dating Service for Lonely Elms."

"In ten to fifteen years," says Sean Fox, the arborist in charge of the Elm Recovery Project since Kock's death in 2005, "these will be ready to reproduce. In a hundred years, we'll have a resistant elm grove, which will look beautiful."

and creating important wetland environments. Their fur is thick and lush, a combination of short underfur (about 2 centimeters or 0.8 inches long), so fine and dense that it provides insulation from cold and waterproofing, topped by long, dark guard hairs (6 centimeters or 2.5 inches in length). The hairs of the underfur are barbed, which makes them ideal for making felt.

Beaver were trapped for their pelts and traded from the beginning of the settlement era. By 1635 they were disappearing from the Montreal area, and trappers were forced to venture westward and northward for furs, extending the trade into the Great Lakes. In 1675, New France was exporting 41,000 kilograms (90,000 pounds) of beaver pelts annually (one pelt weighed between 700 to 900 grams, or 1.5 to 2 pounds). By 1685 that number had leapt to 64,000 kilograms (140,000 pounds), and by the end of the century it was 136,000 kilograms (300,000 pounds). It is estimated that before European contact there were about 10 million beavers in North America; in the last quarter of the seventeenth century, 25 percent of them had been harvested.

The beaver was the ideal animal upon which to base an economy. It doesn't migrate or hibernate, is slow and awkward on land, and lives in lodges 6 meters (20 feet) across containing up to ten animals of various generations. Hunters had merely to smash into the lodge roof and pluck them out. And beaver fur was in strong demand for hats. For a while it seemed that every hat in Europe was made from beaver felt; indeed, in 1679, France passed a law making it illegal to make hats from anything else, or even to make the small hats known as *demi-castors*.

The decline of the Great Lakes fur trade began in the 1670s. By that time, the search for furs had expanded well beyond the Lakes. Montreal voyageurs would paddle to Michilimackinac or Grand Portage, at the junction of Lakes Superior, Michigan, and Huron, to meet convoys coming down through Superior with furs procured as far away as Lake Winnipeg and the Saskatchewan River, and from the Mississippi region in the south. But the quality of these western and southern furs was poor: they were lighter in color with thick skins, when the market wanted dark winter fur with thin skins. The prized pelts came from the north, from the Hudson Bay area, which was controlled by the English.

Furthermore, the trade was at the mercy of European fashion, and then as now nothing remained in style for long. Declining fur quality coincided with a drop in demand; by 1699, hatmakers in Europe were mixing beaver fur with rabbit, and when the trend shifted to smaller hats, the ban on demi-castors was lifted. Then, during the War of the Spanish Succession, 1700–1713, no beaver fur at all was imported from North America; hats were made with *laine de vigogne,* hair from a species of Peruvian llama. The beaver, saved by the whims of eighteenth-century tastes, has made a significant comeback, and in wilderness areas it is now almost as numerous as it was before settlement times.

The muskrat is closely related to the beaver, though smaller; both males and females weigh less than 1.4 kilograms (3 pounds). Like the beaver's, the muskrat's coat is well adapted to life in the water, with a thick underfur and long, glossy guard hairs; its feet are webbed and its tail somewhat flattened and hairless. It will exhibit similar behavior to its cousin, but it doesn't build dams or eat woody materials. It burrows into river and lake banks and builds lodges in the water at the mouth of its den. Where there are no hospitable banks, muskrats make lodges in the centers of ponds or wetlands, using reeds and cattails piled into a mound and plastered with mud. When beavers were scarce, muskrat coats became popular in Europe, where the fur was known first as Hudson seal and later as musquash, from the Algonquin word for the animal, *mussascus,* meaning "swamp dweller." Today, muskrat is a more important fur export than beaver, with nearly 8 million animals trapped annually.

The porcupine is the continent's second-largest rodent after the beaver. Descended from South American forest dwellers, porcupines are adapted for climbing high into the canopy; their hind feet have long, hooked claws and an extremely thick, fleshy pad that allows them to clamp tightly to small branches. But their most obvious feature is their quills, which have developed from hair into stiff, barbed defensive weapons. Each quill is up to 10 centimeters (4 inches) long, with an antibiotic coating in case the animal is pierced by one of its own quills while climbing or fighting off other males during the fall mating season. Females come into heat for only twelve hours, and so competition can be fierce and noisy. Porcupines can't throw their quills, but they can swing their tails with real force. They will advertise their offensive intentions with a strong odor, and the quills themselves contain a fluorescent material that makes the animal appear to glow at night. Because it is a nocturnal creature, that is when it is most likely to run into predators or rival males.

The red squirrel is another creature of the pine, spruce, or hemlock forest. A small rodent with a buff eye ring, reddish pelt, and a short red tail that curls to only halfway up its back, the red squirrel is extremely territorial: its insistent chattering tells everyone, especially other red squirrels, to go away. Unlike gray squirrels, red squirrels store all their winter food supply in one place, usually in a tree hollow, and then guard their caches with their lives. Gray squirrels, on the other hand, bury nuts and seeds individually, so that if an intruder finds one or two, its entire supply isn't threatened. Red squirrels live on pine seeds in the winter—they sit on stumps or low tree branches and drop the discarded cone bracts onto large piles, or middens, at the bases of their trees—and in the spring they eat the new buds of pine and other conifers. With the decline of the eastern white pines, the red squirrel was pushed northward into the transitional and boreal zones, leaving the southern territories to gray squirrels, which are naturally residents of the more southerly mixed deciduous forest. In the Ontario and Quebec portions of the forest, black squirrels appear to outnumber the gray, but black is simply one of several color phases of the species. Gray squirrels come in many colors, including brown, reddish-brown, blond, black, and white. The town of Olney, Illinois, is known for its albino gray squirrels.

THE BIRDS

The pine siskin, a small, olive-brown-striped bird that resembles a goldfinch, is primarily a bird of the boreal forest but is a common winter visitor to the Great Lakes–St. Lawrence region. Its breeding range reaches down to a line drawn from the western end of Lake

FACING PAGE: Flocks of cedar waxwings are often driven south in search of food, a phenomenon known as irruption.

Isle Royale, a 544-square-kilometer (210-square-mile) island in western Lake Superior, is the site of the world's longest-running predator-prey study, begun in 1958 by researchers at Purdue University, Indiana, and still carried on at Michigan Technical University. The focus of attention is the intertwined survival of moose and wolves in this relatively isolated environment.

Moose first swam to the island in 1905 and flourished until a crash in their principal food source—balsam fir—reduced their numbers to a few mating pairs in 1935. A major fire the next year regenerated the forest and the moose, and by the time the first gray wolves crossed the ice from Ontario in the winter of 1949, the moose herd was healthy and numerous.

Wolves now hunt the island in three separate packs, totaling around 21 animals. They usually confine themselves to killing young or elderly moose, because hardy adults can easily fight off a marauding wolf pack. One male held off a pack for three days before the wolves tired and moved on. A plague of canine parvovirus reduced the wolf population on the island from fifty in 1980 to thirteen in 1993, and moose numbers soared: by 1994 there were 2,400, far more than the island could support.

An infestation of winter ticks in 1996 reduced the moose population to 1,200, and a second wave in 2002 cut moose numbers to 900. Ticks attach themselves to a moose's hide and draw blood meals; one adult moose was found to have more than 50,000 ticks. The resulting blood and hair loss often causes moose to die of exposure during the winter, which can bring deep snowfalls and temperatures below -40°C (-40°F).

Even with ticks, cold weather, and a loss of genetic variability (since all the animals are descended from a few individuals), both moose and wolf populations on Isle Royale are thriving, proving that predator-prey dynamics, although far from being a static relationship, work themselves out in the absence of human intervention.

Ontario to Georgian Bay. The pine grosbeak, on the other hand, probably never felt at home in the southern pine forests in summer, but it too is a regular visitor in winter. A burly, heavy finch with a large, seed-cracking beak, a reddish body and head (for the males; the females' heads are mustard-colored), and black wings with white bars, it nests in summer in northern coniferous trees 3 to 4.5 meters (10 to 15 feet) from the ground. In winter it prefers to frequent deciduous trees, especially white and mountain ashes, which keep their fruit throughout the winter. The pine grosbeak is distantly related to the Eurasian bullfinch, one of which is thought to have blown to North America across the North Pacific some 12 million years ago.

All of the warblers found in the Great Lakes–St. Lawrence forest are migrants. About half fly through the basin in spring on their way to their boreal breeding grounds, and in the fall they head south to their wintering regions in the Caribbean and Latin America. The other half nest in the Great Lakes–St. Lawrence forest. The pine warbler, for example, nests exclusively in pines. In its northern range in the Great Lakes basin it will nest in red and pitch pines if white pines are absent, but the loss of the great pineries has undoubtedly sent pine warbler populations into severe decline. Other warblers that breed south of the boreal forest include the Canada warbler and the northern waterthrush, which spends much of its time on the ground, foraging under damp leaf litter for insects, worms, and small snails.

Birds that are more comfortable in deciduous and mixed forests now dominate the Great Lakes–St. Lawrence zone. Of the twenty species that come to our feeder north of Kingston, Ontario, during the winter, the three most common are blue jays, black-capped chickadees, and slate-colored juncos, all birds of mixed woodlands. The junco, a sparrow-sized bird with a black cowl that extends to midchest, is found across northern North America and breeds in the upper Great Lakes states—Minnesota, Wisconsin, and Michigan—as well as Ontario.

Black-capped chickadees are North American members of the tit family. Tits with crests are called titmice (or, some insist,

titmouses), and tits with black caps and bibs are called chickadees, a close approximation to their signal call. They are permanent residents of their home ranges, with an alpha-male-and-female pair that will dominate the feeding stations—including caches of insects hidden under loose bark and in curled leaves—of their central nesting sites. Chickadees dig out nesting cavities in punky trees and line them with moss, or take over holes excavated by flickers or woodpeckers. Although they prefer insects and perform amazing acrobatic feats to extract them from branch tips, in winter they eat oily meats such as sunflower seeds, holding the seeds tightly

against a branch with one foot while expertly pecking them open.

The blue jay is a colorful rogue, not as bold around humans as the gray jay but equally intelligent. When predators are about—merlins or sharp-shinned hawks—every bird in the vicinity remains in hiding until the blue jays come out and give the all-clear with a call that the nineteenth-century ornithologist Alexander Wilson described as the squeaking of a rusty wheelbarrow. Blue jays have been observed in laboratory experiments making use of tools, such as feathers, paper clips, and lengths of straw, to rake food toward their cages. In the wild, they are short-distance migrants found only in North America, which involves them in one of history's most fascinating questions: how much information did Europeans have about North America before Christopher Columbus? The earliest known depiction of a blue jay is found on a decorative panel of the hand-illuminated manuscript of *Les très riches heures,* a breviary produced in France for the Duc de Berry in 1409.

A female moose emerges from Kawagama Lake, in central Ontario. Shallow lakes provide safety from wolves, water plants for food, and a welcome escape from blackflies in spring.

PREDATORS AND PREY

The word *moose* comes from the animal's Algonquin name, *moos,* which means eater of twigs. It is North America's largest ungulate, or hoofed animal, next to the bison, and the largest member of the deer family. The males weigh up to 800 kilograms (1,750 pounds) and stand 2.3 meters (7.5 feet) tall at the shoulder. In the Great

Lakes basin, moose are common in the boreal forest but are also found in great numbers around Lakes Superior and Huron. It is distinguished from other deer (including elk) not only by the size and shape of its antlers—which are more palmate and less tined than those of other cervids—but also by the size and complexity of its nose. The moose's nose is large, flat, and wide, and intricately honeycombed with muscle and sinew, apparently an adaptation to submersion while the animal eats water plants. Also unusual is its habit of foraging for food in water up to its belly in "moose pastures." Ecologists label such areas "pulse-stabilized ecosystems," periodically but regularly flooded riparian wetlands that contain mineral-rich forage plants such as willows, aspens, dogwoods, sedges, and forbs. Moose do not browse the tips of aquatic plants, but pull them up by the roots to eat the new, nutritious growth at the base.

Moose evolved sharing the same habitat as woodland caribou and, because of their size, were able to inhabit areas with deeper snow and colder temperatures than white-tailed deer, to whom they are closely related. This was fortunate, since white-tailed deer carry an internal parasitic nematode, the meningeal worm, a tiny organism with a complicated life cycle. As an adult it lives and lays its eggs in the meninges, the lining between the brain and skull. The eggs travel to the lungs, where they hatch. The larvae are then coughed up in the mouth and swallowed by the deer, to be eventually excreted in the animal's feces. The larvae hook themselves into ground slugs and snails, where they continue to mature for three weeks. Other cervids eat the slugs and snails, and so the parasite enters a new host, traveling from the stomach into the bloodstream and then up the spinal column to the meninges, where the cycle repeats itself.

Although meningeal worms are found in much of North America's white-tailed deer population, the deer are not adversely affected by them. In caribou, elk, and moose, however, they cause serious damage. Moose are especially susceptible, which may be why they are such solitary animals; although males occasionally congregate in small groups during the spring, before their antlers are quite formed, they spend most of their time alone, and the females remain with their yearlings only until the fall rutting season. Symptoms of meningeal worm infection begin with a weakening of the hind legs, resulting in clumsiness, walking in circles, loss of hair, hypermetria (abnormal high-stepping), eventual lameness and blindness, and death. Those who have spotted a "ghost moose" in the dark coniferous woods are haunted by the image of the doomed animal's pale, hairless skin.

Primarily because of their ability to inhabit a variety of habitats and eat a wider range of vegetation—and their ability to tolerate human disturbances—white-tailed deer have the southern portions of the Great Lakes–St. Lawrence forest to themselves. With their small hooves and thin coats, they are unsuited to life much farther north, where deep snow and boggy terrain make them easy prey to wolves. Deer rely on camouflage as their primary defense: the young (often two fawns but sometimes one or three, depending on food availability during winter pregnancy) are light brown with white spots. In cases of multiple birth, the fawns are born separately, in different birthing sites, and remain in place for several days while the nursing mother travels from one to another. After a few weeks they are strong enough to follow her about, and they may stay with her for up to four years before establishing their own territory. Deer can usually outrun predators, jumping over fallen logs to slow their pursuers. The familiar flagging of their white tails is not a warning to other deer of danger nearby, as is sometimes supposed, but a signal to the predator. Animals that prey on deer—wolves, coyotes, and cougars—know that they have little chance of catching an adult in full flight; they hunt by silent stalking or by ambush. When a deer flashes its tail, it is telling the predator that it has been seen, so it might as well give up the chase, which it usually does.

Except for coyotes and foxes, wild canines and felines have been drastically reduced in numbers or, in some cases, extirpated in the Great Lakes basin. Gray wolves thrive farther north on the Canadian Shield but have been hunted mercilessly in most human-inhabited regions of eastern North America; in Ontario, for example, a bounty on wolves was in effect from 1793 until 1972.

A pack of gray wolves patrol their home range on Michigan's Upper Peninsula. Wolves turn gray with age; the alpha male in the foreground is at least twelve years old.

The cougar, or puma, has been eliminated from its eastern range, the last one east of Manitoba having been killed in New Brunswick in 1938. A large, tawny-colored, solitary, highly efficient predator, the cougar once ranged throughout the continent, but hunting and habitat loss soon pushed it into the Rockies and the higher areas of the West Coast, where it is appropriately known as the mountain lion. The late R.D. Lawrence, a naturalist and a reliable observer, claimed to have seen two sets of cougar tracks in northern Ontario in 1954. Since then there have been several unconfirmed sightings of cougars farther south, and many determined people believe that the eastern cougar still exists in remote valleys of the Appalachians or in northern Ontario. But no biologist has verified these recent claims, and no evidence has been put forward that the sighted animals are not western cougars—in other words, former pets or private zoo animals that have escaped or been released into the wild.

But large carnivores still roam the Great Lakes–St. Lawrence forest. Black bears are doing very well in the Great Lakes region, especially since several state and provincial governments have imposed bans on the hunting of bear cubs in the spring. Black bears are found in suitable habitats throughout North America, wherever there is sufficient contiguous forest to provide the 13 to 580 square kilometers (5 to 225 square

Black bear cubs await their mother's return from a foraging expedition.

BEAR FACTS

One strategy for a successful species is not to specialize in a particular habitat or food source, but to be able to benefit from a variety of conditions. The black bear is a good example. It is the most successful of North American bears because it lives in all forest types and feeds on anything from berries and grubs to mice, thus freeing itself from dependence on large game.

There are estimated to be 150,000 black bears living in the Great Lakes basin, with the largest populations located along the southern edge of the Canadian Shield. An increase in human-bear encounters in the past few years has prompted some people to suggest that the cancellation of the spring bear hunt, imposed by the Ontario government in 2001, has resulted in a sudden increase in the bear population. Ontario's Ministry of Natural Resources points out, however, that the no-hunting law has resulted in only 1,500 fewer bears being killed per year in the province, for an increase of about 7.5 percent of the total population in the five years since the hunt was cancelled—not a significant enough increase to account for the higher frequency of bear encounters. The increase is more likely the result of a number of factors, including a rise in the region's human population. A similar increase in human-bear encounters has been reported in Michigan, where bear hunting is still allowed; in 2005, 2,200 bears were killed out of a statewide population of about 19,000.

miles) the males need for their home ranges. Adult males can weigh up to 360 kilograms (800 pounds), females about 270 kilos (600 pounds), and both are omnivorous feeders, gorging on grass in the early spring, eating berries and fruit when in season, and resorting to meat in the fall, when they are putting on fat for the winter.

Bears are the only large predators that hibernate. In the northern reaches of their Great Lakes range, they go into such deep hibernation that their heart rate drops from 40 beats per minute to 10, and their oxygen intake is halved. Their metabolism also slows so that they lose very little body heat during this period of dormancy. The females even give birth in December or January without fully awakening; cubs remain with their mother for the first summer, den with her that fall, and then are driven off to establish their own home ranges during their second summer.

Encounters between humans and black bears are often memorable but rarely fatal for the humans; normally black bears would rather run than fight. Exceptions occur when the female believes that her cubs are threatened, or when bears feel that they are being denied food that rightfully belongs to them. It is difficult to mistake a black bear's track for anything else, but sometimes, for instance when the heel registers in soft mud or sand, an isolated bear print can look deceptively human. Check the big toe: in bears, the big toe is on the outside of the foot.

The gray wolf once ranged throughout North America but in the Great Lakes basin is now found only in northern Ontario, Minnesota, Wisconsin, and upper Michigan, where pack sizes vary from two to twenty individuals, depending on location and the size of game. Wolves are the largest members of the dog family. An adult male wolf can weigh 45 kilograms (100 pounds), measure 2 meters (6.5 feet) from nose to tail tip (the tail itself is about 50 centimeters or 20 inches long), and stand 66 to 82 centimeters (26 to 32 inches) tall at the shoulder. Females are slightly smaller. Both are powerful and intelligent hunters, relying on their keen senses of smell and hearing to locate prey. They often eat animals larger than themselves, although Farley Mowat, in *Never Cry Wolf,* reports that wolves he observed in the Far North ate field mice when caribou were scarce, and wolves are the primary predators of beavers. They can pick up the scent of prey 2.5 kilometers (1.5 miles) away if they are downwind of it, and can hear another wolf howling up to 6.5 kilometers (4 miles) away.

When a pack detects a potential prey, it goes into a kind of huddle: the wolves will stand in a tight group, nose to nose, wagging their tails exuberantly for 10 to 15 seconds, and then take off in pursuit. They can maintain a speed of 40 kilometers (25 miles) an hour for 20 minutes, faster for shorter distances, but even at that most young, healthy deer will outrun them, especially in dense bush or in snow deeper than 38 centimeters (15 inches). The majority of deer caught by wolves are old, and are either chased onto frozen lakes in winter, where they have trouble on slippery ice, or ambushed. Researchers have observed wolves chasing a deer into the waiting jaws of the rest of the pack at a specific point in the deer's trajectory. Not surprisingly, wolves' brains are as much as 30 cubic centimeters (1.8 cubic inches) larger than those of their largest canine cousins.

A species of wolf once thought to be a hybrid of the gray wolf and the coyote, called the Algonquin wolf because it was found only in and around Ontario's Algonquin Park, has recently been shown by DNA analysis to be an isolated, remnant population of the endangered red wolf, the only other wolf species native to North America. Ontario's red wolves are unique outside the southeastern United States, where the species has been artificially introduced. Smaller than a gray wolf but larger than a coyote, the red wolf lives on beavers during the summer (ambushing the rodents while they are on land, cutting trees) and white-tailed deer during the winter.

The identification has been good news for wolf ecologists since, as an endangered species, red wolves are automatically protected from local hunters who traditionally killed all wolves on sight because of the perceived threat to the local deer population. But wolves alone do not lower deer populations. Over a twenty-year study period, the researchers John and Mary Theberge found that the six packs of red wolves in Algonquin Park killed about 110 to 124 deer during the winter, approximately 10 to 12 percent of the total deer population. Since the deer herds increased by about 35 percent during that period, wolf predation obviously does not endanger the health of the herd. When deer numbers plummet, it is more often because of heavy snowfall and resultant starvation, or hunting by humans.

FOREST FLOOR FLORA

Early settlers in the Great Lakes–St. Lawrence forest missed the wildflowers they had known in their native countries. Catharine Parr Traill, for example, writing of her introduction to the Ontario woodlands in 1832, spoke of her "home-longings" for "the old familiar scenes, when the hedges put out their green buds and the Violets scent the air, when pale Primroses and the gay starry Celandine gladden the eye." Fortunately she and her fellow pioneers soon found local equivalents every bit as endearing.

Among the more than four hundred species of wildflowers native to Ontario, Traill found white violets blooming in early April with small, sweet-scented, greenish-white flowers; and then, "on pulling up a thrifty plant late in the summer," she wrote, "it surprises you with a new set of flowers, quite different from the spring blossoms; these are small buds and flowers of a dull chocolate-brown." Another white violet, which she called the "branching white wood violet," now named the Canada violet, grew in the rich, black humus of beech and maple woods and bloomed all summer. She also noted several blue violets, including the wood violet, or early blue violet, and the arrow-leaved violet, a bright, royal-blue flower that grew "in low, sandy, shady valleys or very light, loamy soil."

Of the four species of dandelion (from *dent-de-lion,* or "lion's tooth") now found in the Great Lakes region, only the dwarf dandelion is native. The others (the common, the red-seeded, and the fall dandelion) have been more recently introduced from Europe. All may be eaten: the greens, when young, make a fine addition to salads, tasting like endive (one of its common names is wild endive), and can also be boiled, like spinach. In Traill's time the buds and flowers were pickled. She noted that the roots could be cleaned, dried slowly in the oven until crisp, then ground into powder and made into a tolerable substitute for coffee. She added, however, that

The monarch is the best-known butterfly of the Great Lakes region, and also the least understood. It is the only butterfly that migrates in the fall, massing in September on the north shores of Lakes Erie and Ontario by the millions and flying 3,000 kilometers (1,860 miles) to the Mexican state of Michoacán, high in the Transverse Neovolcanic Mountains.

The mystery isn't why monarchs migrate. They are a tropical species and cannot overwinter where the temperature drops below freezing. The mystery is how they know to return to the same patch of oyamel pines in Michoacán every winter, and how they know where to return to in the spring. No single monarch makes the trip twice, so how is knowledge of the migration route and destination passed on from generation to generation?

Adult monarchs leave their northern range in early September and arrive at one of twelve wintering sites in Michoacán usually on November 2 (the Day of the Dead: indigenous Mexicans used to think they were the souls of the departed returning to their former homes). There they cluster on pines in vast roosts and go into a 135-day diapause, waking in March to begin their return journey. Those adults make it as far as the Gulf Coast of Texas, where they lay eggs on milkweed plants and die. The eggs hatch thirty days later; the caterpillars feed on the milkweed and pupate, and then the next generation of adults continue the northward migration. They get about halfway home and then they, too, stop to lay eggs on milkweed plants. The butterflies that finally arrive in Canada and the northern United States in June and July are three generations away from those that left the previous fall.

Monarchs then reproduce through two or three generations during the summer. The adults that leave in September for Mexico are often six generations from those that made the trip the previous year, and yet the migrating hordes always arrive at the same 3-hectare (7.5-acre) wintering site, usually on the same day, every year. Despite intense study by many entomologists, how the insects manage their flight, writes Sue Halpern in her book about monarch migration, *Four Wings and a Prayer,* "remains one of the great unsolved mysteries of animal biology."

"a small portion of fresh coffee would, I think, be an improvement to the beverage."

Despite its brilliant yellow composite flower and evident utility, this member of the aster family has not become a garden flower, probably because it is too hard to contain: each plant produces hundreds of parachutelike seeds that fill the air each fall and the meadows each spring. The French name for it, *pissenlit,* echoed in the Newfoundland moniker pissabed, refers not to the flower's yellow color but to the fact that an infusion made from dandelion is a powerful diuretic.

Another native plant that has remained a weed is the milkweed, of which there are one hundred species worldwide. Ten are found in the Great Lakes area, although five are quite rare. All display the

An adult monarch butterfly and caterpillar, the latter feeding on the leaves of a milkweed plant.

typical goblet-shaped flower structure, a tiny cup with five petals pointing up and the five divisions of the calyx forming the legs. The swamp milkweed, with its pink or purplish flowers, is found throughout the basin in wet meadows, in ditches, and along shorelines. The butterfly weed and the poke milkweed are Carolinian species. The former has orange flowers, and the petals of the latter are cream-colored, tinged with purple or green. Both prefer sandy meadows and tallgrass prairies. The green milkweed is one of the rare species. It also likes meadows and grasslands but thrives somewhat farther north, along the edges of Lakes Ontario, Erie, and Huron right up to Manitoulin Island.

Other rare species include the purple, Sullivant's, whorled, and prairie milkweeds. All milkweeds have long, pointed, downy, usually smooth seed pods, but those of the common milkweed, which now dominates the basin's fields and roadsides, are quite covered in knobs or warts. The pods are crowned with a silky white down that was carded and woven into candle and lamp wicks and also used to stuff cushions. During World War II there were experimental milk-weed farms in southern Michigan that supplied seed pod silk to the air force, that was meant to be used to line flight suits for warmth and buoyancy.

Perhaps the milkweed's best-known feature is its vital contribution to the life cycle of the monarch butterfly, one of the few milkweed butterflies found north of the tropics. Although temperate zone milkweeds are only mildly toxic, tropical varieties can be highly poisonous. An African milkweed is used to make arrow poison, and milkweed root is mixed with meat and used as bait to kill jackals and hyenas. A few insects, including butterfly caterpillars, have evolved a method of storing the milkweed's poison without themselves being affected; somehow, the adult butterfly retains the poison. Monarchs feeding on North American milkweed species are not exactly poisonous, but they are certainly distasteful, and most insectivorous birds and mammals leave them alone. Monarchs may have learned this trick in the tropics.

The forest is sustaining in many ways, most obviously as a provider of food. In the category of edible forest products, mushrooms reign supreme. Early settlers from Europe, where wild mushroom picking was a popular pastime, found ample opportunity for culinary experimentation in the Great Lakes basin. Of the 160 Canadian species of mushrooms and toadstools described by H.T. Güssow and W.S. Odell in their 1926 guide, *Mushrooms and Toadstools,* only two, they claimed, were poisonous. These were two amanita mushrooms, *Amanita muscaria* and *Amanita phalloides,* known as fly agaric and the death angel, respectively. At least one other should be added to that short list: *Amanita virosa,* known as the death cap. In general, it may be best to leave all amanitas alone. There is, by the way, no scientific difference between a mushroom and a toadstool: the distinction was a folk way of separating edible mushrooms from inedible toadstools. In fact, there are edible toadstools and poisonous mushrooms. "There is only one test to find out whether a mushroom . . . is poisonous and that is to eat it," writes J. Walton Groves in *Edible and Poisonous Mushrooms of Canada* (1962). "If it makes you sick or kills you, it is poisonous."

FACING PAGE: White-tailed deer graze in open grassland but prefer tangled woodlands for outdistancing wolves and other predators.

Bryce Kendrick, in *The Fifth Kingdom,* an encyclopedic work on the world's fungi, classifies Europeans as "pickers" and North Americans as "kickers" when it comes to eating wild mushrooms, and it is true that many in the New World are wary of eating a nything that doesn't come wrapped in cellophane bearing a bar code. But the distinction breaks down in Michigan, where half a million pickers attend the annual National Mushroom Hunting Championship at Boyne City each spring. The chief prey of these hunters is the morel, and two types are highly prized: the black morel, which comes up in mid-May; and the yellow morel, which appears a week later. The morel's wrinkled, phallus-shaped fruiting bodies are the premier edible fungi in the Great Lakes basin. They are common but declining throughout the region, except in Michigan, where they grow in stupefying abundance: the 1970 champion picked 900 morels in one hour. One picker in 2006 gathered 800 morels and didn't even place in the top ten.

The edible yellow morel, highly prized by mushroom gourmets.

Most people who dwell in the Great Lakes—St. Lawrence forest region are also familiar with fairy rings, the precise circles in which some species of mushrooms grow. Superstition has it that these are charmed spots where fairies gather for their nightly festivals. The plainer truth is that each mushroom in the ring grows from a single fruiting body that has exhausted the soil close by and sent fresh shoots out around itself to form a circle. As the soil continues to deplete, the circle becomes larger until it is no longer distinguishable as a circle at all.

But those who wish to hold to the magical explanation are welcome to do so, for even when we are armed with scientific facts, the forest is a place of mystery and

wonder. Catharine Parr Traill, in her *Studies of Plant Life in Canada,* mentions a common weed that grew by her doorstep, a small polygonum known as carpetweed. "It is crushed by the foot and bruised," she writes, "but springs up again as if unharmed beneath our tread, and flourishes under all circumstances, however adverse. This little plant had lessons to teach me, and gave me courage when trials pressed hard upon me." The woods can inspire wisdom as well.

The fly agaric, member of the poisonous amanita group.

FIVE

THE CAROLINIAN FOREST

As ITS NAME SUGGESTS, the Carolinian forest
extends from the Carolinas in the south,
up the Atlantic seaboard through Ten-
nessee and New Jersey to the southern portions of the Great Lakes
region, through New York, Ohio, and southern Michigan and into
southwestern Ontario. Examples of pure Carolinian forest exist in
Canada only in the most southerly regions, such as on Pelee Island
and Point Pelee in southwestern Ontario (with an anomalous showing at the eastern end of Lake Ontario), and in the United States portion of the basin only in pockets in the most northerly part of the
states of New York and Ohio. A transition zone, in which Carolinian species such as prickly ash and northern hackberry mingle with
trees more typical of the St. Lawrence–Great Lakes forest, extends
across southwestern Ontario from Windsor north to a line drawn
roughly from Toronto to Grand Bend, on Georgian Bay.

Although the area occupied by the Carolinian forest in the Great
Lakes basin is small compared with that of the boreal or Great
Lakes–St. Lawrence forest, what it lacks in size it makes up for
in species diversity. As an ecosystem, it harbors 1,600 species of
plants, nearly half of all species found in the basin, and of the 134
tree species native to the basin, 75 are Carolinian. Some refer to the

FACING PAGE: Backus
Woods, near Long Point,
on the north shore of
Lake Erie, is the largest
stand of Carolinian forest
remaining in Canada.

157

The American hardwood forest of history—the domain of the

woodland Indians, the forest which was so dangerous and unlivable in the

eyes of the first English settlers and which we call primeval today—

was in truth a luminous, youthful, supple forest, new-born out of the Ice Age.

In the nobility and quality of its trees, in the number of species of trees, bushes,

vines and flowers; in the purity of lakes and streams, in the abundance

and color of its birds and fish and in the personalities of its animals, no other

forest that ever grew on earth could be compared to it.

RUTHERFORD PLATT, *The Great American Forest*, 1965

Carolinian as the deciduous forest since, except for red cedar, it is dominated by hardwoods. Before settlement, the two most common species were sugar maple and American beech, which together made up 80 percent of the forest canopy. Other hardwoods found in the northern Carolinian zone include American basswood; nine species of oaks (which are actually members of the beech family), including black oak, white oak, and bur oak; and hickories and elms.

The tree that is perhaps most often associated with the Great Lakes—St. Lawrence forest, the sugar maple, actually belongs to the Carolinian forest, one of several broadleaf species that moved northward 10,000 years ago as the continent warmed. The others were the elms and oaks, some of which are now considered to be true northern species. We are surprised to find that when John James Audubon, writing in the 1830s, described a maple sugar camp and its familiar activities—"With large ladles the sugar-makers stirred the thickening juice of the maple"—he was describing an operation located in Kentucky. The maples, elms, and oaks were followed 5,000 years later by butternut, beeches, ashes, and hickories. All these species are still found in the Great Lakes region, although not as plentifully as they once were. Only the sugar maple has become more abundant since its arrival.

Sugar maple trees prefer well-drained, slightly acidic soil covering limestone bedrock, which is what the retreating Wisconsinan glacier left behind, and also do well on Shield soils. They thrive in rich, riverside loams or almost pure sand, on south-facing slopes or in shaded areas. They are highly susceptible to air pollution, which may explain why they are mainly rural and small-town trees. In large cities they can serve as warning signs for industrial gases: across the region, acid rain has caused severe maple dieback, which appears as an early-season browning of the tips of the outermost leaves. When healthy, maples can reach heights of up to 40 meters (130 feet) and trunk diameters of 90 to 120 centimeters (3 to 4 feet). The largest specimen in Ontario, in North Pelham, near Niagara Falls, is 25 meters (82 feet) high and 191 centimeters (6.3 feet) in diameter, though such old-growth sizes are becoming increasingly rare. In the area of my home in eastern Ontario's transition zone, ancient maples occasionally occur in young woods that were once pastures, and one can easily imagine them standing out prominently in a field cleared by early settlers. Today they are the standing dead, leafless and rotting, surrounded by prickly ash and maple saplings, bored through by pileated woodpeckers, offering accommodation to gray squirrels, owls, and raccoons, and slowly returning their centuries of accumulated nutrients back to the forest.

Canada's Pelee Island, the largest of the twenty-one islands in the Lake Erie Archipelago, is one of the most biologically diverse islands for its size in North America. Fish Point, its southern tip, supports 430 plant species, 52 of which are nationally rare.

A sugar maple dominates a field of hawkweed. Maple sugar provided sweetener, nutrition, and industry for early Great Lakes settlers.

The grayish-brown bark of the sugar maple is deeply furrowed, with the edges of its vertical plates curling slightly away from the trunk. The wood is extremely hard, 30 percent stronger than white oak, and polished maple floors are comparable in hardness to marble. Its famous leaf is deeply palmated, consisting of five lobes on five main veins emanating from the base, dull green on top and paler, somewhat hairy beneath. Pre-Contact Aboriginal people discovered that maple sap contains such high levels of glucose—stored in the roots during winter and vacuum-pumped up into the canopy in early spring—that it could be boiled down to make sugar. European settlers learned the trick from them, and nearly every farmstead had its well-managed sugar bush. Maple syrup production is still a major industry in Quebec, Ontario, and the eastern states, and a highly beneficial one, since maple syrup is the only sweetener except honey that contains the phosphates necessary for calcium retention in bones. It was once used medicinally as a treatment for rickets and tuberculosis in children. In many ways, the sugar maple is to Canada what the eastern white pine was to the colonial states: the emblematic spray of copper leaves on the Canadian penny and the red leaf on the Canadian flag can only be those of the sugar maple.

The leaves of most deciduous trees turn from green to yellow or red before dropping in the autumn; staghorn sumacs, birches, elms, basswoods, and some oaks all brighten up a forest hillside in September and October. But the sugar maple is particularly spectacular when weather conditions are favorable. Hot, dry summers followed by early fall rains, which keep the leaves green and delay leaf fall, make for the most varied and vivid colors later in the season. Deciduous leaves always contain yellow carotenoids, but in high summer they are eclipsed by green because the leaves' cells are filled with chlorophyll, the compound that makes photosynthesis possible. In the fall, chlorophyll is withdrawn from the leaves, and then the yellow shows through.

Why leaves turn red is a little more complicated. The inside of a deciduous leaf in autumn has been compared to the inside of the *Titanic* after it struck the iceberg: according to the biologist Susan Milius, writing in *Science News,* "Metabolic pathways start to fail. Compounds break apart. Doomed cells rush to salvage the valuables, especially nitrogen, by sending them off to safer tissues." After a dry summer, trees are less able to take up nitrogen from the soil, and therefore must get it from the air in order to store up enough for the winter, when they are without leaves and in deep metabolic rest. Even after leaves lose their chlorophyll they continue to absorb nitrogen, but they are also still exposed to sunlight: too much ultraviolet light falling on leaves bereft of chlorophyll inhibits the intake of nitrogen, and so the tree manufactures a red compound called anthocyanin to protect its dying leaves from the sun. In 2001, William Hoch of the University of Wisconsin showed that plants adapt to cold autumns by manufacturing more anthocyanin than those growing in more temperate climates, and the more anthocyanin the leaves contain, the redder they become, especially on the

SUGAR MAPLE

BUR OAK

MAPLE OF THE MARSHES

The silver maple, a Carolinian species named for the silvery undersides of its leaves, does well in soggy areas (its alternative names are river, water, creek, and swamp maple) and is often found growing in wetlands and along streambanks in association with white elm, also a forest swamp species. It grows in profusion in the Ohio River valley and bravely holds its own in its northern outpost within the Great Lakes basin. When the Ontario government passed its Ontario Tree Planting Act in 1893, under which it paid farmers 25 cents for every tree planted and still alive after three years, silver maples were sown by the thousands in the province's swamps and marshes.

Unlike the winged keys, or samaras, of most other maples, which must overwinter on the ground and dry out to a reddish-brown the following summer to be viable, silver maple samaras will sprout the summer they fall, when they're still green, providing that they fall in swampy soil or along a wet riverbank or lakeshore. One of the fastest-growing species in the forest, mature silver maples can reach 30 meters (98 feet) rapidly. But they live only half as long as sugar maples, about 125 years, which means that many of the silver maples planted in the frenzy of 1893 are just now beginning to die off.

Silver maples, like these in Ontario's Minesing Swamp, are among the fastest-growing hardwoods, and are often found near water.

The citruslike flowers of the tulip tree, the tallest tree in the Carolinian forest and a member of the magnolia family.

side of the tree exposed to the most sunlight. It is also thought that anthocyanin plays a role in repairing leaves damaged by insects. The deciduous tree's brilliant fall display is thus a measure of how well the species has adapted to higher latitudes.

Most Carolinian trees have exotic-sounding names to northern ears: cucumber tree, pawpaw, Kentucky coffee. In 1898, the geographer C.H. Merriam defined the Carolinian zone as that area "in which the sassafras, tulip tree, hackberry, sycamore, sweet gum, rose magnolia, redbud, persimmon and short-leaf pine first make their appearance," and according to Gerry Waldron, author of the definitive *Trees of the Carolinian Forest,* most of those species are found (and have been found by Waldron) up to the Toronto–Grand Bend line in southwestern Ontario. The exceptions are persimmon and sweet gum, which have their northern limits in southern Ohio. Perhaps they are still to be discovered farther north: as Waldron reports, the swamp cottonwood, though common in Michigan, wasn't known in Ontario until he and two other dendrologists discovered a stand of them in a buttonbush swamp near Sarnia in November 2002.

The tulip tree is the northern Carolinian forest's tallest species, growing to more than 35 meters (115 feet). A wide-ranging tree (it is the state tree of Indiana, Kentucky, and Tennessee), it prefers dry, sandy soils with lots of light. Its leaves are oddly lobed, almost square, with the two bottom lobes wider than the two top, and strangely patterned veins, some of which run parallel to the edges. The flower resembles a yellowish-orange tulip. Its near relative the magnolia, or cucumber tree, though common in the mountain valleys of Tennessee and the Carolinas, is an endangered species in its northern range. It grows in association with trees that are still doing quite well—white oaks, white ashes, sugar maples, hickories, and sassafrases—but like the tulip tree is intolerant of shade. A tallish (20 meters, or 65 feet) tree with 18-centimeter (7-inch) tapered, many-veined leaves and yellow flowers, the magnolia (named for Pierre Magnol, the seventeenth-century French botanist who first studied it) has soft but close-grained wood and a deep, wide root system suitable for its preferred habitat: wet, sandy loam such as is found at Lake Erie's Long Point and Niagara regions.

Another Carolinian species at risk is the Kentucky coffee tree; although common as an ornamental, it is listed as threatened in the wild. It is a member of the legume family: its name derives from the fact that Aboriginal people and settlers dried the beans contained in its long, brown pods, which often remained on the tree all winter, and made a tolerable substitute for coffee. (Beware of the unroasted beans, which are highly toxic.) As with all legumes, the roots of the Kentucky coffee tree produce bacteria that fix nitrogen into the soil upon decaying and so are of great benefit where they grow in large stands. Like alders, such stands can be all clones stemming from a single root, and hence all of the same sex. Unless there are opposite-sex trees nearby, no new seeds will be produced.

CREATURES OF THE CAROLINIAN

The basin's Carolinian forest is host to several mammals more commonly associated with the southern United States. The opossum, for example, which can hardly be thought of in the north with its first syllable intact, is North America's only marsupial. It has continued to expand northward, taking advantage of global warming as well as human garbage and a lack of predators. Its young are delivered while still embryos after only thirteen days' gestation. Sightless, hairless, lacking hind limbs and tails, and weighing about as much as a grain of rice each, the young grope up the female's belly and into her marsupial pouch, where they spend the next sixty days nursing and maturing to the stage at which placental mammals are born. The adults have long, white guard hairs—the word *opossum* comes from the Algonquin *apasum,* meaning "white animal"—with black ears and markings, especially on their undersides. They are arboreal creatures, and their dark undersides make them difficult to

TULIP TREE

KENTUCKY COFFEE TREE

The opossum, North America's only marsupial, is becoming more common in the Great Lakes basin.

spot from the ground. In their northern range, as far north as southwestern Ontario and throughout most of the Great Lakes states except northern Michigan and Minnesota, they are omnivorous, eating everything from carrion to carrots. Samples of opossum scat taken in November in southern Michigan revealed that 50 percent of their diet consisted of mammals and birds, 30 percent of fruit, and 16 percent of insects; the rest was made up of snakes, frogs, crawfish, and snails. Opossum females have only one litter of about a dozen young per year. Both males and females spend a great deal of time building up a supply of fat for the winter. This they store in their prehensile tails, which they also use for climbing and, reportedly, for carrying clumps of leaves and other material to their dens, either on the ground in hollow logs or in tree cavities.

The red fox is ubiquitous throughout the Great Lakes region, indeed throughout the northern hemisphere; it is the world's most widely distributed carnivore. There is some question, however, as to whether the red fox we know today is the same red fox that was native to North America. From fossil evidence it seems there were red foxes here long before European settlement, but they were outnumbered by gray foxes, which are about the same size and weight as their red cousins and once occupied similar territory. Whereas the red fox is predominantly red with a bushy, white-tipped tail, the gray fox is mostly gray, especially in the face and across the shoulders, with some red in its underparts. Its bushy tail is gray with a dark gray dorsal stripe along the top. The gray fox has several feline characteristics: it has retractable claws, for example, and not only can climb trees (in some areas it is known as the tree fox) but will leap from one tree to another, leaving no trace on the ground for possible pursuers.

This so frustrated the New England gentry, whose foxhounds could not follow the gray fox's scent trail, that in 1750 American fox hunters began importing and releasing red foxes from Britain

In the Carolinian zone, the red fox often shares habitat with the gray fox. The red fox may in fact be a hybrid of the European fox.

(Vulpes vulpes), which were apparently far more sporting. These British foxes either edged out the native red variety *(Vulpes fulva)* or, more probably, interbred with them. Some authorities now refer to the North American red fox as a subspecies of the European fox, designating it *Vulpes vulpes fulva.* Others call it flat-out *Vulpes vulpes.* In any case, the red fox is now far more numerous than the gray *(Urocyon cinereoargenteus),* although in the Lakes basin their ranges overlap.

The endangered blue racer is probably a remnant of the prairie habitat that once extended deep into the Great Lakes basin.

The blue racer, a snake with a slender tail, elongated head, large eyes, and a shiny, bluish-green body with whitish undersides and lips, is one of the region's largest snakes. Adults may reach up to 1.5 meters (5 feet) from the tip of the snout to the anus vent, excluding the tail. Its distribution in the basin is limited to south of the Lakes from Iowa east to Ohio and north into southwestern Ontario: in Canada, blue racers are found only on Pelee Island with a suspected remnant population near Windsor.

In summer, blue racers live in open, prairielike habitat with abundant cover, such as dense woody or herbaceous vegetation, rock outcrops, or hedgerows. They hibernate in winter in quarries and cisterns and in areas such as alvars where limestone bedrock is close to the surface. Active and alert during the day, they hunt rodents, frogs, and other snakes and will even climb shrubs to catch small birds. They in turn are preyed upon by raptors—red-tailed hawks, great horned owls, and northern harriers—as well as by raccoons, foxes, and coyotes. Mating takes place in the spring, after which females lay an average of fourteen eggs, usually in decaying wood or sandy loam or under rocks. Nests are sometimes shared with other blue racers or eastern fox snakes, and egg mortality is high.

But the species's gradual decline in its northern range is due more to changing climate and dwindling prairie habitat than to natural causes. Compared with other racer populations in North America, blue racers require an extremely wide area; the average range on Pelee Island is 75 hectares (185 acres) for females and 140 hectares (346 acres) for males. Natural prairie habitats in the Great Lakes basin are dwindling, as is the blue racer population: in 1995 there were about 205 adult blue racers on Pelee Island; recent counts suggest the number has declined since then.

The red fox, however, prefers open spaces such as clearings, farmers' fields, and golf courses, where it hunts grassland species such as white-footed mice and meadow voles; whereas the gray fox spends more time in dense brush and deeply wooded areas (hence its increasing rarity, since its habitat is also dwindling), preying on rabbits and rodents but also eating a lot of vegetative matter, such as berries, fruits, grasses, and even insects. In some areas, insects can make up 40 percent of the gray fox's diet. The gray fox is a Carolinian species, little known north of the Lakes; the red fox, with its stout British genes, is found anywhere south of the Arctic Circle.

The fox squirrel is also a Carolinian species. Its natural range extends from Florida and Texas up to the Great Lakes, having expanded recently into Minnesota and the Dakotas. The Canadian ornithologist Percy Taverner, who spent some time in 1912 at the University of Michigan in Ann Arbor, wrote that the fox squirrels there were highly intelligent and easily tamed, which seems a contradiction but, upon reflection, is not. In Canada they are found in pure stands of Carolinian forest, which means mainly on Pelee Island, where there are between two hundred and three hundred individuals, all descended from fox squirrels introduced to the island in 1893 from southern Ohio.

They are larger than gray squirrels (confusingly called *Sciurus carolinensis*): the average mass of a gray squirrel is around 500 grams (a little over 1 pound), whereas fox squirrels regularly weigh in at 800 grams (about 1.8 pounds), and one hefty individual, collected by the naturalist Ernest Thompson Seton in 1899, registered 1116 grams (nearly 2.5 pounds). Fox squirrels come in three color phases—black, salt-and-pepper, and red—but in their northern range they are primarily beige-gray with somewhat rufous undersides and large, mottled black-and-orange tails. Being omnivorous, they consume beechnuts, berries, and rosehips (all seeds) as well as insects, caterpillars, and birds' eggs. They bury acorns like gray squirrels but are better at finding them in the spring. For reasons perhaps unknowable to us, both gray and fox squirrels are seemingly wasteful nut eaters; they almost always take a single bite from an acorn and toss it away, then pick another acorn, take another single bite, and toss it away. The ground around oak trees is often liberally strewn with partially eaten acorns. Whatever the squirrel's motivation, the habit does serve nature's purpose, since in order to germinate, acorns need to have their shells opened.

Pelee Island and Point Pelee, at the western end of Lake Erie, are a mecca for birders, as each spring and fall more than 200 species of birds fly over on their annual migrations to and from their northern breeding grounds. Both island and peninsula are at the confluence of two major bird flyways—the Mississippi and the eastern—and most birds stop to rest and fatten up either before attempting the long lake crossing heading south (in the fall) or after accomplishing it (in the spring), when they arrive exhausted and depleted.

The chestnut-sided warbler song is a rich, whistled *zee zee zee meet-meet ya.*

The warblers are typical as a group of Carolinian songbirds. Small, quick, colorful birds, warblers take their name from the quality of their singing. They are perching birds; their feet are adapted to grip small branches, and their principal diet consists of insects, spiders, and mites. Their migrations coincide with the emergence of these arthropods in the spring and their move into diapause, or winter dormancy, in the fall.

The most common is the yellow warbler, a small (12 centimeters, or 4.7 inches long) songbird that is almost completely yellow except for reddish streaks on the breast of the male. The blackness of the eye stands out in sharp contrast to the yellow face. Yellow warblers are voracious insectivores that prefer wet, deciduous shrublands, usually of willows or alders, and so are often found in riparian zones or reclaimed areas where those species are the first to move in.

Their nests are deep cups built on the upright forks of short trees, rarely more than 2 meters (6.5 feet) from the ground, well insulated in the north with fine grasses, feathers, and down. Unfortunately, the tiny birds are often victims of the parasitic brown-headed cowbird, which is nearly twice warbler size, and which lays its eggs in other birds' nests and lets its unwitting hosts incubate and raise its young. Since the cowbird hatchling is far bigger and thus more demanding than the yellow warbler chicks, the warbler parents spend most of their time, often to the point of exhaustion, feeding the cowbirds and ignoring their own offspring. After a few thousand years of this, however, the yellow warbler seems to be catching on: parents now seem to be able to recognize a cowbird egg and will either tip it out of the nest or build a second nest over top of it (and sometimes over their own eggs as well), and lay another clutch. Yellow warbler nests have been found with up to seven layers of buried cowbird eggs.

The northern yellow warbler builds deep, cuplike nests in wet deciduous thickets in the Carolinian zone.

However, recent studies suggest that brown-headed cowbirds retaliate when host birds eject cowbird eggs from their nests. The biologists Jeffrey Hoover and Scott Robinson observed cowbird predation on 182 prothonotary warbler nests in southern Illinois and found that when the warblers ejected the cowbird eggs, cowbirds attacked the nests and destroyed the warbler eggs and usually the nests as well. When the warblers rebuilt their nests, cowbirds were more likely to parasitize them. The researchers suggest that warblers accept cowbird eggs and the onerous task of raising cowbird chicks because they fear "mafia-like retaliatory behavior" from cowbirds. As with so many aspects of nature, the scientists conclude, the interaction of these species is "even more sophisticated than previously thought."

Other typical warblers of the northern Carolinian include the blue-winged warbler, with yellow body, bluish-gray back and wings, and dark stripe connecting its eye and longish, black beak; the cerulean warbler, a striking bird with white underparts and throat and blue head, back, and wings, two white wing bars, and a blue collar; the less common but closely related Blackburnian warbler, whose bright orange throat, white wing patches, and dark cap light up the woods in spring; and the hooded warbler, with its deep, black cowl and bright yellow cutaway around the eye. The ovenbird is also a member of the warbler family; a small, grayish bird with two black stripes running over its head from the beak, and thick black stripes on its whitish underparts, it spends most of its time on the ground and is noted for its distinctive call, which sounds like "Teacher, teacher, teacher!"

Wild turkeys remain in small family groups during the summer but form large flocks in fall and winter, often comprising up to thirty birds.

WARBLERS AND WATER LEVELS

The prothonotary warbler is one of the most elegant birds of the Carolinian forest. A small, long-beaked warbler with yellow front and head, grayish-blue wings, and white rump patch (a prothonotary is a religious or legal clerk who wears a gold hood and a blue cape), it migrates north from its wintering grounds in South America each spring to nest only in deciduous swamps. The male arrives first, in early May, claims a territory of about 2 hectares (5 acres) usually with silver maples or birch and at least 1 hectare (2.5 acres) of water, selects four or five cavity nest sites, and fills them with green moss. The female arrives in June and chooses one of the dummy sites for her real nest. She lines it with grasses and rootlets before laying as many as eight eggs.

The population of prothonotaries has declined seriously since the 1960s, largely because of loss of habitat in South America but also because of fluctuations in lake levels in the Great Lakes basin, which has compromised Carolinian wetlands around Lake Erie, the warbler's home base. In Ontario, where 150 mating pairs were counted in the 1930s, the population plummeted to only 10 pairs in 1996. Fortunately, designation as an endangered species has led to habitat protection in Ontario and nesting-box programs in Ohio and Michigan that have helped nearly to double the population in the past decade.

The prothonotary, also known as the golden swamp warbler, is one of the few warblers to nest in tree cavities.

The chestnut-sided warbler has a yellow crown, variegated black-and-white upper parts, and a whitish belly with a reddish line running under each wing along its flank. Its preference for brushy or disturbed habitat means that it has increased in number with the cutting of mature deciduous stands and is now found throughout the Great Lakes basin.

The Carolinian zone is also the home of the Carolina wren, a year-round resident that makes its nest in holes in trees. It is reddish-brown on top, buff below, with a distinct white eye stripe, or super-cilium, reaching all the way to the back of its large head. Carolina wrens establish permanent territories, which the males defend by singing: each has a repertoire of more than forty different songs, some of them borrowed from other species. Studies suggest that female wrens choose their mates on the basis of the number and variety of their songs, possibly because a wide selection of songs requires a high degree of intelligence. Since Carolina wrens from one area are known to have songs—a sort of dialect—that differ from those of Carolina wrens in another area, it may be that the female judges the male's repertoire to determine how familiar he is with his habitat, and therefore with its best nesting sites and food sources.

In the transition zone between the Carolinian and Great Lakes–St. Lawrence forests, wild turkeys have been reintroduced and are flourishing. A foraging group of thirty or more, the red-wattled males up to 1.2 meters (4 feet) tall, wander through our property every few months, terrorizing our free-range chickens and stirring guilty thoughts in us of Thanksgiving dinners. In upstate New York and Pennsylvania they are still indigenous, although sometimes hybridized with escaped or released domestic turkeys. Hybrids are heavier than wild turkeys—wild males average about 7 kilograms (15 pounds), females just under 4.5 kilograms (10 pounds)—and have white-tipped tail feathers. Wild turkeys are powerful fliers in short bursts and can be found at night roosting in the tops of the highest trees in the forest. Benjamin Franklin thought they should be America's emblematic bird, but others found the bald eagle a nobler species. Perhaps they objected to having an American emblem that bore the name of another country; *turkey* probably referred originally to guinea fowl imported from Africa, which arrived in Europe via Turkey. The Europeans brought the name with them, along with *robin, groundhog,* and *elk,* and transferred them to similar but usually unrelated North American species. There are accounts of settlers confusing turkeys with turkey vultures, at least until the bird arrived at the dinner table.

THE SLITHER FACTOR

The Carolinian forest is the natural home of the third-largest snakes inhabiting North America, the rat snakes. So called because their principal food items are small rodents, rat snakes are from the south, where they are sometimes called chicken snakes. The two northern species are the black rat snake and the fox snake. Both are constrictors and can be distinguished by their flat abdomens, which nearly form right angles with their sides.

The black rat snake is an imposing creature to encounter, as I can attest from having lived in a cabin, the attic of which was regularly patrolled by a large black rat snake that kept the red squirrel and white-footed mouse population in check, albeit rather noisily. Black rat snakes are noted for their ability to climb trees and rob birds' nests: I've watched one climb almost vertically up a thick maple to get at a chickadee nest. Mostly black with a hint of darker blotches, it can grow up to 2 meters (6.5 feet) in length. Its usual habitat is open fields and the edges of woodlots. When disturbed, it coils like a cobra, rears its neck, hisses, and will even strike, although it is not poisonous and rarely inflicts a wound. It mates in June, the male flicking its sensitive tongue along the female's body and aligning his length with hers. One day while I was splitting wood at the cabin, a pair of entwined black rat snakes rolled off the roof and continued their intensely muscled constriction at my feet; at first I thought they were a mating pair, but in fact they were two males in competition for a female, each trying to out-constrict the other.

Immature black rat snakes are buff-gray with brownish patches and look a lot like mature fox snakes, which are pale brown to yellowish, with brown patches; fox snakes, however, have a regular row of smaller brown blotches down either side. They are rarely found

BLACK RAT SNAKE

in attics as they are not skilled climbers. When handled, they emit a pungent, musky secretion that smells like a fox's den, hence their name. They are woodland snakes, most common along the shores of Lakes Erie, Ontario, and Huron, and on the islands in Georgian Bay—although they are now considered at risk in Ontario. Their maximum length is around 1.5 meters (5 feet), which is still quite large, especially when they coil and vibrate their tails like rattle-snakes—a case of mimicry that can be quite effective, even though they clearly do not have rattles. The fox snake also eats small mammals, from mice and voles to young rabbits and squirrels. As with the black rat snake, mating takes place in June and the females lay 10 to 20 eggs, usually in the hollow of a rotting log or stump. The eggs adhere together, absorbing moisture from the surrounding wood and increasing in size by a third or a half before they hatch in late August or September.

SOUTHERN BELLES

The dense canopy of the Carolinian forest discourages a lot of undergrowth during the summer, but in the wet meadows and swampy clearings there are numerous late-blooming wildflowers. The flowering spurge is a tall, delicate plant that flowers from June through October and exudes a milky juice when the stem is broken; Catharine Parr Traill warned that this juice "is highly acrid and poisonous" and noted that the starchy parts of the plant were ground and sold as cassava flour. It was used as a purgative, or diarrhetic, so powerful that it was commonly known as "Go-Quick," and an 1817 medical text refers to it as "one of the most efficient medicines of the evacuating class."

The tall bellflower also blooms in June; it is a member of the bellflower family, as are the harebells and lobelia. It is the only campanula that does not produce bell-like blossoms: its five-lobed, blue flowers are flat but have the long, protruding, tonguelike style that is typical of the species. Although many other bellflowers were introduced to North America from Europe—Canterbury bells, for example, which are now ubiquitous—the related cardinal flower has had the opposite history. Native to the St. Lawrence and Great

FACING PAGE: The brightly hued cardinal flower flourishes in the dark margins of streams and swamps.

Lakes basin, its seeds were sent back to England, France, and Italy, where it quickly became a favorite. It is named not for its color but because the first European seedling flowered in the seventeenth-century Roman garden of Cardinal Barberini. In its native habitat, its vivid, intense red flowers, glowing like flames on the wet margins of streams and swamps, were no doubt encouraging to settlers who saw so beautiful a plant thriving in such forbidding surroundings.

The dense button snakeroot, also known as dense blazing star, is a tall, thistlelike plant with a spike of small, purple blossoms that grace the Carolinian floor from July to September. Purple foxglove is sometimes cited as a Carolinian wildflower, but true foxglove is a foreign import, a member of the Mediterranean snapdragon family. The native foxgloves are all "false" foxgloves, members of the Gerardia family, named for the sixteenth-century English botanist John Gerard, author of the earliest herbal written in English. Traill's "Oak-leaved Gerardia" is probably downy false foxglove, which has oaklike leaves and grows 1.8 meters (6 feet) tall, with large yellow bells appearing in August. Fern-leaved false foxglove, also a tall, yellow-flowering plant with bell-shaped flowers, has leaves that look like ferns; it thrives in dry, upland oak woods from Minnesota to Ontario.

The Carolinian forest floor is best seen in spring, before the leaves are out and while early-blooming wildflowers receive dappled sunlight. The forest is a riot of spring perennials. These include the pond plant the yellow, or American, lotus and the mayapple, which is also found in the southern parts of the Great Lakes—St. Lawrence forest. Traill called it the mandrake, although the true mandrake is a European member of the nightshade family. She reported that its medicinal value "has superseded the use of calomel in complaints of the liver," but that "ignorant persons have been poisoned by mistaking the leaves for those of the Marsh Marigold," which was used as a potherb by settlers.

The best known of the spring wildflowers is the white trillium, the largest, showiest, and most widely distributed of the trilliums and the one that has been designated the floral emblem of Ontario. With its three white petals framed against three dark green, ribbed leaves, it lights up the forest floor for two weeks in early May before turning slightly pinkish and then fading away altogether. The purple trillium, with flowers that are either red or maroon, is found in the sunlit woods of Minnesota, Michigan, and Wisconsin, where it is sometimes called wake-robin—possibly because its early appearance in spring seems to summon the robin back from its southern haunts, or, more intriguingly, because the trillium's roots once enjoyed a reputation as an aphrodisiac. According to the botanist Geoffrey Grigson, the moniker *wake-robin* originated in England and refers "to the use of Robin as a pet name for the penis." There are no trilliums in England; the English wake-robin is the arum,

The delicate flower of the purple trillium, sometimes called the ill-scented trillium, rises above its stem on a slender stalk.

another suspected aphrodisiac. The family is represented in the Great Lakes region by the water arum or wild calla, a lily with heart-shaped leaves and a very suggestive golden spadix protruding from a delicate white spathe.

To our northern senses, the Carolinian forest is an exotic incursion of tropical lushness into the temperate zone, an intriguing hint of the southern bayou country. Thick Virginia creepers depend from unfamiliar branches; the floor is a tangle of growth on moist and pungent soil. Birds making their way north from Florida or Louisiana in May, or south from their breeding grounds in September, must find this distant outpost of their winter homes irresistible. The murmur of Atlantic waves fretting a sandy shore is never far from the Carolinian forest in the Carolina states; in the Great Lakes basin, it is the soft, relentless sound of an inland sea.

SIX

LIFE
IN THE
MARGINS

MOST ORGANISMS HAVE TWO BASIC requirements for life: air and water, and in the
Great Lakes basin those elements are
abundantly present just about everywhere. But often the *quality* of
life depends on other, secondary needs—sunlight, soil, nutrients,
the companionship and interaction of other individuals and species—
and these ingredients are not always available in equal measure. In
some habitats, there might be ample sunlight but thin soil; in others,
the soil may be rich but poorly drained, or too loose to hold water, or
heavily shaded, or too exposed. Such habitats still support life, but
plants, animals, birds, insects, reptiles, and amphibians have had to
adapt their requirements to fit their environments.

The ecosystems in this chapter exist between the simple cat-
egories of forest and lake, some quite literally: wetlands and sand
dunes, for example, are situated at the interface of water and land,
exhibiting aspects of both and supporting life that exploits that
dual inheritance. Alvars, those strange areas of extremely thin or
nonexistent soil atop layers of flat, sedimentary bedrock, are unique
to the Great Lakes basin in North America and produce fascinating ecological communities found nowhere else on the continent.
And urban forests, struggling to survive in the unnatural context

FACING PAGE: The
bullfrog's booming call
attracts females and warns
off rival males. It also
attracts such predators
as great blue herons and
snapping turtles.

The muskeg lying over the bog was springy and at times seemed as though
it must surely give way and let me down into the water and muck underneath.
Labrador tea, swamp laurel, Andromeda, sedges, and sphagnum, all woven
through with the tiny grass-like stems of cranberry; here was a stable ecological
community, more ancient perhaps than the forests surrounding it.

SIGURD OLSON, *Runes of the North*, 1963

of concrete, debris, and the enforced monoculture of our major cities, are often the last remnants of the great natural forests that once covered the continent. While each of these ecosystems exists in the margins of the major realms discussed earlier, none of them is "marginal" in the sense of being inferior or achieving less than its full potential: all are rich in biodiversity and highly important for the creatures and plants that inhabit them.

SWAMPED

The word *swamp* has an unhealthy sound to it, something suggestive of death and decay. Malaria is called swamp fever because the disease was contracted by people who lived or worked in swampy areas where mosquitoes bred. In the Sherlock Holmes story "The Speckled Band," the most venomous snake in the world is the Indian swamp adder. The word comes from the Old Scots, where it meant "sunken" or "subsided"; a seventeenth-century Scottish medical text warned that "if in a woman with childe the breasts suddenly fall swampe, then will shee abort or miscarry."

Pilgrims in New England were the first to use the word to refer to wetlands: they called tree-covered wetlands "swamps," meaning ground that supported vegetation but was too low and wet to be plowed. To the Pilgrims, however, swamps weren't all bad. Captain

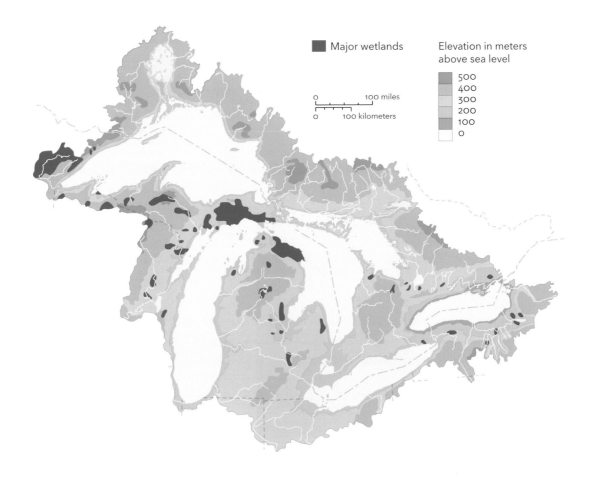

Major wetlands

Elevation in meters above sea level

500
400
300
200
100
0

0   100 miles

0   100 kilometers

John Smith, leader of the Virginia Colony, wrote in 1624 that "some small Marshes and Swamps there are, but more profitable than hurtfull." They were profitable because they could be drained and cleared and turned into workable farmland.

As the continent's western regions opened to colonization, swamps were considered impediments to settlement. In 1850, the United States passed the Swamp Lands Act, which ceded 64 million acres (26 million hectares) of publicly owned land that was deemed "wet and unfit for cultivation" to state governments on condition that those governments drained them and made them fit for farming. In the Great Lakes area, Minnesota received 2 million

MAJOR WETLANDS OF THE GREAT LAKES BASIN

Life in the Margins | 183

hectares (5 million acres), Illinois 600,000 (1.5 million acres), and Wisconsin 1.4 million (3.5 million acres). In most cases, any citizen who went to the trouble of draining the swamps could assume title to the land. By the 1930s, virtually all of the huge wetlands in Illinois, Pennsylvania, Michigan, and Wisconsin had been drained. Similar attitudes to swamps existed in Canada; more than 70 percent of southern Ontario's wetlands have been drained since pioneer days. Drained wetlands are often referred to euphemistically as "reclaimed land," as though wetlands originally belonged to us and were somehow stolen by water, but have now been returned to their rightful owners.

Occasionally, wetlands suffered a different fate: instead of being drained, they were turned into lakes or reservoirs. Northern Pennsylvania's Pymatuning Swamp, for example, was a 10,000-hectare (25,000-acre) wetland that was once the home of the mysterious Mound Builders, a people who are thought to have lived at the time of the Paleo-Indian culture, 10,000 years ago. In 1934 it was flooded to make a reservoir lake 25 kilometers (15.5 miles) long and 10 meters (33 feet) deep, to help control spring floods on the Shenango River. Although this former swamp still provides resting space for migrating Canada geese and other waterfowl, in general much biodiversity is lost when wetlands disappear.

After the retreat of the glaciers, the Great Lakes shorelines were fringed by extensive coastal wetlands. The basin of the western end of Lake Erie, between Point Pelee and the tip of the lake, was a vast, soggy plain bordered by massive swamps and marshes. The twenty-one islands (six Canadian, fifteen American) that make up the Erie Islands today were then high points of land surrounded by reeds and low shrubs. As water levels rose, the islands remained as a corridor for many southern species of plants, birds, and animals working their way north with the warming climate. Similarly, only a few hundred years ago, the south shore of the Detroit River and much of the land surrounding Lake St. Clair and the St. Clair River was marsh and prime wild-rice habitat. The Great Black Swamp in northern Ohio comprised nearly 4,000 square kilometers (1,500 square miles) of fertile, life-giving wetlands. In 1922, the naturalist Elliot Rowland Downing described the tamarack bogs at the southern end of Lake Michigan as "one of the most striking associations of plants and animals to be found in the Chicago area," fascinating because they were remnants of an ecosystem that was widespread in the region immediately following the glacial period, and still containing organisms not usually found so far south. Downing encountered a subarctic mosquito species, for example, trapped in water held by the leaves of a pitcher plant.

Wetland is an imprecise term. It refers to any one of four types of transitional zones in which the water table is at the same height as or slightly higher than the surrounding land, and where there is persistent water less than 2 meters (6.5 feet) deep. A *marsh* is usually associated with a pond or a stream or the shallow edge of a lake, is typified by shallow standing water, and contains bulrushes, cattails, reeds, and water lilies. *Swamp* still denotes its original meaning: a wooded area of standing water or saturated soil that may or may not dry up in summer, often with cedars and low conifers or hardwoods such as swamp white oak that like wet feet. *Bogs* are stagnant and acidic vessels of trapped water, an environment that supports sphagnum moss and such shrubs as blueberries, cranberries, and some orchids. Finally, *fens,* which are like bogs but less acidic (that is, more alkaline), enjoy some minimal water flow and

FACING PAGE: A typical coastal wetland of Ontario's Bruce Peninsula provides important wildlife habitat and acts as a settling pond for spring runoff.

encourage sedges, grasses, and low shrubs throughout, rather than just around the edges.

All wetlands are important wildlife habitats for fish, reptiles, songbirds, and amphibians, as well as vital links in the routes of migrating waterfowl, offering resting places, food sources, and protection from predators during stopovers. In the Great Lakes basin, more than a dozen species of ducks, grebes, and geese nest in wetland habitats and feed on the tender roots of aquatic plants. One species of water plantain is called the duck potato, since its tubers are a favorite of ducks and muskrats. The health of waterfowl is so closely tied to that of wetlands that in Lakes Erie, Michigan, and Huron the populations of American coots, least bitterns, marsh wrens, pied-billed grebes, soras, and swamp sparrows rise and fall with fluctuations in the lakes' water levels, which naturally affect the depth and extent of coastal wetlands.

Wetlands are the spawning grounds for as many as a hundred species of Great Lakes fish, from muskellunge and northern pike to minnows and deepwater sculpins, and the breeding grounds for many species of birds. Great blue herons, black-crowned night herons, and ospreys build nests in the (often dead) trees standing in swamps and feed on frogs and small fishes. Such at-risk species as the king rail and the least bittern shelter and nest among the reeds. And dabbling ducks such as pintails and blue-winged teals are often

MUSKELLUNGE

NORTHERN PIKE

seen with their tails in the air and their heads beneath the surface as they search the shallow bottom for shoots.

Southern Ontario's Minesing Swamp is a major wetland that has been spared the drainer's trench, one that gives a glimpse into what wetlands must have been like when settlers first arrived. Situated between Lake Simcoe and Georgian Bay, it is southern Ontario's largest wetland, 6,000 hectares (15,000 acres) of water, aquatic plants, and standing forest in an 80-meter (260-foot) depression left by the retreating Wisconsinan glaciers. At its center is a vast waterfowl staging area, where, when spring floodwaters inundate large areas of grassy fens, a swaying expanse of sedges and cattails provides ideal habitat for a diverse array of migrating birds. Soras, which are small, short-billed rails, pad about silently in the dense vegetation, foraging for seeds and snails. More than 220 species of

Minesing Swamp, southern Ontario's largest remaining wetland, is home to dozens of species of birds, reptiles, amphibians, and plants.

birds have been recorded in the swamp, 66 of which are spring and fall migrants: whistling swans, snow geese, and ducks and duck-like birds of many kinds—pintails, wigeons, gadwalls, buffleheads and scaup, goldeneyes and redheads—all pass through on their way to their northern breeding grounds. Sandhill cranes stop over on their spring migration to western and northern Canada. Many other wetland species nest here, including wood ducks, American black ducks, mallards, grebes, and several members of the heron family, including American and least bitterns.

The swamp also contains one of the oldest great blue heron colonies in the Great Lakes basin. The herons, large, gray, long-legged, long-necked, gracile wading birds, build their stick nests atop the trunks of flooded silver maples. They fly down from their aeries to stand motionless in the shallow water at the swamp's edge, blending with the greenery, waiting for unsuspecting small fish or frogs to swim by. Underwater, their legs must look like plant stems. Herons also eat snakes, small birds, and even young muskrats. In the air, they look like feathered pterodactyls. They hold their necks in a tight S position when flying, and their black feet trail visibly behind them. During breeding season, the heads of both males and females are adorned with long black plumes that hang down along the backs of their necks. (These plumes, or *aigrettes* in French, provide the name of the heron's closely related cousins, the egrets.)

In the 1980s, great blue herons were placed on the American Audubon Society's Blue List, suggesting that they were in decline. Though it is not officially endangered, the bird's status still bears watching. According to Byron Wesson, director of land management and stewardship services for the Nottawasaga Valley Conservation Authority, the number of heron nests in Minesing Swamp has gone down in recent years, for reasons unknown. Similar declines have been observed in Minnesota's Peltier Lake, which in 1989 was home to 1,137 nesting pairs of great blue herons, black-crowned night herons, and great egrets. By 2003 those numbers had dropped alarmingly, with few chicks reaching maturity and many nests abandoned. Cameras placed in the marsh caught evidence that the damage was being done by marauding raccoons and great horned owls.

There are raccoons in Minesing, as well as great gray owls, but herons may be declining because their food is becoming scarcer. The swamp is home to thirty fish species and ten frog and toad species, including the delightfully named pickerel frog, the mink frog, and the northern chorus frog. But frog populations are falling in many waterways; in the Great Lakes region, the Fowler's toad and the Blanchard's cricket frog are at risk. And, as Wesson says, "something is happening to the walleye population" as well.

Jack's Lake, north of the swamp, contains a unique variety of walleye that lays its eggs on lake-bottom vegetation, like its close cousin the yellow perch, rather than on bare gravel, as walleyes normally do. In 2000, a survey of the lake found only sixteen specimens and no clue to the cause of the decline. Another variety, the blue walleye, once abundant in Lakes Erie and Ontario, has been extinct since 1985 because of overfishing and declining water quality. Trouble in the frog and fish populations could account for trouble higher up, in the heronry.

Frogs are amphibians—from Greek words meaning "two lives," in this case lives spent on land and in water. Sometimes these habitats are occupied sequentially, in different stages of the animal's life cycle. The yellow-spotted salamander, for example, another common Great Lakes basin amphibian, lays its eggs in water but spends its adult life on the forest floor, keeping cool and moist under leaf litter and in rotting logs, and returning to its natal pond in the spring to mate and spawn. Frogs are in and out of water all their lives but deposit their eggs in water and spend their first few tadpole stages entirely in water, breathing through fishlike gills. The most common frogs in the Great Lakes basin are the bullfrog, he of the bulbous vocal sac; the spring peeper, a thumbnail-sized frog whose high, piping chorus is one of the first signs of spring; and the northern leopard frog, whose vocal sacs appear to bulge between its ears and its shoulders. Although all three are still common, pollution and habitat loss are taking their usual tolls, and numbers are down.

A healthy wetland is a botanist's dream. Many prize plants are found on the spongy ridges that form string fens, a boreal-like network of sedges and grasses studded with long, thin stands of cedars,

OVERLEAF: Spring peepers breed as early as March in temporary woodland ponds formed by melting snow or rain.

Frogs, fish, and mammals share many of the same types of genes that regulate reproduction, and consequently biologists look to frogs for the early warning signs of genetic change brought on by exposure to pesticides.

Globally, frogs have been in decline since the early 1990s, and scientists have been searching for a cause. In 1997, Tyrone Hayes of the University of California, Berkeley, conducted a series of experiments with African clawed frogs, subjecting them to increasing concentrations of the universal herbicide atrazine. He found that 80 percent of adult male frogs reared in water containing atrazine in concentrations greater than 1.0 part per billion (ppb) had smaller than normal laryngeal dilator muscles—the muscles that control the frogs' mating calls—and 30 percent had deformed reproductive organs. Some had both testes and ovaries. When he repeated the experiments using northern leopard frogs, he found "sex reversal" in males reared in water with only 0.1 ppb atrazine; some of these had eggs growing in their testes. He also found similar deformities in frogs in the wild. Hayes believes that atrazine triggers genes that cause male frogs to convert testosterone into estradiol—a naturally occurring form of estrogen—turning them into hermaphrodites, and he refers to the effect of atrazine as "chemical castration and feminization."

Atrazine is one of the world's most ubiquitous herbicides and has been found in most waterways bordering agricultural land, including those flowing into the Great Lakes. Water quality tests in the Great Lakes have shown concentrations of atrazine ranging from 1.0 to 1.2 ppb in Lakes Erie, Ontario, and Michigan. The current concentration of atrazine in water for human consumption considered acceptable by the United States Environmental Protection Agency is 3 ppb, but water with up to 350 ppb atrazine is deemed safe for aquatic life.

tamaracks, and alder thickets growing between long, narrow ponds, like a miniature version of New York State's Finger Lakes. The trees grow on hummocks formed by the root-balls of predecessor trees that have fallen and decomposed; the holes left by their falling have filled with water and support aquatic plant life such as the broadleaf arrowhead, a water plantain whose edible roots were harvested by First Nations peoples and used as a poultice for wounds, and bog buckbean, a member of the striking gentian family.

Fens are less acidic than bogs but still support a number of orchid species, all of them beautiful when flowering and some of them rare. In the fens in Minesing Swamp, there are Hooker's orchids, prairie white-fringed orchids, and small purple-fringed orchids. Arethusa, also called dragon's mouth, which Roger Tory Peterson calls a "bizarre flower, with its three erect sepals and the hood over its blotched and crested lip," looks a bit like a pink lady's slipper (which, though rare, is found in some swamps, as is the extremely rare ram's-head lady's slipper), except the slipper appears to have been mangled by an overzealous puppy. In all, ten orchid species, ten different violets, and twenty-three types of grasses are among the more than four hundred plant species found in wetlands throughout the Great Lakes basin.

The decline in populations of amphibians like the leopard frog may be caused by exposure to herbicides.

A female snapping turtle lays up to forty eggs in holes dug in sand with her powerful forelimbs.

Wetlands are home to a large number of rare and sensitive reptiles, including the globally threatened spotted turtle, at under 10 centimeters (4 inches) in length one of the basin's smallest and daintiest turtles. The wood terrapin, or wood turtle, is a heavily chiseled, 20-centimeter (8-inch) brownish turtle once found throughout eastern North America except in Indiana and Illinois, but now scarce. So too is the Blanding's turtle, the only box turtle of the genus *Emys*, in fact referred to as a "semibox." Box turtles are so called because their plastron, the underside of their shell, is divided into two movable halves, hinged in the middle by ligaments. When threatened, the turtle can draw in its head, limbs, and tail and close up its plastron like a box, so tightly, writes one herpetologist, that not even a broom straw can be inserted between the halves. Wood turtles are largely terrestrial, and have been for so long that they retain traces of webbing only on the hind feet. Indifferent swimmers, they prefer damp woods or the margins of swamps, half burying themselves in mud. They are herbivores and love berries but will occasionally eat insect larvae, snails, slugs, and earthworms.

All turtles are fairly long-lived; some box turtles don't reach sexual maturity until they are fourteen years old. Generally speaking, the larger the animal, the longer it lives, and the largest reptile in any swamp, in fact the largest terrestrial reptile in the northern part of the continent is the common snapping turtle. Snappers can live for a hundred years. Adult snappers grow to about 20 kilograms (45 pounds), and really old ones grow so fat on their diet of fish that their flesh oozes out through the openings in their plastrons and carapaces—at which point they were once considered a delicacy. They certainly don't look delicate; they look like armored tanks.

A snapper can measure 71 centimeters (28 inches) in length with head and tail outstretched, and its encrusted brown-to-black shell and yellow plastron seem too small for its body, which in fact is the case, since the adult cannot withdraw its enormous head or long tail into them. It is a strong swimmer, able to remain submerged for long periods and, some say, unable to eat except underwater: it forages for food by lying on the river or swamp bottom ready to dart its head out to grab passing fish. The snapper is lightning fast, especially when it senses danger; it can strike with the speed, if not the range, of a rattlesnake, and its head can reach halfway back along its shell. It is not wise to pick up a snapper by the shell: experts recommend lifting it by its tail, and if it's too big to be picked up that way, leave it alone. Seasoned turtle watchers keep large grain shovels in their cars for sliding recalcitrant snappers off the roads.

In April and May, females leave the water to lay their eggs, preferably in sand or rough gravel in riverside sand spits or along country roadsides. They scoop deep holes with their strong, clawed forelimbs, then turn and wiggle their way into the holes and cover themselves with sand to deposit their eggs in peace. About forty eggs are laid, sometimes as many as eighty, looking like bright white ping-pong balls; on average, 65 percent of them hatch in August or September. (Deflated ping-pong balls on the roadside mean

a skunk or raccoon has found the clutch.) Hatchlings claw their way up through the natal sand and migrate instinctively to water, crawling the gauntlet of raccoons, skunks, crows, and great blue herons as they go.

Because they are so long-lived, have large amounts of fat, and feed principally on fish, snapping turtles have been studied as indicators of local contamination in rivers and wetlands. Swamps and marshes act as water filters, and many of the fertilizers and pesticides picked up by runoff through farmland end up in sediments at the bottom of wetlands. In coastal wetlands, high levels of PCBs bioaccumulate—that is, collect in progressively higher concentrations—in the turtles' flesh, causing severe reproductive problems. In one study, conducted in Wheatley Harbour on Lake Erie, only 12 percent of snapping turtle eggs hatched and only 2 percent of those lived to become adults. Those adults were found to have reduced concentrations of calcium and globulin. Snapper populations are not threatened, but only because they are doing much better in inland wetlands, such as Minesing Swamp, than they are in those connected directly to the Great Lakes.

The small swamp near a cabin we once rented, not far from eastern Ontario's Charleston Lake, was home to muskrats, painted turtles, damselflies (similar to dragonflies except that, when at rest, their wings remain in a dihedral, or V formation), and many birds.

Damselflies are unusual in the insect world, having short antennae, superb eyesight, and long wings that cannot be folded out of the way when resting or, as seen here, mating.

A pair of wood ducks regularly broke into panicked flight whenever we walked near their nest. Unlike most ducks, which are open-water birds that nest in aquatic vegetation, wood ducks prefer shallow water and nest in the hollows of trees (or, sometimes, in large man-made nesting boxes), close to the ground or as much as 15 meters (50 feet) above it. Migrating wood ducks arrive in the Great Lakes area in April, where they congregate in swamps and on beaver ponds, choose mates, and select nesting sites. They do not bring material to the nest but soften whatever they find in the cavity with down feathers. More than one female may lay eggs in a nest; up to thirty-one eggs have been found in a single brood. The young have sharp claws on their webbed toes and a hook at the end of their bills, useful at fledging time for climbing out of the nest cavity and jumping to the ground, where the female (the drake having long abandoned the nest) leads them to water. Apart from eating tree, sedge, and water lily seeds that float in the water, wood ducks wander into the woods in search of berries and nuts—especially acorns, which they swallow whole. Their gizzards are capable of crushing and grinding chestnuts, beechnuts, acorns, and even bitter pecan nuts, which are as hard as hickory nuts. They are also very fond of spiders.

The adults are brightly and conspicuously patterned, especially the male, with its white-striped, crested head, bright red and white bill, white throat, and iridescent green plumage. The wood duck's beauty has worked against it in the past, as it was one of the most popular birds in the feather trade of the late nineteenth century, when it almost became extinct. It was protected from hunting from 1918 to 1941 in the United States, and there are now estimated to be 3 million in North America; the population is considered secure.

Another marsh or surface-feeding duck, and perhaps the most recognizable member of the duck family, is the mallard. Again, the predominant color of the male's head is iridescent green with purplish highlights, with a white neck ring, brownish back, and white tail feathers. Mallards are often seen close to human habitations and are so easily tamed that they are the progenitors of almost all domestic ducks. In the wild they frequently interbreed with other duck species, including pintails, gadwalls, and their nearest relative, the American black duck. (The females of mallards and American black ducks are difficult to tell apart, so that may account for the interbreeding.) In the east, the Great Lakes basin is the northern extent of their breeding range, although in the west they breed as far north as Alaska. Like wood ducks, mallards eat acorns and hickory nuts but subsist mainly on seeds: the stomach of one specimen contained 102,400 primrose willow seeds. Vegetation provides 90 percent of their diet, but the other 10 percent is varied and even includes meat. They have been known to eat salmon carcasses in the Northwest and also, presumably, in the Great Lakes area, and they will perform a "rain dance" in which they pat their feet rapidly on wet ground, making a sound that imitates the patter of rain and brings earthworms to the surface. A report published in Pennsylvania in 1914 noted that twenty mallards completely cleared a large pond of mosquito pupae and larvae in forty-eight hours. Ironically, wild mallards could be the solution, rather than the spark, to the spread of avian flu.

There are two species of marsh wrens in the Great Lakes basin, the long-billed (now known as the marsh wren) and the short-billed (now called the sedge wren). Although their ranges overlap, they are not even the same genus. The marsh wren is found in the Great Lakes region but is more a western bird, and is slightly larger than the sedge wren. Both weave small, ball-like nests of dry grass in wet areas (marsh wrens usually nest in cattail marshes, sedge wrens in sedge marshes and wet meadows). The males of both species build a number of dummy nests, sometimes as many as twenty-two, of which only two or three are occupied—by different females; wren males are polygynous (that is, they have more female mates). This may be meant to deceive predators and nest parasitizers, such as cowbirds, or it may simply be the males' way of showing the females how industrious they are.

Marsh wrens are further divided into western and eastern subgroups, differentiated by their singing. Eastern marsh wren males have a song repertoire of 30 to 70 songs each, while their western counterparts sing up to 210 songs; the divide between these two populations is Lake Superior. In *The Nature of Birds,* Adrian Forsyth notes that western marsh wren males devote 50 percent more brain area to vocalization than do their eastern conspecifics: "This fits with what we know about polygynous mating systems," Forsyth writes, "which favor males with the most developed courtship and territorial displays." Western males are more polygynous than eastern males, which suggests that eastern males are chosen by females not so much for their song repertoires as for their competence as providers. "A diverse repertoire is less useful [in a less polygynous system], and the valuable brain space that could be devoted to a large repertoire would be better employed in other tasks, such as finding food."

However, females of some other wetland bird species are attracted to males with large repertoires, just as female moose respond well to male moose with large antlers. If a male has enough brain space to devote a large part of it to learning new songs, he must have the intelligence that also makes him a good provider. Female red-winged blackbirds, at least in captivity, show a more vigorous courtship display when a recording of multiple song types is played to them, and female swamp sparrows go into a frenzy of nest building when they hear a male with a seemingly inexhaustible repertoire of songs. As studies of the Carolina wren, described in the previous chapter, suggest, choosing a mate on the basis of his musical repertoire means that birdsong is more than an expression of contentment; it's also a language that communicates intelligence and therefore knowledge of the territory's optimum food sources and nesting sites.

Creeping or flitting about the margins of wetlands are many smaller birds, either spring and fall migrants or breeding residents adapted to swampy conditions. Two species of waterthrushes are found in the Great Lakes region. One of the most common, the northern waterthrush, is a small warbler (waterthrushes only *look* like thrushes), dark brown above with a pale yellowish, black-striped underbelly and a ringing voice. They prefer densely wooded swamps with slow-moving water, and spend most of their time on the ground, foraging under the leaf litter for insects and other invertebrates. The Louisiana waterthrush, a southerly species that barely extends its range into the Great Lakes basin, is very similar to the northern, but it is whitish behind the streaked breast rather than yellowish. Both species continually bob their short tails, in the manner of phoebes, while walking or perching.

The spotted sandpiper breeds across North America and has been found to nest in the Great Lakes region. A robin-sized, plain brown shorebird, found usually on mudflats and beaches but also in shallow wetlands, it is distinguished by the large spots on its white breast and throat (in breeding season, which is April to August) and the small hook of white that appears on its shoulder ahead of its wing. It is the most common sandpiper in the region

FACING PAGE: A male sedge wren delivers its repertoire of songs atop a narrow-leaved cattail flower.

during breeding season, but during the spring and fall migrations it may be mistaken for the similar solitary sandpiper, although the solitary lacks the dark spots on the breast. Its legs are slightly longer than those of the spotted, and the spotted bobs continuously, even when it appears to be resting.

Recently, increased awareness of the importance of wetlands to the environment—they are the kidneys and liver of the Great Lakes ecosystem—has many groups working to restore ailing wetlands to health. Part of healing a wetland involves removing organisms that are contributing to their decline. A project begun in 1995 to restore the Cootes Paradise Marsh, at the western end of Lake Ontario, called for the expulsion of Asian carp, an introduced species of large, bottom-feeding fish that disturbs the natural breeding habitat of smaller, native fish by constantly rooting out aquatic plants and stirring up sediments. Within two years of their exclusion, phytoplankton—microscopic aquatic plant material that provides much of the food for small fish and many benthic, or lake-bottom, organisms and, incidentally, contributes roughly half of all the oxygen produced on the planet—increased from about 2 individuals per liter (quart) of water to more than 400 per liter. A total of twenty-five fish species were found to be using the marsh, the most common being pumpkinhead sunfishes and brown bullheads in the vegetated sections, and gizzard shad and alewives in the open areas. As well, some populations, such as yellow perch, fathead minnows, and emerald shiners, increased in number.

Similar projects are taking place around the Great Lakes shores and offer hope that the Lakes' delicate aquatic habitats will once again flourish as the spawning and breeding grounds for many of the region's native species.

SUN ON ROCK

From a distance, the Stone Road alvar on Pelee Island looks like an ordinary meadow, perhaps a former pasture that has been recently reclaimed by nature. Low shrubs and an occasional red cedar dot the savannalike landscape. The few trees around the edges are low and stunted and full of birds. There's an indigo bunting and a rufous-sided towhee in the grove of Carolinian chinquapin oaks and hickories at the start of a graveled path that curves off through the field, passing more Carolinian tree species, some of them quite rare. The hoptree, the seeds of which may have floated to the island from Point Pelee or been dropped to the ground in the guano of a migrating bird, is found only along the shores of Lake Erie and on the Erie Islands, and its presence here promises a sighting of a giant swallowtail butterfly, which in its caterpillar stage feeds on the hoptree's trifoliate leaves.

Signposts along the path soon make it apparent that this is no ordinary meadow. The plaques draw attention to the plants, many

ALVAR COMMUNITIES
IN THE GREAT LAKES BASIN

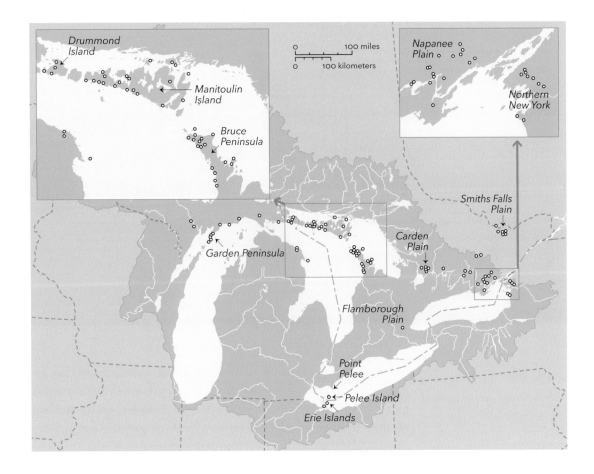

of which are scarce even in the Carolinian zone: hoptree, so unusual it's not listed in *Peterson Field Guide;* corn speedwell, so called
because it grows beside paths to greet the traveler; small skullcap,
which is a mint; and false pennyroyal, which also has a minty fragrance. There are also a few blue ashes, among the rarest trees in

the Great Lakes basin and an endangered species. Though an ash, the blue ash grows so slowly (on Pelee Island, a growth rate of about 2 millimeters a year, or less than a tenth of an inch, is common) that its wood can be as dense and heavy as oak. Savanna sparrows and yellow-billed cuckoos feed on its seeds.

In fact, the Stone Road Alvar is a 220-hectare (540-acre) ecological wonderland at the center of the island, one of the most biologically diverse habitats in all of Canada and the United States. It is a close association of six different kinds of communities: oak-hickory woodland; oak savanna; red cedar savanna; old-field thicket; prairie; and open alvar. According to Mary Celestino's definitive *Wildflowers of the Canadian Erie Islands,* it is home to 396 plant species, including 44 that are provincially rare and 33 regionally rare. At least four species occur nowhere else in Canada: downy wood mint, corn salad, yellow horse gentian, and Leavenworth's sedge.

Alvars themselves are rare. Defined as ecosystems of grasses and other herbaceous plants and sparse, shrubby vegetation growing in extremely thin soil on beds of limestone or dolostone, they exist in North America only in the Great Lakes basin. The International Alvar Conservation Initiative, working with the Nature Conservancy, has identified and assessed 121 alvar sites, comprising a total of 11,000 hectares (27,200 acres), or about a fifth of one percent of the total Great

Though nearly without soil, alvars, like this one on the Bruce Peninsula, support an amazing variety of plants, including grasses, mosses, and trees.

Lakes basin landmass. Two-thirds of the alvars are in Ontario; most of the rest are equally divided between Michigan (on Drummond Island and nearby areas) and New York (Jefferson County), with a few small sites distributed throughout the Erie Islands and Marblehead Peninsula in Ohio. They form an arc from Michigan's Upper Peninsula, across Drummond and Manitoulin islands, down the Bruce Peninsula, and in patchy areas of exposed limestone in southern Ontario and upstate New York—roughly following the limestone and dolostone cuesta of the Niagara Escarpment.

There are alvars in northern Europe: the word is from Sweden, where they were first described, and is applied to sites on several islands in the Baltic Sea. Wherever alvars are found, they are important and endangered habitats; with the harsh growing conditions they offer, the plants found on them have to be tough. Celestino calls them "disjuncts," because they exist on alvars often far from their native habitats, such as on the western plains. They are capable of surviving the extreme freezing and thawing, floods and droughts, that are the usual alvar cycles.

Alvars haven't always been valued, which partly explains why they are so rare today. In eighteenth- and nineteenth-century land surveys, designed to encourage agricultural settlement, areas with less than 10 centimeters (4 inches) of soil over solid bedrock were variously described as "prairies," "plains," or "meadow," if the alvar was of the grassland type, or "rocky barrens" if the limestone pavement was exposed. In 1845, the Maxton Plains alvar on northern Michigan's Drummond Island was uninvitingly described as "naked rock with scattering of small trees in crevices"; an 1856 survey identified Flamborough Plains in southern Ontario as "broken land." Carden Plain, also in southern Ontario, was described in 1856 as "soil burned off to rock."

Fire has played a significant role in the formation of some alvars. At the best of times, alvars are extreme environments—extremely hot in the summer, when the sun can heat the underlying limestone to 43°C (109 °F), nearly hot enough to fry an egg, and extremely cold in the winter, when ice crystals fragment and perturb the unlayered soil. They often flood in the spring, sometimes retaining meltwater for weeks, and parch in late summer, when the water has evaporated and the plant and animal life in the soil sizzles. Fire can exacerbate these conditions by destroying microbes and root systems that would otherwise nourish and hold the soil together.

But fire can also create alvars. Judith Jones, a botanist living on Manitoulin Island, has studied the fire history of most of the alvars in the Great Lakes basin. She became interested in the subject when she heard a native oral history account of an episode from the early 1600s when a group of Iroquois seized possession of Manitoulin Island from the Ottawa nation that had been living there seasonally for many generations. To discourage the Iroquois, the Ottawa set fire to the island, and much of its cover of northern hardwoods and spruce was destroyed. Jones wondered if the legend explained the extensive alvars on Manitoulin, and if fire had played a role in creating other alvars in the basin.

Assessing charcoal found in alvar soil, and cores from trees still growing in the limestone crevices, she found that several types of alvars were, in fact, initiated by fire. Alvars originally covered by trees all seemed to have been associated with burning. All the bur oak–limestone savannas she investigated, all the white cedar–jack pine–shrubby cinquefoil savanna alvars, and 83 percent of the mixed conifer-juniper alvars showed signs of fire initiation. The grassland alvars, however, seemed always to have been alvars. The grasslands alvar on Great La Cloche Island, between Manitoulin Island and the mainland, for example, had existed for 4,000 to 5,000 years and in that time had accumulated only 12 centimeters, or less than 5 inches, of soil. It showed no signs of having been started by fire.

Virtually all of the Lake Huron side of Manitoulin Island, from the shore to up to 4 kilometers (2.5 miles) inland, is a series of alvars. Two of them are forested with jack pine and white cedar interspersed with open spaces sporting such rare but exquisite wildflowers as lance-leaved coreopsis, a yellow-flowered daisy that grows as high as 60 centimeters (2 feet) above unusual, grasslike leaves. Alvar woodlands often don't look like alvars at all, with such large trees as white pine, white spruce, and white cedar growing up to 40 meters (130 feet), until a tree falls and exposes the shallowness

The Belanger Bay Alvar on Manitoulin Island is heavily treed, despite being watered only by rain and spring runoff.

Manitoulin Island—the name means "spirit island" in Ojibway—is an oasis of plenty in the north end of Lake Michigan. A long, narrow chunk of the Niagara Escarpment between Michigan's Upper Peninsula and Ontario's Bruce Peninsula, Manitoulin Island was created when Lake Algonquin, the geologic precursor of Lake Superior, drained eastward through Lake Nipissing and the Ottawa Valley, thereby scouring out the North Channel that now separates Manitoulin from the mainland. The island shelters more than 1,200 of Canada's 5,000 species of vascular plants.

LAKESIDE DAISY

"We have a great diversity of habitat," says the Manitoulin botanist Judith Jones. "We have shoreline, cliffs, bogs, fens, alvars. We are a microcosm of southern Ontario that hasn't been developed—yet."

Many of the threatened or endangered plant species on the island are alvar species, including dwarf lake iris, Lakeside daisy, Gattinger's agalinis, cylindric blazing star, and Houghton's goldenrod. The endangered loggerhead shrike still nests some years in the low shrubs, red-headed woodpeckers bore holes in the island's red pines, and sharp-tailed grouse form leks, or breeding congregations, on remnant prairie meadows, which are often covered with prairie dropseed grass. Other plants, such as Pitcher's and Hill's thistles, are dune and open sand plants found on one of the island's nature reserves at Misery Bay.

PITCHER'S THISTLE

"Of the twenty-six sites in Canada with Pitcher's thistle," says Jones, who is a spirited island enthusiast, "twenty-two of them are on Manitoulin Island. Gattinger's agalinis is found naturally only on Manitoulin and the North Channel Islands. And the Lakeside daisy, which is named for Lakeside, Ohio, should be called Manitoulin gold, because we have far more of them here than there are in Ohio and Michigan combined."

of its roots and the bare rock on which it was growing. And alvar grasslands such as are found on Great and Little La Cloche Islands are treeless meadows in which field mice and voles delve beneath the tall grasses and sedges.

Another species that favors alvar grasslands is the loggerhead shrike, a largish (20 centimeters, or 8 inches) gray, black, and white bird with a hooked beak and a peculiar predatory habit. Shrikes nest in hawthorn or red cedar trees and hunt mice and insects in the grass, then impale their prey on the thorns of their nest trees before eating them, because their weak songbird feet cannot hold them. Native to the prairies and the southern United States, loggerhead shrikes migrated east as early settlers cut down forests and created savanna grasslands—which they called farms—and allowed thorn trees to grow along the fencerows. Encroaching suburbs have subsumed much of this habitat, and the loggerhead shrike is now listed as endangered in its eastern range. It can still be found on the Carden and Napanee alvars, where extensive ranchlands create short-grass prairie conditions and thorn trees provide nesting sites and larder posts.

As is the case with Pelee Island's Stone Road Alvar, the rich species diversity and distinctive life-forms that alvars maintain have come to the attention of many citizens' groups in the basin, and steps are being taken to preserve and restore these unique and significant habitats. No longer dismissed as "broken land," alvars are now recognized for their vital contribution to the life of the region.

THE URBAN FOREST

One day in the winter of 1872, the historian Henry Scadding stood on Toronto's Queen Street bridge, which spans the Don River slightly to the east of the city's center, and recorded what he saw. The frozen river, he wrote in *Toronto of Old* (1873), reminded him of a rural English lane. Horses and sleighs were using it as a thoroughfare, and it was "bordered on each side by a high shrubbery of wild willow, alder, wych-hazel, dog-wood, tree-cranberry, and other specimens of the lesser brushwood of the forest." Up the slope there grew "numerous elm trees, very lofty, with gracefully-

FACING PAGE: Toronto's urban forest, covering more than 17 percent of the city, cools and cleans the air and preserves diminishing native tree species.

drooping branches." Looking higher he saw that oaks and "pines of a great height and thickness crowded the tops of the hills."

The population of Toronto at the time was about 35,000, and so it is understandable that much of the city seemed rural. It was situated between two rivers, the Don and the Humber, that meandered into Lake Ontario. Their valleys were joined by a great number of deep ravines that remained treed well into the mid-1900s. The valleys are still wooded and the view from the Queen Street bridge is not so different from that of 1872. The pines are gone—even in Scadding's day many of them had been blown down by tornadoes—and the white elms have succumbed to Dutch elm disease. But to a remarkable degree, Toronto's urban forest has remained intact since the city was founded. If a modern Scadding were to look over Toronto from the top of the CN Tower, he would see a city built around more than 1,000 treed parks, comprising 10,000 hectares (nearly 25,000 acres) of land, or 17 percent of the total city area. The city's residential areas are also hidden under an almost continuous canopy of green.

Toronto is not unique. The urban forest in Buffalo, New York, maintained in the park system and broadened tree-lined avenues designed by Frederick Law Olmsted in 1868, covers about 1,600 hectares (4,000 acres) in the heart of the city. Milwaukee,

also hit hard by Dutch elm disease in the 1960s (the city lost 200,000 elms), is once again 42 percent covered by forest canopy in some areas, and urban foresters are working toward increasing that figure. Chicago can almost be described as a forest with buildings scattered among the trees: it has 50.8 million trees, roughly twenty for each citizen. The average American city is 33 percent shaded by its urban canopy. Twenty-five percent of the forested area in the United States, one out of every four trees, is found in cities. In many cases, the trees in city parks, along waterways, and on boulevards represent all that is left of the original forest that existed in presettlement days. Remnants of the virgin forest that once covered all of New England still exist in downtown New York City, for instance: one tulip tree in Queens is estimated to be 450 years old.

"Urban forestry is not just about looking after trees," says a former chief forester of Toronto, Willem Morsink, one of the pioneers of a scientific field that until recently sounded, to many ears, like an oxymoron. "We look after all aspects of the natural environment: water, wildlife, as well as the people who live in the forest." Before moving to Toronto, Morsink was the chief forester in Windsor, Ontario, where less than 2 percent of the original forest remained in the countryside surrounding the city, and most of that was in hedgerows. The forest canopy was denser within city limits than outside them. Many of the urban species, however, were European imports, either accidentals or ornamentals, like the horse chestnut. When the ancient elms along Windsor's Ouellette Avenue died in the 1960s—the first diseased elm in Canada was identified in Windsor in 1958—Morsink replaced them with the rare but native Kentucky coffee tree. On other sites he favored such native shade species as silver maple and sycamore, whose hollow trunks were used by settlers as food storage coffers.

Part of an urban forester's job is to restore to areas within the city the kind of trees that naturally grew there, by

Raccoons have adapted well to city life: they are larger and have different social habits than their wilder counterparts.

Urban sewer systems now do two jobs: they direct both sewage and stormwater, or spring runoff, into a city's water treatment plant. During storms or after heavy snows, so much water can flow into a sewer that the treatment plant floods and overflows; raw sewage as well as runoff contaminated with salt, oil, lawn fertilizers, and other chemicals spills directly into the nearest lake or river.

With precipitation expected to increase as a result of climate change, federal, state, or provincial, and municipal governments are investing in stormponds, artificial wetlands situated between storm drains and sewage plants. The stormponds handle runoff, leaving the treatment plants to deal only with sewage. Wetlands hold water for days and weeks, directing it by means of constructed swales and weirs into a series of sedimentation ponds, where contaminants settle out before the cleared water is allowed to continue into the natural system. The area is planted with native species of plants and attracts birds, rabbits, amphibians, and other wildlife—including local citizens seeking contact with a relatively natural environment. And the city saves millions of dollars in cleanup and treatment costs.

In 2000, the governments of Canada and Ontario allocated more than c$2.5 billion for urban water treatment improvements around Lake Ontario, and stormponds feature prominently in the planning. The city of Toronto is spending another c$1.5 billion on waterfront regeneration, including upgrades to Grenadier Pond, in the city's High Park, which already functions as a stormpond.

The citizens of Duluth, Minnesota, are lobbying for a stormpond to be built in Bayfront Park, between Duluth's downtown and its harbor. The city has allocated 0.2 hectare (0.5 acre) for the project, but the planners want at least 0.8 hectare (2 acres), enough to contain a wetland designed in the shape of the Great Lakes, with each lake planted with wetland species native to that lake. They anticipate the pond will cost us$1 million per acre, but they expect the cost to be offset by much lower expenditures on sewage treatment improvements. "What the stormpond will do is educate people to the importance of wetlands," says Kurt Leuthold, a project engineer. "With awareness comes protection, and that's the ultimate goal."

matching soil and drainage types to specific tree species. In Toronto, Morsink identified six forest ecosystems: wet, swampy forests on poorly drained soil and bottomlands, where willows and alders do well; wet-moist elm-ash forests on loam and clay soils that become saturated in the spring; sugar maple forests on sloping clay and loam terrain, which held enough water to maintain the trees' supply in the summer without drowning them in the spring; dry oak-pine forests, on well-drained sandy soils with less than 10 percent water retention by soil volume, such as the black oak savanna in High Park; edge-of-forest species, such as yellow and paper birches; and Carolinian-zone trees that do well in dry, sandy areas, such as hoptree, shagbark hickory, and sassafras. By planting native trees in the kind of habitat they prefer, Morsink and his successor, Richard Ubbens, have created a variety of habitats that are as close to natural as it is possible to come in a man-made environment.

Toronto's urban forest supports a full complement of forest wildlife. More than a thousand red foxes live within the city limits, cruising the golf courses and the ravines, as does an entire deer herd and a pack of eastern coyotes that keep the deer in check. At least two hundred species of birds have been spotted in the Don Valley, including thirty-five species of waterfowl at the river's mouth in Toronto Harbour. In some years 30,000 birds have been counted feeding in the shallow nearshore water. There are more skunks per square kilometer in downtown Toronto than there are in Algonquin Park, and the city's urban raccoons may be evolving their own separate subspecies: they are bigger, live longer, and have different feeding, denning, and reproductive habits than their wild counterparts.

When Willem Morsink began working in Toronto in 1985, he was an oddball adjunct to the city's parks division. Today Richard Ubbens heads a department with 230 full-time employees; more foresters work for him than for the provincial government's Ministry of Natural Resources, "and we're still underresourced," he says.

Urban forests benefit cities in many ways. Some of them are simply aesthetic: real estate agents know that a house with a tree in the yard will sell for more than an identical house without one. But, as is often the case, there are links between aesthetics and psychological health: people may want trees in their yard because trees make them feel better. As E.O. Wilson puts it in *The Future of Life,* "What we call aesthetics may be just the pleasurable sensations we get from the particular stimuli to which our brains are inherently adapted," and our brains are adapted to natural, not artificial, habitats. Results of a nine-year study published in 1984 in *Science* magazine by Roger S. Ulrich of the Harvard Cancer Center reported that surgery patients in a Pennsylvania hospital recovered faster and required less medication if their rooms afforded a view of trees rather than of brick walls.

When researchers from the University of Illinois looked at the role of trees in Chicago's Robert Taylor Homes—the largest public housing project in the world, consisting of twenty-eight highrise apartment buildings, some on treed lots but most on land that was paved—they found that residents who lived among trees experienced better relationships with their neighbors and a stronger sense of community. They felt safer; they gathered at night more and their children played outside more often, forming relationships with other children. The researchers also found that there was significantly less domestic violence in homes in areas where there were trees. "Without vegetation," said Frances Kuo, one of the researchers, "people are very different beings."

Urban trees benefit the environment as well as the soul. During summer months, the cooling effect of trees reduces the need for air-conditioning, and therefore the demand for electricity, which in turn decreases carbon emissions from coal-burning power plants. A recent study in Milwaukee determined that shade trees saved the city's homeowners $650,000 a year in energy bills and calculated that if a tree were planted beside every house in the city so that its shade fell on air conditioners, the annual savings would be more than $1.5 million. A similar study in Chicago found that while deciduous trees provided shade in the summer, coniferous trees reduced wind speed in the Windy City, and that increasing both types of tree cover by 10 percent would save each resident $50 to $90 a year in heating and cooling costs.

GREAT LAKES SAND DUNES

Coastal sand dunes around the Great Lakes constitute vital and distinctive environments that support more unique species of plants, insects, and animals than any other ecosystem in the Great Lakes basin. The dune system on the eastern shore of Lake Michigan is the largest in the world, covering more than 111,000 hectares (275,000 acres); the eastern shore of Lake Ontario also contains an extensive dune system, stretching 27 kilometers (17 miles) along the New York State coastline, as does the south shore of Lake Superior. Sand dunes in the basin support 315 species of vascular plants; 36 species of mites as well as flies, beetles, springtails, book lice, and fungi; 32 species of mammals; and 68 species of shorebirds and passerines.

Dunes are made of sand deposited in the basin 10,000 years ago by melting glaciers. They are found primarily at the mouths of rivers, which carry sand from the higher land to the lakeshores. High water levels 6,000 to 4,000 years ago sifted and sorted the sand particles, pushing the smaller grains inland and leaving larger pebbles at the water's edge. Over the past 3,000 years, lake currents, meltwater, and wind have formed the sand into the four basic dune types found in the basin: parabolic, or U-shaped dunes; perched dunes sitting atop glacial moraines; linear dunes running parallel to the shoreline, formed by rising and falling lake levels; and transverse dunes, from sand deposited in shallow bays along the glaciers' retreating edges.

Without vegetation, sand dunes would quickly be dispersed by wind. The Great Lakes dunes have become the habitat for a number of grass species specifically adapted to survival in the dunes' rugged environment, where nutrients are few, moisture is low, and temperatures at sand level can soar to 82°C (180°F). American beach grass, or marram grass, for example, actually requires burial by sand to propagate. Its rhizomes, or root tendrils, extend 3 meters (9.8 feet) into the sand, and can absorb silica to strengthen the plant's stalks and render them resistant to blasting sandstorms. Great Lakes wheatgrass

Lakeside dunes in Hiawatha National Forest, Michigan.

also reproduces by means of rhizomes, flourishing on the leeward sides of dunes on Lakes Huron, Superior, and Michigan. Long-leaved reed grass, sand cherry, and wormwood are other hardy species found around the Great Lakes.

More than 2,000 hectares (5,000 acres) of Lake Michigan's unique dune system have been mined since the 1900s, and many of its more famous locales—Pigeon Hill, Creeping Joe, and Maggie Thorp dunes, to name a few—have disappeared. Dune sand is nearly 80 percent quartz and is used primarily in foundries and for glass production; it sells for less than US$11 per tonne (US$10 per ton). Efforts by the Lake Michigan Federation and the West Michigan Environmental Action Council to preserve the dunes have heightened public awareness and slowed the dunes' human-caused erosion. A 1991 study, for example, found that more than 1 million people visit Sleeping Bear Dunes National Park every year to see the dunes, and the park has generated US$39 million since its creation. As appreciation for these magnificent and ecologically significant habitat increases, so do chances for their long-term survival.

Trees also act as retention reservoirs for water. They are constantly transpiring water vapor into the air, and an average-size 12-meter (40-foot) tree holds 67 liters (17.7 gallons) of water in its roots, trunk, branches, and leaves. During rainstorms, then, trees absorb water that would otherwise enter storm drains or urban creeks, eroding soil and flushing pollutants into the Lakes. The Milwaukee study found that the urban forest in that city reduces stormwater flow by 22 percent, saving the city $1.5 million a year by eliminating the need to build extra stormwater retention facilities.

Trees live by turning carbon dioxide into carbohydrates (which they ingest) and oxygen (which they exhale). Carbon dioxide is a greenhouse gas, produced by the burning of wood and fossil fuels, and so in removing carbon from the air, trees reduce the buildup of carbon dioxide in the atmosphere and slow global warming. The amount of carbon sequestered by a single tree can be astonishing. A 1993 study found that a 12-meter (40-foot) tree with a crown area of 113 square meters (1,216 square feet) sequesters 47 kilograms

(104 pounds) of carbon from the atmosphere per year—that's 2,350 kilograms (5,180 pounds) of carbon over the fifty-year average life span of a tree.

Morsink has measured the amount of carbon a tree takes from the air and the amount of carbon its shade saves a power plant from having to produce. He has calculated that one urban tree cleans 149.2 kilograms (329 pounds) of carbon each year from the air. Since each person in the Great Lakes basin produces approximately 4.3 tonnes (4.7 tons) of carbon dioxide emissions each year, it takes about twenty-eight trees per person (slightly more than there are in Chicago) to offset our annual carbon contribution to the atmosphere. Cities are where the most carbon is produced; therefore, urban forests are our first lines of defense against carbon dioxide buildup in the atmosphere. Chicago's trees take 141,000 tonnes (155,000 tons) of carbon out of the Chicago's air per year and turn it into life-giving oxygen. They also remove more than 5,400 tonnes (6,000 tons) of air pollutants, saving the city $9.2 million a year in atmospheric cleanup.

It's partly for the body, but also largely for the soul that urban forests are attracting so much attention among town planners, administrators, and even developers. People—including people who vote and buy houses—are beginning to understand that trees are more than accessories to an urban building lot. Richard Louv, the child development guru whose book *The Last Child in the Woods* is subtitled *Saving Our Children from Nature-Deficit Disorder,* charted the growing movement toward increasing the amount of natural habitats in cities. "A denatured urban or suburban environment," he writes, "is not good for children or the land." Truly grassroots initiatives such as green urbanism, landscape urbanism, and the "zoopolis movement"—which seeks to integrate wild animal populations into city cores by means of wildlife corridors—are gaining in popularity with urban planners and architects, and urban forestry is becoming a vital component of these trends. "We're getting to the point at which we can tell the city planners what we want the city to look like four or five decades from now," says Richard Ubbens. And the city planners are beginning to listen.

FACING PAGE: Urban green spaces, such as Toronto's High Park, provide city residents with important links to nature.

SEVEN

WATER
WORLD

THE PRESENCE OF WATER IN all its forms—liquid, solid, and vapor—distinguishes our planet from the others in the solar system and makes life on Earth possible. As the French hydrologist Robert Kandel bluntly put it: "No water, no life." Mammalian bodies, including ours, are about 78 percent water, and water accounts for 50 percent of the mass of even the driest plants. Without the continuous presence of water—in the air, in the ground, in our cells—we will die.

But water hasn't always been here. Four and a half billion years ago, waterless Earth was buffeted by a series of huge comets that originated in the Oort cloud beyond the orbit of Pluto. The force of one explosive collision tore off an enormous chunk of Earth, roughly a quarter of the planet, and the resulting debris became our satellite moon.

Comets are composed primarily of ice and frozen carbon dioxide, and it is this bombardment of ice balls, vaporizing on impact, that accounts for most of the water on Earth. In a sense not intended by ufologists, life really did arrive from outer space. The idea that the amount of water on the planet is constant, that the same water just keeps cycling and recycling, is not entirely accurate, since ice comets are coming at us all the time, vaporizing when they enter

FACING PAGE: Water ripples over glacial deposits at Lake Ontario's Whitby Marsh. Only 1 percent of Great Lakes water is renewed each year.

223

Seen from the sky, Erie's elliptical mirror

Flashes ten thousand square miles of mercurial glass...

ROBERT FINCH, "Lake," from *Sail-boat and Lake,* 1988

Earth's atmosphere and adding about 270 million tonnes (300 million tons) of new water to the existing water cycle every year.

At first, water molecules circled the earth as vapor, but eventually the clouds condensed and fell on the planet as rain—centuries, perhaps millennia, of rain. Freshwater filled every depression on the earth's surface, including the Pacific basin, which, some geologists believe, is the result of the impact that created the moon. A secondary effect of that collision was a crack in the earth's lithosphere that encircled the planet like a gaping wound, spewing molten lava and dissolved gases up to the earth's surface. Where that rift was underwater, the vents heated the water to about 700°C (1,300°F), and minerals were released into the oceans in clouds, so-called "black smokers." In some of the deepest parts of the oceans, these vents are still smoking, and it is now thought that life on Earth originated at such sites. Life-forms found near black smokers are bizarrely different from, and yet eerily reminiscent of, modern animal assemblages: 2-meter (6-foot) tubeworms, pale clams the size of melons, white crabs, yellow mussels, jellyfishlike organisms, eyeless shrimp. These creatures live in complete darkness, metabolizing hydrogen sulfide instead of oxygen. Not only do they resemble marine fauna found everywhere today, including the Great Lakes, but their existence underlines the property of water that was essential for life: its ability to dissolve minerals, to turn rock into food.

Of the 1.36 billion cubic kilometers (326 million cubic miles) of water on the planet, only about 2.6 percent of it, 36 million cubic kilometers (8.6 million cubic miles), is freshwater, and only about a

third of that is available to us. The rest is trapped in underground aquifers or frozen in polar and glacial ice. That still leaves a lot of freshwater, about 11.5 million cubic kilometers (2.8 million cubic miles). And about a fifth of that is stored in or recharges through the Great Lakes.

LOW-LEVEL HEADACHES

The Great Lakes are large enough for the moon's gravitational pull to cause tides, albeit small ones. The largest is recorded in Lake Michigan, where tides at Chicago and Milwaukee have an oscillation of 4.3 centimeters (1.7 inches). Spectacular short-period fluctuations, unrelated to tides, occur on all five lakes. These result from the tilting of the lake surfaces caused by wind or differential barometric pressure associated with storms, phenomena known as

The tiny pumpkinseed, or yellow sunfish, spawns in wetlands and inhabits shallow bays and ponds, where it is preyed upon by herons, loons, and larger fish.

seiches. Lake Erie has the highest seichal fluctuations, because it is the shallowest; its axis lies parallel to the prevailing winds and its basin is as regular and smooth as the bottom of a bathtub. Strong winds blowing along Lake Erie often raise the downwind water level as much as 2.6 meters (8.4 feet) and lower the windward end by the same amount. When the wind stops, the water slops back and forth for the next fourteen to sixteen hours, in imitation of tides. In June 1954, a seiche caused by a sudden squall and its related pres-

sure jump blew into Lake Michigan, raising water in Chicago's harbor by 3 meters (10 feet) and killing eight bystanders.

Longer-period fluctuations in lake levels also occur as the result of rainfall, evaporation, and the flow of water from one lake to another. As everywhere on earth, water in the Great Lakes is constantly evaporating and precipitating as rain or snow. The average annual rainfall over Lake Superior is 73.5 centimeters (29 inches), and the average amount of water lost through evaporation is about 45.7 centimeters (18 inches). In the lower Lakes, rainfall averages 86 centimeters (34 inches) per year and evaporation claims 91 centimeters (36 inches). The Lakes receive a great deal more water from their contributary rivers and from underground aquifers than from direct precipitation (rain and snow account for less than 1 percent of the Lakes' annual renewal of water), but they are more or less offset by the rate of flow from one lake to another and eventually into the St. Lawrence River, so that the actual fluctuation of lake levels is about 1.2 meters (4 feet) over a five- or six-year period in Lake Superior, and up to 2 meters (6.5 feet) over the same length of time in Lake Ontario.

These changes can occur rapidly, in some cases alarmingly so, when seasonal conditions conspire against the status quo. And it can take several years for normal levels to reestablish themselves after an unusual fluctuation. For example, Lake Huron's all-time high of 177.19 meters (581.36 feet) above sea level was set in 1986 and was almost reached again in 1997. However, low precipitation in the Lake Superior region and extremely high temperatures in the lower Lakes in 1998 caused Lakes Michigan-Huron water to drop 64 centimeters (25 inches) in 1999. In 2000, the lakes dropped again, for a total of 127 centimeters (50 inches). The level rose slightly the following year, but in 2003 it fell to only 175.73 meters (576.57 feet)— a drop of nearly a meter and a half (almost 5 feet) in six years.

Fluctuating water levels have eroded a series of high-water marks on this shoreline outcrop on Ontario's French River. Historically lake levels rise and fall more than 1 meter (3 feet) over a seven-year period.

Residents, mainly cottage owners whose properties are accessible only by boat, expressed concern, worried that either global warming or increased dredging of the St. Clair River was causing Lakes Michigan-Huron to drain too quickly into the lower Lakes. According to Geoff Peach, coastal resources manager at the Lake Huron Centre for Coastal Conservation, the current level of Lakes Michigan-Huron is "hovering around 176 meters [577 feet], which is about 40-45 centimeters [about a foot and a half] below the lake's long-term average." However, it is still above its record low of 175.7 meters (576.5 feet), set in 1961. The effects of dredging were felt most strongly in the 1950s, he says, and although climate change might account for the dip, "we don't have a long enough data set to say with confidence that it is not simply a normal low-level fluctuation similar to what has been experienced historically." In other words, one of the main characteristics of any body of water as large as a Great Lake is unpredictability.

The Great Lakes exhibit both lacustrine and oceanlike currents; because of their size, their currents are affected by the Coriolis force, an effect caused by the earth's rotation on its north-south axis. In the northern hemisphere, the Coriolis force causes large-body water currents to veer to the right. Investigators on the Lakes have reported on "the apparent tendency of wind-driven surface water to move to the right of the wind direction," which means that lake currents tend to revolve around the Lakes in a clockwise direction. The Lakes also exhibit localized upwellings and sinkings of massive volumes of water, another oceanic trick. Otherwise the Lakes' strong currents are influenced by the prevailing westerly winds that create surface waves, the flow-through of water from lake to lake, and the shape and topography of the individual lake basins. Generally speaking, surface currents in all five lakes circle near their shores at a rate of between 1.6 and 3.2 kilometers an hour (1 to 2 miles per hour) before draining into the next lake basin and eventually into the St. Lawrence River.

One further consequence of the Lakes' size is a deviation from the phenomenon general to lakes known as thermal stratification. During the summer, the water at the surface of a lake is warmer

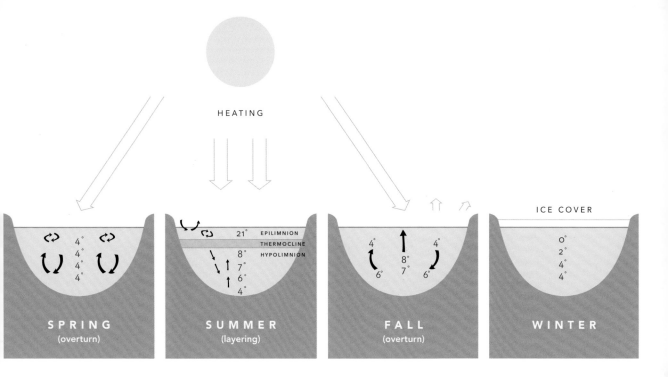

HEATING

ICE COVER

4°	21° EPILIMNION		0°
4°	THERMOCLINE	4°	2°
4°	8° HYPOLIMNION	8°	4°
4°	7°	7°	4°
	6°	6°	
	4°		

SPRING
(overturn)

SUMMER
(layering)

FALL
(overturn)

WINTER

than the water at the bottom, and in colder months it is not. Stratification has to do with water density, which is a factor of its temperature: denser water sinks to the bottom of the lake, and less
dense water rises to the top. The temperature of maximum density
of fresh water is 4°C (39.2°F); anything colder or warmer will be less
dense and so lighter. In the spring, in lakes of moderate dimensions,
all the water from top to bottom is the same temperature—4°C—
and is circulated evenly by wind and current. This is called spring
overturn. As summer progresses, however, the surface water warms,
becomes lighter (and therefore less dense), and so does not sink to
mix with the lower layer. This surface layer—the epilimnion—may
be as warm as 21°C (70°F), while the lower layer—the hypolimnion—
remains at 4°C or only slightly warmer. Between them lies the thermocline, the depth at which the temperature change is greater than
1°C per meter (0.55°F per foot) of depth, and a zone that may be 20
meters (65.6 feet) thick where the temperature drops suddenly as
depth increases. No water can pass through it to mix with the layers
above or below. In the fall, when the epilimnion gradually cools until it is the same temperature as the hypolimnion, the thermocline

disappears, and once again the shallow and deep layers mix. This is the fall overturn. Then winter sets in, and the upper layer begins to lose its warmth. As it cools to below 4°C (39.2°F), however, it actually becomes lighter, and so remains above the lower, denser layer. Thus the upper layer can freeze over, and the lower layer will remain 4°C above the freezing point.

In each of the Great Lakes, this ideal stratification model is skewed by sheer size. The thermocline does not occupy the same depth or have the same thickness evenly throughout the lake; instead it fluctuates, rising and falling under the influence of currents, seiches, high waves, and even the Coriolis force. This has enormous implications for the distribution of nutrients and of pollutants, for only the epilimnion circulates while the hypolimnion remains dormant and stagnant. It also decreases the amount of habitat available to cold-water fish species, while increasing the habitat for warm-water species.

The Lakes are subject to another, related phenomenon. During the summer, shallow inshore water warms much more rapidly than surface water near the center of the lake, so the Great Lakes tend to warm in the summer from the shore out, creating a vertical thermocline known as a thermobar. As William Ashworth notes in *The Late, Great Lakes*, "This change from a horizontal to a vertical interface has profound effects on the life within the waters, the breeding cycles of wetland-dependent animals, and even the climates of nearby coastal cities." In other words, much of the natural history of the Great Lakes is unique to the Great Lakes.

CLEAR, COOL WATER

One of the chief questions asked by limnologists of the nineteenth century was whether the water at the bottom of the Lakes, in the hypolimnion, might be salty, either from dissolved salt from the Paleozoic salt beds that underlie the Detroit River (the source of Windsor Salt) and Goderich, Ontario (Sifto Salt), or from some prehistoric encroachment of the Atlantic Ocean. After all, 10,000 years ago marine fish such as Atlantic cod and Atlantic salmon were commonly found in the basins that became Lakes Ontario and Erie.

Investigations proved that neither was the case; of all the many dissolved minerals found in Great Lakes water, sodium chloride exists in only trace amounts. The Lakes are low in minerals generally: on average, uncontaminated Great Lakes water contains dissolved minerals in concentrations of 110 parts per million (ppm), whereas ocean water contains about 35,000 ppm, and rainwater between 30 and 40 ppm.

The composition of these dissolved minerals varies from lake to lake. For example, although iron is present in all five in small quantities, its concentration in Lake Superior (0.16 ppm) is three times that of other Lakes because of high iron deposits in the Canadian Shield. Lake Michigan is relatively high in magnesium (7.01 ppm), an essential element needed by plants for photosynthesis, because of a large deposit of magnesium sulfate in southwestern Wisconsin. Other factors contributing to disparities among the Lakes include their size in relation to the size of their respective drainage areas. The surface of Lake Superior occupies 40 percent of its drainage area, which means that 40 percent of the rain falling on the Lake Superior watershed falls directly on the lake and therefore absorbs no minerals from the surrounding land. Lake Erie, on the other hand, occupies only 28 percent of its drainage area, and Lake Ontario 22 percent; in the lower Lakes, there is much more rainfall annually, and almost 80 percent of it falls on land before draining into the lakes, picking up and dissolving great amounts of minerals as it goes.

These mineral concentrations, it should be remembered, are historical; they represent the Lakes in their pristine states. Many date from studies conducted in the early half of the twentieth century and measure only naturally occurring minerals, such as calcium, carbon, magnesium, iron, sodium, and potassium, and natural compounds such as carbon dioxide and nitrous oxide. They don't take into account the increase in dissolved minerals entering the Lakes from agricultural, industrial, and municipal wastes. Instead, they set the baseline for the era of intense pollution that was to come. As early as 1950, the concentrations and kinds of compounds entering the Lakes were very different from historical norms.

Studies conducted in 1951 at lake-water intakes in several Ohio cities, for example, showed mineral concentrations up to 367 ppm; as we shall see, this figure leapt astronomically during the second half of the century.

DEADLY BLOOMS

Throughout the 1950s and '60s, the most serious problem affecting water quality in the Great Lakes was nutrient loading, a superabundance of nutrients in the water causing a shift in the Lakes' algal population. Before settlement, all the Great Lakes were oligotrophic, meaning there was very little production of organic material, such as algae, in their waters. The Lakes were nearly as clean and clear as rainwater, and the quality was almost that of distilled water. Phytoplankton varieties were few, primarily diatoms, microscopic algae that had adapted to the Lakes' cold temperatures and low phospho-

rus levels. Diatoms lived primarily at the summer thermocline, the interface between the epilimnion and the hypolimnion, and relied mainly on silicon dioxide, a nutrient the lakes had in abundance. Positioned at the bottom of the food chain, they flourished in the Lakes' shallow embayments, such as the western end of Lake Erie, Lake Ontario's Bay of Quinte, Lake Michigan's Green Bay, and Lake Huron's Saginaw Bay—which, as the early settlers found, attracted fish and were therefore prime areas for commercial fishing.

When the same settlers cut down trees along the rivers that fed the Lakes, however, they allowed more sunlight to warm the river water, and the temperature of the Lakes began to rise. Then, with the growth of cities, water taken out of the Lakes for industrial use was returned at warmer temperatures. Detergents containing phosphates were discharged into the Lakes, and runoff from agricultural regions carried more and more inorganic fertilizers. Algal growth began to explode. Records kept in Cleveland tell the story: hydrologists at the Cleveland waterworks had been recording algal counts at the city's intake pipes since 1919, when the tally was around 100 algae per milliliter of water (2,960 per ounce). By 1945 the count had risen to 800 algae per milliliter (23,700 per ounce), and in 1964 it was 2,500 algae per milliliter (74,000 per ounce), high enough to make the water look like pea soup.

Huge diatom blooms were depleting Lake Erie's store of silicon dioxide, and eventually diatomic algae were replaced with forms that relied more on nitrogen than on silicon, in particular green and blue-green algae, also known as cyanobacteria, the oldest living organisms on the planet. As more phosphorus entered the Lakes, even dissolved nitrogen began to disappear, and blue-green algae, which can extract nitrogen from the air, gradually dominated all other kinds. Unprecedented amounts of blue-green algae bloomed at the surface, shading the thermocline and cooling the waters below. When the algae died, it sank to the bottom, where it blanketed the sediment as it decomposed, consuming large amounts of oxygen in the process. So much oxygen was used up that the lake bottoms became chronically anoxic, entering an oxygen-deprived condition known as hypereutrophication that is inimical to animal life.

FACING PAGE: High levels of phosphorus from agricultural and urban runoff create dangerous algal blooms in Lakes Ontario and Erie.

MAYFLY ADULT (*above*)
AND NYMPH

The consequences of eutrophication in Great Lakes water were heralded in the early 1950s by insects so ubiquitous the warning could hardly have gone unheeded: the mayfly. Belonging to the family Ephemeridae, mayflies (also known as shadflies) commonly inhabit ponds, streams, and lakes. The adults of the genus *Hexagenia* lay their eggs in deep water, and the nymphs live in the detritus on the lake bottom for several years before rising to the surface, molting into preadult form and floating for a few hours until their four wings dry. During this brief interval they are feasted upon by frogs and fish, particularly walleye and blue pike. Come night, the surviving subimagos swarm to shore, where they attach themselves to cattails or poplar leaves, or to street lamps, cottage porch lights, and shop signs. In the morning they molt and swarm again—they are the only insects known to molt after their wings are functional. Many are scooped up by bats.

At this stage they are practically transparent, their internal organs visible within their wraithlike bodies. "No doubt it was these strange, pale insects dancing in the moonlight," the entomologist A.H. Verrill wrote in the 1930s, "that gave rise to the tales of fairy dances, for no lovely fairies in gowns of spiders' silk move with more rhythmic grace or greater abandon." They mate, the male dies and falls to the ground, and the female flies back out over the lake, where she wraps her wings about her body and plunges into the water to lay her 4,000 eggs on the rocky bottom before dying in her turn.

For thousands of years, mayfly nymphs were the most common lake-bottom creatures in Lake Erie, and every June adult mayflies had swarmed Lake Erie's shoreline on a single night before dying. In the 1940s, they appeared on shore in such numbers that snowplows were sometimes brought out to clear the roads of the bodies of the dead males. In 1953, however, no mayflies appeared at all. That September the nymph count in Lake Erie's sediment plunged from around 500 nymphs per square meter (46 per square foot) to fewer than 50 (5 per square foot). A few returned the following year, a few less in 1955, but by 1956 the mayfly was entirely extirpated from Lake Erie. Studies found that the lake bottom was so low in oxygen that mayfly nymphs were not surviving until the first molt; they

Algal blooms in Lake Erie were common in the 1970s, producing the infamous "dead lake" effect, but they declined substantially when the International Joint Commission imposed cutbacks in the discharge of phosphorus under the terms of the Great Lakes Water Quality Agreement of 1978. Phosphorus is the limiting factor—the nutrient that controls the abundance or scarcity—of algae: excess phosphate results in excess growth. The agreement aimed to lower phosphorus discharges in Lake Erie by nearly 50 percent, from 20,000 tonnes (22,040 tons) per year to 11,000 tonnes (12,122 tons). By the time the agreement was amended in 1987, the load had been reduced to 13,000 tonnes (14,326 tons). Indeed, Lake Erie had become so relatively free of algae that some groups, including the Ontario Federation of Anglers and Hunters, suggested deliberately dumping phosphorus into the lake in order to increase fish production.

They needn't have worried. In its biennial report for 2000, the IJC noted with alarm that "for lakes Superior, Huron, Michigan and Ontario, concentrations [of phosphorus] indicated that progress has been sustained. In the case of Lake Erie, however, open water concentrations... often exceed the guideline, indicating that phosphorus is being released into the lake by sources or processes not fully understood." By 2002, eutrophication was again a problem and media reports were again decrying the critical state of the lake.

The return of runaway algal blooms, which are now spreading into Lake St. Clair, is especially worrisome since one of the returned algae is *Microcystis*. Studies in the 1990s suggested that *Microcystis* produces a toxin that can promote liver cancer and may be responsible for bird and fish die-offs in the 1970s that were formerly blamed on pollution.

During the Great Lakes' brief respite from eutrophication, the mayfly was found in Lake Erie once again. In a bizarre twist, however, its renaissance may be one of the causes of the lake's renewed difficulties. Much of the phosphorus that had been in the water had settled into the sediment. A study conducted by Ohio State's Stone Laboratories has found that mayfly nymphs can actually increase the amount of buried phosphorus in the water by burrowing into and disturbing lake-bottom mud. The study found that the water column above mayfly colonies contained twenty-six times more phosphorus than water measured in other parts of the lake.

had been completely displaced by a species of oligochaetes—sludge worms—that fared better in nearly anoxic conditions. Indigenous fish species such as chub, cisco, and lake herring, which like mayflies required high amounts of oxygen, began to die off as well, replaced by invasive species, especially alewives and carp, that could live with almost no oxygen.

By the early 1960s, concerns about eutrophication were making headlines. In 1965, *Newsweek* called Lake Erie "the Dead Sea" and *Maclean's* magazine declared that "Lake Erie is dying." But that was not quite accurate. Eutrophication is the opposite of oligotrophism, or lack of productivity: Lake Erie and the other Great Lakes were actually producing too much organic material; algal blooms were choking the indigenous life out of the lakes and allowing new species, many of them nonnative, to take hold.

In 1969, however, an event occurred that drew the spotlight away from the problem of nutrient loading and eutrophication. That year, the U.S. Food and Drug Administration seized 29,000 kilograms (64,000 pounds) of coho salmon from commercial fishers on Lake Michigan on the suspicion that the fish were contaminated with a pesticide called DDT.

RATTLING THE FOOD CHAIN

Before the settlement era, 177 species of fish could be found in the northern waters of North America, 150 of them in the Great Lakes. Seventy percent of those fell into just five major families: the Salmonidae (salmon, trout, grayling, whitefish, and cisco); the Cyprinidae (carp, minnows, chub); the Catostomidae (thirty-nine species of suckers); the Percidae (perch, walleye, darters, and sauger); and the Cottidae (sculpins). These cool- and cold-water species—cool-water fish prefer water temperatures between 15°C and 25°C (59°F and 77°F); cold-water species favor water less than 15°C (59°F)—existed in a fragile food web, fragile because of the relative youth of the Great Lakes system: 10,000 years is too little time for species to adapt to a habitat and to one another. A much older lake, Lake Baikal, has existed for 50 million years, and despite massive assaults to its ecosystem from industrial pollution, its fish popula-

WALLEYE

YELLOW PERCH

tions have remained fairly stable. But Great Lakes species lack the resilience needed to bounce back from environmental stresses, and it doesn't take much to tip the scale from abundance to extirpation.

In general, fish represent an enormous proportion of the world's biota, with 28,500 species worldwide, more than half of all known vertebrate species. Among these, the Perciformes—perch and their kin—are the largest of vertebrate orders, with Cypriniformes, which include carp and minnows, the second largest. Whereas Perciformes dominate the oceans, cypriniform fishes predominate in freshwater lakes and streams. Minnows, including carp, dace, shiners, and true minnows, are primarily prey species (most are insectivores), and despite being eaten by just about any fish bigger than 7.5 centimeters (3 inches), they exist in vast numbers. They have acute senses of hearing and smell, and so are able to identify predators quickly. If an individual is attacked, its broken skin secretes a chemical that acts as a fear stimulant to other minnows: this chemical is detected immediately and a school of several thousand minnows can turn as one and disappear in an instant.

Perhaps they are successful too because of a peculiarity in their spawning ritual. Minnows spawn at various times of the year, depending on the species, but usually in a swift-moving stream with a pebbly bed. The male makes a nest on the stream bottom by picking up pebbles in his mouth and depositing them to form a cave-like mound, with the opening facing downstream. He then guards the nest until a female comes along to make use of it. If, while he is guarding it, another male approaches, the guardian male joins the newcomer beside the nest, and the two males swim upstream, side by side, tails moving in unison, for 4.6 to 6 meters (15 to 20 feet), whereupon both stop and settle on the bottom with their noses touching. After a few moments they separate, the guardian male returns to the nest, and the intruder swims off. Behaviorists call this "deferred combat," but it might easily be called "declined combat." Given the enormous amounts of energy some species exert defending their mating territories, often at the expense of their ability to mate, minnows seem to have come to a resourceful solution.

The redbelly dace prefers the tea-colored, acidic waters of bogs and ponds, where it dines on algae and is an important prey of brook trout.

Minnows common to the lower Lakes include brassy minnows and cutlips minnows, both phytoplankton eaters that spawn in cold streams and wetlands around Lakes Ontario and Erie but not farther north. Any other Great Lakes fish referred to as a minnow is probably either a dace, a chub, or a shiner. Lake chub are found across Canada and into Alaska and the midwestern states. They are about 7.5 centimeters (3 inches) long when mature, although some can grow to 15 centimeters (6 inches), and live off insect larvae (mostly mayfly and caddisfly), zooplankton, and sometimes smaller fish at the stream or bog bottom. Like minnows, they are eaten in turn by lake trout, northern pike, and walleye, as well as by birds such as belted kingfishers, loons, and mergansers. Emerald shiners and spottail shiners are also commonly referred to as minnows; the spottail is the more northerly of the two, being more tolerant of cold water and spawning earlier in the season, in May or June.

Another important food source for larger fish is the freshwater sculpins, of which four are prevalent in the Great Lakes. Although ocean sculpins are often large, lake sculpins rarely grow much longer than 7.5 or 10 centimeters (3 or 4 inches). The most common is

the slimy sculpin, named because of the mucous coating that covers its scales to reduce friction in the water and to protect its body from pathogens. The slimy sculpin, the similar mottled sculpin, and the little-known spoonhead sculpin spawn in spring by swimming up streams to deposit their eggs. The male chooses the nest site under a rock or a ledge, the female enters the cavity, turns upside down, and deposits her eggs on the ceiling. The male remains behind to defend the nest from predation, mostly by brook trout,

BRASSY MINNOW

LAKE CHUB

SLIMY SCULPIN

but when the eggs hatch, neither parent stays around to look after the fry. The habits of the deep-water sculpin are less known, as it inhabits water at much greater depths than the other three: they have been found as deep as 365 meters (1,200 feet) in Lake Superior. They, too, are nest builders, probably spawn year-round, and eat copepods and other zooplanktonic creatures. At such depths they are eaten primarily by lake trout and burbot.

At the other end of the food chain are the large fish. The largest is the lake sturgeon. A member of the sturgeon and paddlefish family, sturgeons are an ancient species, barely changed since the age of dinosaurs; indeed, fossil remains of *Acipenser* sturgeons date from the Early Cretaceous. A scaleless, torpedo-shaped, cartilaginous fish, it has five rows of large, bony scutes embedded in the skin along its flanks, and its head is covered by plates; with its long, protruding snout it looks more like an ichthyosaur than anything modern. Sturgeon live for more than a hundred years, can weigh up to 136 kilograms (300 pounds) and, if left long enough, will grow to 2.4 meters (8 feet) or more, although those found today average 27 kilograms (60 pounds) and less than 1.5 meters (5 feet). They are anadromous, which means they spend most of their time in the warm, marginal shoals of the Lakes, then migrate at spawning times up fast-moving natal streams. They are slow-moving, bottom-feeding fish. Barbels, like the whiskers on catfish, hang from their lower jaws to detect food on the sandy lake bottom. The sturgeon sucks up everything—sand, pebbles, sticks, as well as food—grinds it in its gizzard, filters out the debris, and eats the rest, mainly crayfish, mollusks, insect larvae and nymphs, leeches, and even algae.

These primitive monsters shared the Great Lakes with three members of the salmon family: Atlantic salmon, lake trout, and lake whitefish. The anadromous Atlantic salmon (*Salmo salar*—*salar* is from the same root as the French *sault,* and means "to leap") entered Lake Ontario shortly after the last glaciation, when direct access to the lakes from the Atlantic was still possible. As the glaciers retreated and the land rebounded, salmon trapped in Lake Ontario survived and became freshwater fish, although they remained taxonomically identical to the saltwater variety. Landlocked salmon stay in the deeper part of the lake until ready to spawn in November, then migrate up tributary rivers and streams to deposit and fertilize their eggs. Atlantic salmon do not die after spawning, as Pacific salmon do; the females rest in deep pools for a week or two and then return to the lake, and the males usually spend the winter in the river. Niagara Falls prevented Atlantic salmon from spreading into Lake Erie and beyond, and the last native Atlantic salmon was caught in Lake Ontario in 1890. Its demise as a species was caused by overfishing as well as by the construction of mill dams on contributary streams, which blocked fish from reaching their

LAKE STURGEON

EMERALD SHINER

DEATH OF A MONSTER

The lake sturgeon, once the largest and longest-lived species in the Lakes, has declined sharply in recent years.

Female lake sturgeon don't reach sexual maturity until they are more than twenty years old, and even then they spawn only once every two to four years, making them extremely vulnerable to environmental stresses. Native fishers speared them in vast but sustainable numbers. The first Europeans to frequent the lakes were amazed by their great size and ubiquity. Pierre Radisson marveled at "sturgeons of vast bigness" in Lake Superior in 1658. A later account from Lake Erie, probably written during a spawning migration, described fishers "standing in a flat-bottomed boat killing numbers of them by hitting them on the head with an axe."

For most of the nineteenth century, however, sturgeon were killed because it was wrongly supposed they ate the eggs and young of other, more valuable, fish. Sturgeon carcasses were fed to pigs or used as fertilizer; they were even dried and burned in the boilers of steamboats on the Detroit River. That ended, however, when a fish plant in Sandusky, Ohio, began selling smoked sturgeon and lake sturgeon caviar in 1860. (Russian caviar comes from a closely related fish, the beluga sturgeon.) That year the plant sold 8,200 kilograms (18,000 pounds) of Lake Erie sturgeon in New York City; by 1880, the catch was 3.2 million kilograms (7 million pounds).

Because they spawn so infrequently, the females carry a lot of roe. And the number of eggs and intervals between spawns increase with age and weight, so that a fifty-year-old, 45-kilogram (100-pound) female can hold 3 million eggs: one caught in 1911 contained 13.7 kilograms (30 pounds) of caviar, which sold for $1.50 per pound—for a fisher, two months' wages from one fish. Sturgeon were also prized for the quality of the gelatin isinglass in their swim bladders. Isinglass was used as a clarifying agent in wine and beer and as a setting agent in glues, jams, and jellies: the word is from the Dutch *huysenblase,* which means "sturgeon bladder."

By the 1880s, the sturgeon population had shrunk considerably, and despite a brief comeback in the 1930s they are now listed as threatened or endangered throughout the Great Lakes. Beginning in 1999, commercial fishers in Lake Huron's Saginaw Bay were asked by the U.S. Fish and Wildlife Service to tag all lake sturgeon caught as a bycatch in their nets. Only 129 sturgeon were tagged in four years, and these averaged 112 centimeters (44 inches) in length and fourteen years in age.

An anonymous poem in *The Methodist Magazine* in 1828 had lauded the Great Lakes as a boundless cornucopia:

> These waters plenty fish afford,
> The perch, and pike, and cat;
> And there the spotted salmon swims,
> And sturgeon stored with fat.

Today, as Peter Unwin notes in *The Wolf's Head: Writing Lake Superior,* "most people in North America have never seen a sturgeon and never will."

habitual spawning beds. Deforestation also resulted in a considerable increase in temperature in the spawning and nursery streams of this cold-water species. With the disappearance of Atlantic salmon, lake whitefish and lake trout became the mainstays of the Great Lakes fisheries.

"I have eaten tunny in the gulf of Genoa," wrote Anna Jameson, a British officer's wife who visited Lake Superior in 1836, "anchovies fresh out of the bay of Naples, trout of the Salz-kammergut, and diverse other fishy dainties rich and rare, but the exquisite, the refined white-fish exceeds them all." The same year, the explorer John Richardson, who had accompanied Franklin on his overland trek to the Arctic Ocean in 1822, declared that "a diet of whitefish alone, with no other food, can be eaten for days without losing its appeal." Both writers were describing the lake whitefish, so called because of its silvery color reflecting a pinkish iridescence; those in the Great Lakes have a greenish brown shading down their backs, and almost clear fins.

Not large fish, adults seldom being more than 51 centimeters (20 inches) long and weighing on average 1.4 to 1.8 kilograms (3 to 4 pounds), they existed in such numbers that the fisheries thought them inexhaustible. Their presence in the northern hemisphere dates at least from the periods between the last two glaciations; closely related to salmon and trout, they flourished in the cold waters of melting glaciers, swimming right up to the ice margins. Lake whitefish spawn in the fall, the females laying up to 26,500 eggs per kilogram (12,000 eggs per pound) of body weight; then both parents abandon the eggs to return to deep water. The eggs hatch the following spring and live on zooplankton until they mature enough to survive in the open lake, where their principal food is a species of amphipod, *Diporeia hoyi*, which was once the most abundant macroinvertebrate in the Great Lakes. In cool, deep water, below the summer thermocline, these tiny, shrimplike creatures made up nearly 70 percent of

The shrimplike *Diporeia*, far right, and the *Lumbricidae* worm, also shown, are part of the freshwater food chain now under attack by invasive species.

all benthic organisms, and where *Diporeia* thrived, so too did lake whitefish populations.

The American Fur Company opened the first commercial fishing station on the Great Lakes at Grand Portage, Minnesota, at the mouth of the Pigeon River, in 1835. Within three years the company was making more money from whitefish than it was from furs. The Hudson's Bay Company soon set up rival stations at Sault Ste. Marie, Michipicoten (on Lake Superior's north shore), and Fort William. Catches, consisting of lake trout, cisco or lake herring, and lake whitefish, were salted, barreled, and shipped to Chicago and New York. Soon all five lakes supported enormous inland fisheries, and commercial harvesting of lake whitefish continued heavily throughout the nineteenth century and into the twentieth. During much of the last century, Port Dover on the north shore of Lake Erie was the largest freshwater fishing port in the world.

Whitefish populations have been in steady decline since the 1920s, however. In Lake Huron, the total catch in 1920 was 11,000 tonnes (12,100 tons); by 1970 it had declined to 3,000 tonnes (3,300 tons), and that year studies showed that rainbow smelt and alewives—both introduced species, both predators of whitefish young—constituted 60 percent of the lake's biota. Whitefish populations increased during the 1980s and '90s, when fishing quotas were lowered and other introduced species, such as lake trout and chinook salmon, fed heavily on smelt and alewives; but since then they have declined again. In Lake Ontario, the two major whitefish communities, one in the Bay of Quinte and the other along the southern shore of Ontario's Prince Edward County, crashed in the 1960s, resurged in the 1980s, and reached historic levels in the early 1990s, but have since fallen to record lows.

ATLANTIC SALMON

LAKE WHITEFISH

On small lakes in the Great Lakes basin, especially Lake Simcoe, ice fishing for lake whitefish is still a popular sport, and whitefish remain the mainstay of the Lake Michigan fishery. On that lake, the commercial catch of whitefish has actually increased by 7 percent per year since 1985, and is now about 7 million tonnes (7.7 million tons) per year. Recent studies, however, show that although the whitefish population seems to be stable and even increasing in number, individual fish are smaller than they should be. The reason may be that their principal food, the shrimplike *Diporeia,* is being outcompeted by yet another nonindigenous invader, the zebra mussel (of which much more later), which feeds on the same diatoms as *Diporeia.* The days of an inexhaustible whitefish fishery are over.

For decades, the most important species in the Great Lakes fishery was the lake trout, one of the largest freshwater fishes in North American waters. Officially classified as char, lake trout is the second

A famous hunter discovered that, while he was out hunting, his wife was seeing another man. One day he hid by his lodge, and when he caught his wife in the arms of her lover, he dispatched her with his war club, buried her under the ashes of his fire, and with his two young sons fled to a distant part of the country. But the spirit of his wife haunted the children, terrifying them in their dreams and plaguing their imaginations. After traveling many days along the Lake Superior shoreline, they came to a place called Pauwateeg (today, Sault Ste. Marie).

There at the falls, they saw the woman's skull rolling along the beach. A sandhill crane was sitting on a rock in the rapids, and they called to it: "Grandfather, take us across the falls, so we can escape this spirit." The crane took them across on his back, telling them not to touch the back of his head, which was sore from a wound and had not healed. After delivering them to the other side, the bird returned to his rock in the rapids.

Then the skull called out to the crane, asking him to take her across the falls. The crane obliged, telling the skull not to touch the back of his head. But the skull was curious and touched the sore spot, and the crane dropped her into the rapids. "You shall be changed into something for the benefit of your people," said the crane. As the skull bounced from rock to rock, the brains scattered into the water like fish roe. They assumed the shape of a new species of fish, white in color, with a peculiar flavor that has caused it, ever since, to be a great favorite with the Indians.

Adapted from Henry Rowe Schoolcraft's *Algic Researches*, 1839. Schoolcraft, the Indian Agent in Sault Ste. Marie, Michigan, in the 1850s, published several collections of Ojibwa legends, which he learned from his Ojibwa wife, Jane Johnston. Many of them influenced Longfellow's epic poem *Hiawatha*.

LAKE TROUT

NINESPINE STICKLEBACK

largest of the salmonids, behind only chinook salmon of the Pacific Ocean. It averages 4.5 kilograms (10 pounds), but records of much larger lake trout abound, including one caught in Lake Superior in 1952 weighing 28.6 kilograms (63 pounds). They are a cold-water fish, favoring the deepest regions of the Lakes, and migrate to warmer, shallow, graveled shoals to spawn from September to November. The adults are carnivorous, feeding on small fish, especially young ciscoes but also whitefish, smelt, perch, alewives, sculpins, shiners, and sticklebacks. They will eat plankton, freshwater sponges, blackfly larvae, and even small mammals when fish are unavailable. The fat content of lake trout is very high; one type of lake trout, the deepwater, slow-moving siscowet found in Lake Superior, is almost 50 percent fat and is only palatable when smoked.

The abundance of lake trout in the Great Lakes can be discerned from fishing statistics. In 1879, 454,000 kilograms (1 million pounds) of lake trout was taken from Lake Ontario, which is the least fish-productive of the Great Lakes. In 1900, Lake Erie alone produced 15 million kilograms (33 million pounds), mostly of lake trout, lake whitefish, and sturgeon. Lake Huron fishers caught 3.6 million kilograms (7.4 million pounds) of lake trout per year throughout the 1890s, and those in Lake Michigan averaged 1.4 million kilograms (3 million pounds) per year. But Lake Superior, with its chill water, was the true home of the lake trout. Charles Penny, a Detroit merchant who accompanied Michigan's state geologist on a mineral expedition to Lake Superior in 1840, noted in his journal that the expedition members "had great sport catching trout. We took fifty in little over an hour."

ALEWIFE

Lake trout are caught mainly by sport fishers these days, although a commercial fishery still operates in Lake Superior, and almost all are hatchery stock or stock from lakes in the Northwest Territories. From 1965 to 1990, more than 50 million lake trout were released into Lake Michigan alone, "in a seemingly fruitless attempt," writes the Wisconsin fish ecologist Lee Kernen, "to go back in time to when lake trout was the dominant predator in the lake." For reasons not clearly understood, introduced lake trout do not spawn in sustainable numbers, and so fresh stocks must be poured into the Lakes each year to keep the sport fishery alive. A few spawning beds in Lake Superior—near Isle Royale, Stannard Rock, Gull Island Shoal, and Sinclair Cove—support native stocks, as do a few places in Lake Ontario, but the number of eggs remains small, and recruitment of subadults without the adipose finclip signifying a hatchery-raised fish is too low to maintain a natural population. Overfishing and siltation on spawning grounds were partly to blame for the decline of all three major species, but in the case of lake trout, predation by the invasive sea lamprey was also responsible.

In the absence of large, predatorial fish at the top of the food chain, populations of prey species began to explode, especially the alewife, a 15-centimeter (6-inch) fish that is now found throughout the Great Lakes. A member of the herring and shad family, it made its way from the Atlantic into Lake Ontario in the nineteenth century, either via the Erie Canal or as an accidental inclusion in a planting of American shad fry that had been put in the lake in 1870. The alewife increased in Lake Ontario until the 1930s, when it entered Lake Erie through the Welland Canal. It was common in that lake in the 1940s, but did not dominate; it is a deepwater fish and Lake Erie is shallow and relatively warm. Lake Huron, however, was another matter. It appeared there in 1933, and by the 1950s was a significant part of the Lake Huron fish community. Similarly, it was first recorded in Lake Michigan in 1949 and quickly became one of the most abundant fish in that lake. William Ashworth records in *The Late, Great Lakes* that by the early 1960s, "over 90 percent of the fish in Lake Michigan by weight—*by weight*—were alewives." It spread to Lake Superior in 1945, where it became the principal food of the lake trout. In the shrinking Great Lakes fishery, it is still netted by the millions and used to make pet food and fish meal.

The alewife has become a landlocked species, inhabiting the open lake waters most of the year and migrating to shallow beaches and river mouths to spawn in the spring and early summer. Females in freshwater become sexually mature at three years. They roll into the shallows at night, each female laying up to 12,000 eggs, and return to deeper, cooler water during the day. The young hatchlings remain in the shallows as larvae and migrate into deeper water in the fall, when they are about 5 centimeters (2 inches) long.

Alewives feed on zooplankton and some insect larvae, and are preyed upon in turn by burbot, walleye, and particularly lake trout and other salmonids. They have not fully adapted to freshwater, however: their kidneys, which evolved in saltwater, have remained too small to pump freshwater out of their bodies. This makes them extremely sensitive to abrupt changes in water temperature, and sudden spring upwellings of cold bottom water can cause massive die-offs, with mounds of dead alewives washing up onto Great Lakes beaches in June, to the general annoyance of everyone except herring gulls and ring-billed gulls.

The coho salmon seized in Lake Michigan in 1969 had been feeding heavily on alewives. They were found to contain twice as much DDT as the FDA had recently set as a safe level for human consumption. Contaminants in water tend to accumulate in fat tissues and bioaccumulate up the food chain: from copepods in zooplankton to alewives, the toxic level increases fortyfold. According to Dennis Konasewich, then a chemist at the International Joint Commission (IJC) office in Windsor, Ontario, the discovery of DDT-contaminated coho was "the turning point in the history of the Great Lakes." That year, pollution in the Lakes suddenly changed from being a relatively simple dilemma to a virtually insoluble problem.

SILENT SPRINGS

When the International Joint Commission published its report *On the Pollution of Boundary Waters* in 1951, private companies were already dumping 7.6 million cubic meters (268 million cubic feet) of industrial waste into the lakes every day, including 3,600 kilograms (8,000 pounds) of cyanides, 5,900 kilograms (13,000

Shallow embayments such as Julian Bay on Wisconsin's Stockton Island are ideal spawning grounds for warm-water fish, but are threatened by lake-level fluctuations and organic pollutants.

pounds) of phenols, and 11,400 kilograms (25,000 pounds) of ammonium compounds, not to mention assorted oil by-products. But since the chemicals weren't turning up in alarming concentrations in water samples, the IJC assumed there was enough water in the lakes to dilute them. The report's main concern was raw sewage. Four million people were drawing their drinking water directly

from the Lakes, coliform counts were high
on public beaches, and phosphorus from detergents and bacteria from untreated sewage
were contributing to algal blooms and the eutrophication of the Lakes.

But the appearance of Rachel Carson's
Silent Spring in 1963 put an end to the belief
that water pollution was a question of sewage, something the IJC could clear up by re-
quiring cities and businesses to reroute their
discharge pipes through water treatment facilities. The problem wasn't coliform, it was
agricultural pesticides. Carson, a marine biologist, warned that "the problem of water
pollution by pesticides can be understood
only in context, as part of the whole to which
it belongs—the pollution of the total environment by mankind." She focused her concern
on chlorinated hydrocarbons, a wide group
of pesticides that included DDT, heptachlor,
dieldrin, endrin, aldrin, mirex, and chlordane.
Although she mentioned the Great Lakes only
in passing, Carson—who worked for the U.S.
Bureau of Fisheries—knew that what she had
to say about agricultural runoff had obvious
implications for the world's largest inland
waterway, where many of the pesticides were
manufactured and much of the water was
surrounded by farmland.

Carson documented the cases of heptachlor
and mirex, widely used in the southern United
States to control fire ants. Heavy rains in the 1950s in areas where
the chemicals were sprayed had had disastrous effects on aquatic
life: fish died by the thousands in creeks and rivers running through
treated fields. She mentioned bass, sunfish, catfish, shad, and carp—
all species found also in the Great Lakes. Mirex was manufactured

Unable to lay eggs
because their body calcium
was reduced by DDT, bald
eagles declined drastically:
by the 1970s, only two
dozen pairs inhabited the
Great Lakes basin.

outside Buffalo, New York, by the Hooker Chemical Company, and research sparked by *Silent Spring* found that great quantities of it had leached from the plant into the Niagara River and thence into Lake Ontario. Similarly, Carson cited studies showing that DDT sprayed to control salt-marsh mosquitoes along the Florida coast—as it was sprayed on wetlands in the Great Lakes region—was causing reproductive failure in Florida's bald eagle population, which had declined to such an extent that it "might well make it necessary for us to find a new national emblem." This alarm prompted researchers to look at the bald eagle population around the Great Lakes, which they found to be equally under threat.

The bald eagle had enjoyed iconic status in the United States since Titian Peale, the foremost American bird artist of his day after Audubon, featured a soaring eagle on coins he designed for the U.S. Mint in 1848. It has been associated with the Great Lakes region even longer: the background in the wildlife painter and poet Alexander Wilson's portrait of the bald eagle, published in the fourth volume of *American Ornithology* in 1811, showed a frothful Niagara Falls tumbling beneath an auspicious rainbow. Nonetheless, throughout the nineteenth century the eagle was hunted for its feathers and killed as vermin by farmers who thought it preyed on lambs and chickens. Habitat loss also played a role in the eagle's gradual decline. In 1890, Ontario's Fish and Game Commission drafted the province's Fish and Game Act, which partially protected raptors, including the eagle, and in 1940 the United States Bald Eagle Act further restricted direct killing of the bird, but the population continued to decline.

The bald eagle's generic name, *Haliaeetus,* means "sea eagle," because its principal diet consists of fish, although it won't hesitate to eat mammals and reptiles or, in winter, to scavenge dead deer frozen in lake ice. Eagles don't dive into the water after fish, as ospreys and Caspian terns do, but skim along the surface hoping to snag a fish that has come up to feed. They thus require large expanses of water, with tall trees nearby on which to perch as they feed, and to house their huge, untidy-looking nests of interlocking sticks. The females lay one to three whitish eggs and incubate them for thirty-five days; when the chicks hatch, they remain nestlings for ten to twelve weeks. The fledglings remain juveniles for four to eight years, during which time they are a uniform brown color, not unlike a golden eagle; usually only one survives to maturity, when their heads and some of their tail feathers turn white.

Under normal circumstances, a bald eagle lives for twenty-eight years in the wild. They mate for life, migrate south in September, and in March and April return to the same nest year after year, unless something happens to the mate, or to the nest. Despite their fierce appearance, eagles are not particularly aggressive to other birds. The Ontario ornithologist Murray Speirs recalls "the odd sight of a hummingbird dashing at a young eagle riding the updraft along the shore cliff near Port Ryerse, on Lake Erie," and eagles are often seen migrating in company with broad-wing hawks.

During the first half of the last century one pair of bald eagles inhabited every 8 to 16 kilometers (5 to 10 miles) of Great Lakes shoreline. There were two hundred mating pairs along the St. Lawrence River between Montreal and Kingston, and at least fifty mating pairs on Lake Erie. But, as had happened in Florida, by 1950 their numbers had begun to decline. Speirs, in his *Birds of Ontario,* noted that in 1978 there were "only three pairs nesting in recent years in southwestern Ontario," and surveys in the 1970s showed that only two dozen pairs remained on the entire Great Lakes. The culprit was DDT and its breakdown product, DDE, which in vertebrates interferes with the body's ability to retain calcium. The eagles' eggshells were often too thin to bear the weight of the adult during incubation. DDT bioaccumulates in fat, and egg yolks contain lipids meant to sustain embryos before hatching, so that even the eagle chicks that hatched already carried high levels of contamination; many of those that survived were unable to reproduce.

By the time Canada and the United States signed the Great Lakes Water Quality Agreement in 1972, which gave the IJC the job of investigating and monitoring pollution and water quality issues in the Great Lakes, researchers had determined that a total of 26 million kilograms (58 million pounds) of toxic chemicals was being discharged into the Great Lakes every year. The chemicals were coming not only from the five hundred industrial facilities situated on or near the lakeshores, but also from runoff from agricultural field crops throughout the Great Lakes basin. This was a sobering realization: those worried about water quality in the Lakes could no longer take comfort in the knowledge that 44 percent of the land use in the Lake Michigan basin, for example, and 67 percent in the Lake Erie catchment area was farmland. Much of the sediment washing into the Great Lakes annually was laced with contact poisons. Although the spraying of DDT had been curtailed, fish in the Lakes still registered counts higher than 5 ppm—the level at which liver cells begin to disintegrate and the level deemed safe by the FDA. In 1980, eagles and other waterfowl were still showing high levels of DDT and experiencing total reproductive failure.

The largest member of the tern family, the Caspian tern, is making new inroads on the Great Lakes.

Although the spraying of DDT has been banned in North America since the 1970s, the effects of the insecticide era will be with us for decades to come. Many target insects developed a resistance to chemical pesticides by altering their genetic makeup, in some cases within a matter of two or three generations. In 1940, there were only 8 pesticide-resistant species of insects in the world; today there are more than 125.

Rachel Carson warned in 1962 that resistance to DDT and other pesticides was widespread and permanent: *Culex* mosquitoes, the most common genus in the world, showed resistance to DDT in 1946; by 1948, it was necessary to use chlordane as a supplement to DDT. The first chlordane-resistant *Culex* mosquitoes appeared in 1950. Within a year, *Culex* mosquitoes were resistant to methoxychlor, heptachlor, and benzene hexachloride as well. West Nile fever, St. Louis encephalitis, and avian flu are carried by *Culex* mosquitoes. By 1960, twenty-eight species of *Anopheles* mosquitoes—those responsible for malaria—were unaffected by DDT and chlordane, and sixty-five species of crop-destroying insects were DDT-resistant, including the codling moth, a major pest in apple orchards.

Culex pipiens, the basin's most common mosquito, can be a vector for such diseases as West Nile Virus.

"Darwin himself," Carson wrote, "could scarcely have found a better example of the operation of natural selection than is provided by the way the mechanism of resistance operates." And natural selection is irreversible.

DDT wasn't the only chemical to raise concern. Dioxins—highly toxic compounds produced as by-products in the manufacture of other chemicals, especially in processes involving chlorine such as pulp and paper bleaching, and in the burning of plastics in municipal waste incinerators—had been pouring into the air above the Great Lakes since the 1930s. Production peaked in 1959, two years after a huge outbreak of chicken edema killed millions of chickens in the United States and Japan. The cause was traced to dioxins in chicken feed, but the link wasn't made between dioxins and the environment until the 1970s, when the biologist Michael Gilbertson of the IJC noticed that deformities in the embryos of bald eagles, cormorants, Caspian terns, and other fish-eating birds greatly resembled the effects of chicken edema. In 1981, dioxin was found in Lake Ontario fish.

A flock of herring gulls in Presqu'ile Bay, on Lake Ontario: since being hard hit by PCB contamination in the 1970s, the species is slowly regaining ground lost to ring-billed gulls and cormorants.

Dioxins (and related toxins called furans) are what researchers call "hydrophobic and lipophilic," meaning they hate water but love fat. In 1989, Gilbertson published his study of Great Lakes wild birds. Airborne dioxins settle on both land and water: when they settle on farmland they are eaten by grazing cattle, and Great Lakes basin cattle showed low levels of dioxin poisoning. But when dioxin settles on water, it seeks immediately to get out; when fish ingest water through their gills, the dioxins stay behind in the gill membranes, which are extremely fatty. Since fish filter water through their gills all the time, it doesn't take long for dioxin levels in their fatty tissues to soar: Lake Ontario fish tested in the 1980s had dioxin levels 100,000 times higher than it was in the water. When eagles, cormorants, and gulls ate the fish, their fatty tissue also became saturated with dioxins, resulting in gross birth defects, kidney and liver failure, and eventually death. Humans eating a normal North American diet receive most of their dioxins from the consumption of beef, but that's only because we eat more

beef than fish. In 1994, dioxin levels in North American beef averaged 0.4 parts per trillion (ppt), whereas in fish it was 1.73 ppt.

There were also new chemicals in the mix: aroclors, for example, although they were not exactly new. Aroclors had been described as early as 1881 by German chemists investigating the by-products of coal tar. The chemists, looking at benzene used in artificial dyes, found other stable, insoluble, and heat-resistant organic compounds, which they called aroclors, but since they could find no use for them they merely described them in scientific journals and forgot about them. By the 1920s, however, technology had advanced to the point at which fluids that could withstand high temperatures without breaking down were useful as lubricants, and aroclors were rediscovered and renamed. Chemically speaking, they were benzene rings with several hydrogen atoms replaced by chlorine atoms. That made them polychlorinated biphenyls, or PCBs for short.

The Monsanto Corporation began manufacturing PCBs in St. Louis, Missouri, in 1930, marketing them under the trade name Aroclor. It was used primarily as a lubricant and hydraulic fluid in industrial machinery, and as an insulator in electrical transformers. One of its more pernicious applications, however, was to extend the kill-life of certain insecticides. A little Aroclor 1242, for example, prolonged the effectiveness of chlordane and aldrin against mosquito larvae. Aroclor 5460 improved the performance of lindane against the elm leaf beetle. Aroclor 1221 added to DDT increased fruit fly mortality by 33 percent.

The first indication that PCBs were an environmental problem came in 1968, when a mysterious respiratory illness killed 400,000 chickens in Japan. The chickens had been fed oil from the Kanemi Company, a producer of rice bran, and humans who had eaten the rice bran itself also became ill. More than 14,000 patients developed skin rash and organ diseases, called "yusho" in Japanese, that were subsequently linked to dioxins produced by the deterioration of PCBs. Nearly 600 kilograms (1,323 pounds) of PCBs had been inadvertently added to the rice-bran deodorizing process. When the Kanemi Yusho case became known, investigators looked for evidence of PCB and dioxin contamination in Great Lakes waters. Just as the biosentinal species for DDT had been the bald eagle, that for PCBs was the herring gull, then the most numerous gull in the basin.

The herring gull was especially at home on the Great Lakes because it prefers coastal habitats to open water. It is a large gull—66 centimeters (26 inches) in length (ring-billed gulls, by comparison, are only 51 centimeters, or 20 inches long)—with a pearly-gray mantle, extensive black wing tips, and a yellow bill with a bright red spot near the tip of the lower mandible. Herring gull chicks apparently target this red spot to peck at when wanting to be fed by their parents. They eat lots of fish but are omnivorous—they'll open their rather large gullets and swallow whole mice, voles, and even rats— and are principally scavengers, doing most of their foraging on foot. They also readily eat the newly hatched chicks of other gull species; most gulls quickly remove broken eggshells from their nests, since that is what herring gulls look for.

Already in decline because of the influx of ring-billed gulls and double-crested cormorants, herring gulls were hard hit by pollution. As with the eagle, the herring gull's reproductive rate sank dramatically. Whereas normally ten pairs of herring gulls would produce 12 to 15 chicks a year, in 1975 they produced an average of only 1.5, and those that hatched were often deformed and died within hours. Reports of nests near Kingston, Ontario, tell the story of the herring gull's decline. On Pigeon Island, which sheltered the largest local herring gull colony, ninety nests were active from 1961 to 1970, when the first collapsed eggs were found; the following year the number dropped to seventy-eight, and by 1973 there were only thirty-five nests. In a 1974 study, herring gull flesh was found to contain fifty-seven different toxic contaminants, including chlordane, dieldrin, mirex, heptachlor, and PCBs. The FDA set a tolerable limit of 5 ppm of PCBs in fish, which was later dropped to 2 ppm; in 1975, Lake Ontario herring gulls were found to have PCB levels of 3,530 ppm.

All the Lakes were contaminated with PCBs. Zooplankton species in Lake Michigan were found to contain 480 ppm of PCBs. Alewives that fed on them contained over 6,000 ppm. The worst case was in Waukegan, Illinois, where the Outboard Marine Company, which used PCBs in the manufacture of outboard motors, had dumped 90,700 tonnes (100,000 tons) of the chemical into Waukegan Harbor since 1954. Researchers found that sediment at the bottom of the harbor was composed of as much as 500,000 ppm—the sludge was 50 percent PCBs. Coho salmon in the harbor contained 77 ppm.

Heavy metals also came under scrutiny. Because most Great Lakes municipalities were adding chlorine to their drinking water and chlorine was a principal component of PCBs and other synthetic organic chemicals, the production of chlorine in the United

OVERLEAF: Herring gull hatchlings on University River, Lake Superior. Gulls on the upper Lakes suffered less from pollution than those in more industrialized areas.

States increased by 600 percent from 1947 to 1969. Chlorine itself is not particularly toxic, but it combines with other elements in sometimes deadly ways: chlorine atoms in the atmosphere react with oxygen to kill the ozone layer, and recently it has been determined that in water, chlorine combines with leaf mold to produce complex carcinogens.

The association of chlorine with mercury is also nefarious. Chlorine is produced by passing an electric current through a solution of salt, which separates the sodium from the chloride. Sodium is then precipitated out of the solution by the addition of mercury. As a result of the rise in chlorine use, the production of mercury in the United States increased by several thousand percent after 1946. Most of the mercury was recovered for reuse, but much of it was flushed out into the Great Lakes. Two chlorine plants in Sarnia, for example, had been dumping mercury into Lake St. Clair at the rate of 14 kilograms (30 pounds) a day. Mercury is highly toxic, but it is extremely slow-acting: Isaac Newton is thought to have died from mercury poisoning as a result of years of experimenting with quicksilver, which is liquid mercury.

In lake sediments, especially if the mud is rich in bacteria and low in oxygen—as it is in a heavily eutrophied lake—bacteria convert mercury into methyl mercury, which is picked up by filter feeders in zooplankton and biomagnified up the food chain to fish, birds, and humans. Mercury poisoning was known to cause chromosomal aberrations and to affect the nervous and reproductive systems: 5 ppm of mercury in fish had caused Minamata disease in Japan in the 1950s. In 1970, Canada banned the sale of fish caught in Lake St. Clair because of their high mercury content. In 1973, coho salmon in Saginaw Bay were found to contain up to 10.9 ppm.

Other heavy metals identified as problematic in the Lakes included zinc, lead, cadmium, and copper. Their degree of toxicity was influenced by several factors, including water temperature, alkalinity, and oxygen concentrations. In summer, for example, when oxygen levels in the deep waters are low, copper remains stable in the sediments; as the thermocline sinks and oxygen becomes more available, the copper ions oxidize and become soluble. Throughout the 1970s, industries in Detroit discharged 600 kilograms (1,300 pounds) of chromium, a powerful carcinogen, and lead into the Detroit River daily.

The study of lead pollution introduced a fresh area of concern: the precipitation of toxic elements from the air. In the 1940s and '50s, lead was a common component of paint and gasoline, and it is still used in batteries. Much of that lead ended up in the atmosphere: in 1970, a core sample from a Greenland glacier showed that there was lead in the air before the Industrial Revolution at the level of about 20 micrograms per tonne of ice, or 2 parts per billion (ppb); by 1860, the level had risen to 5 ppb; five years after the end of World War II, when cars were increasingly in demand, the ice indicated 12 ppb, and in 1965 the figure had nearly doubled, to 21 ppb. By that time, lead consumption in the United States amounted to 900 grams (2 pounds) per person per year. If atmospheric lead was falling on Greenland, it was certainly falling on the Great Lakes. A study of the pollutants in Lake Superior found that 1 kilogram (2.2 pounds) of lead per day was entering the lake from municipal discharges, 9 kilograms (20 pounds) a day from industries, and 720 kilograms (1,600 pounds) a day from atmospheric precipitation of lead originating as far away as Cincinnati and Pittsburgh.

As well, fifty percent of the PCBs in Lake Michigan settled into it from the air. Some of the precipitate might have come from Lake Michigan itself, since one study determined that the lake was actually exhaling PCBs: sediment at the bottom of the lake was so heavily laden with PCBs that the chemicals were rising up through the water, being expelled into the atmosphere, and remaining airborne until they precipitated out, sometimes back into the lake itself, sometimes onto land.

The more researchers discovered, the more rethinking had to be done. For example, the decline of the Lake Erie fishery was assumed to have been caused by the eutrophication of the bottom water—mats of decaying algae using up too much of the oxygen below the thermocline. But the disappearance of the lake's stocks of cisco, whitefish, sauger, and walleye, although primarily associated with temperature changes, also coincided with the accumulation of chemical pollutants in lake sediments, pollutants now known to affect an organism's ability to reproduce. The blue pike may have been a case in point. Extinct since 1970, the blue pike, a subspecies of walleye, was found in Lakes Erie and Ontario and in the Niagara River. For years it was one of the most abundant fishes in those waters, making up as much as 50 percent of the total catch in Lake Erie from 1885 until 1957, with an annual catch averaging 6.8 million kilograms (15 million pounds). The population crashed in 1958 and never recovered. Significantly, the majority of the mere 450 kilograms (1,000 pounds) of blue pike caught in 1962 were adults over ten years old. If eutrophication were the sole culprit, adults as well as juveniles would have been affected by the lack of oxygen. The inability of the blue pike to produce young, however, sounded so much like that of the bald eagle, herring gull, and double-crested cormorant that toxic contaminants could not be ruled out. Overfishing was certainly a factor, but it is significant that the blue pike was one of the few large fishes to spawn in the sediments in the deepest parts of the lake, where contaminants tend to accumulate.

By 1978, when the IJC announced its revised Water Quality Agreement, more than 350 organic contaminants and heavy metals had been identified in the Great Lakes. Some of the news was encouraging. Concentrations of many chemicals had begun to drop: DDT and DDE, dieldrin, mirex, and PCBs were slowly disappearing from lake water. With the construction or upgrading of many sewage treatment facilities, phosphorus loads had declined appreciably. The IJC set a discharge target limit of 1 part per million, and the Canadian and U.S. governments committed US$7.6 billion toward the construction of sewage plants to meet that goal. By 1983, only

IN DEFENSE OF CORMORANTS

Double-crested cormorants are gaining in numbers and losing in popularity on the Great Lakes. The lighter-plumaged cormorant, second from the right, is a first-year juvenile.

Double-crested cormorants began moving into Lake Superior from Lake of the Woods in 1913, and by the 1940s had spread throughout the Great Lakes watershed. Despite a decline in the 1970s caused by high levels of PCB pollution, cormorant numbers in the basin have grown to nearly 500,000, about 25 percent of the total North American population.

There have been calls for a reduction in the Great Lakes cormorant population. Environmentalists say the birds are threatening vegetation on their nesting sites and several native shorebird species, and fishers claim that a single cormorant eats 450 grams (1 pound) of fish per day; fewer cormorants would mean more fish. But cormorants are one of the few bird species that eat the round goby, which means they are not really in competition for food with ring-billed gulls. And their voracious appetites may be helping to keep the alien round goby in check, a factor that might be kept in mind when contemplating future cormorant culls.

nine facilities in the Great Lakes basin failed to reach the 1-ppm mark: one in Michigan (at Wyandotte, on the Detroit River); three in Ontario (London, Toronto, and Hamilton); two in New York (Niagara Falls and Buffalo); and two in Ohio (both in Cleveland). As a result, algae growth was reduced by more than 30 percent. Although algae are still a problem in Lake Erie and Lake St. Clair, where "dead areas" continue to turn up, studies show that little new phosphorus is entering the Lakes. Fish are able to breathe again, and water clarity has also improved.

Recent bird studies also show cause for cautious optimism. Through the efforts of a great many wildlife officials and naturalist federations in both Canada and the United States, bald eagles are once again breeding along the Great Lakes shorelines. In 2000, there were 104 active nests on Lake Superior and along the lower reaches of the Nipigon River; Lake Erie had 14 nests, from which 21 young eagles fledged. Altogether, a total of 193 eaglets fledged that year, or about 1.3 per nest, easily enough to maintain the population. During the fall migration around the western end of Lake Superior, broad-wing hawks still predominate at observation points like Hawk Ridge and Wisconsin Point, but bald eagles are among the thousands of large raptors that make the annual trek.

Gulls are also making a comeback. The Canadian Wildlife Service, which had been monitoring contamination in herring gull eggs around Lake Ontario since 1974, found in 2000 that toxic levels had "declined dramatically since the late 1970s and have continued to do so." PCB levels in herring gull eggs were down by 93 percent; DDE (and hence DDT) by 92 percent; mirex by 95 percent. As a result, bird populations have increased proportionally. The most numerous birds on Lake Ontario were ring-billed gulls; in 1990, they occupied 253,000 nest sites, and although by 1999 that figure had dropped to 211,514, it was because cormorants were stealing their nesting sites, not because of collapsed eggs.

During the same period, cormorant nests increased by 137 percent. Cormorants eventually ousted entire gull colonies from some islands, yet in areas where no cormorants invaded, ring-billed gull nests actually quintupled. Elsewhere other species were seriously affected by the invading cormorants. Black-crowned night herons, for one: in 1994, they occupied 226 nests on the Leslie Street Spit, a man-made peninsula jutting out into Toronto Harbour; three years later, when cormorants began moving onto the spit, the number fell to 63 nests, and by 2001 there were no nests at all. Cormorant nests, however, shot up to 4,173.

Archaeological evidence from Burlington Bay, on Lake Ontario, shows that double-crested cormorants have been on the Great Lakes for thousands of years, but they have never been as abundant as they have lately become. A new wave of cormorants began colonizing the western end of Lake Superior in 1913, probably from Lake of the Woods, indicating that the current population is an eastern extension of birds from the Great Plains. They quickly spread to Lake Huron and Georgian Bay, and by the 1930s they were seen on Lake Erie; by the early 1940s they were on Lake Ontario. Despite their decline from 1950 to the 1990s, there are now more cormorants on the Great Lakes than ever before. As we shall see, this pattern of species invasion—and entrenchment—is a familiar one in the Great Lakes basin, one that threatens to become even more prevalent in the future.

Cleanup programs have helped the Lakes become beautiful and welcoming habitats once again, but not always to native species.

EIGHT

INVASIONS

THE GREAT LAKES HAVE ALWAYS been attractive to invaders and colonizers: they are relatively young and their waters support less biodiversity than older lakes. And wherever there is room in nature, something is bound to move in. Those organisms that arrived naturally, without any help from us—the Atlantic salmon or the herring gull, to name two—seem to have settled into the Great Lakes ecosystem without causing serious disruptions. Invasion isn't always a destructive force; it is the way species expand and ecosystems mature and evolve.

Some organisms that have arrived in the Lakes region through human intervention, on the other hand, have caused tremendous changes in the makeup of the region's biota, not all of them beneficial. Unfortunately, examples abound. Of the 278 species of plants found growing in 1980 on Toronto's Leslie Street Spit—a 5-kilometer (3-mile) artificial arm protruding into Lake Ontario that has been allowed to grow wild—only 122 were native to southern Ontario. No one knows who brought dandelions over from Europe, or why, since there were two species of dandelions here already. Garlic mustard was sown as cattle feed with seeds imported from Europe in the nineteenth century, as was lamb's-quarter, a wild variety of

FACING PAGE: Zebra mussels, invaders from a distant sea, adhere to any hard surface, including dock pilings, rocks, and even one another.

The Great Lakes...darkly reflect how a global tradefest can turn into an ecological makeover. What was once a distinct North American body of water...is now little more than a degraded multicultural aquarium.

ANDREW NIKIFORUK, *Pandemonium*, 2006

spinach. We had to introduce forage plants, such as alfalfa, to feed our domestic animals, because they too had come from Europe and were more accustomed to eating European crops. Dodder, a rootless, leafless, parasitic plant that squeezes nutrients out of host plants with its long, stringlike vines, made the crossing in sacks of alfalfa seeds, which dodder seeds strongly resemble.

So many invasive aquatic plant and animal species have moved into the Great Lakes ecoregion that a 1998 report by the Illinois Natural History Society's Center for Aquatic Ecology stated that "some biologists argue that it is now a man-made aquaculture system." Whereas before the settlement period there were 150 native fish species in the Great Lakes, nearly half of those have since declined or vanished, and 162 new, nonindigenous species have taken over their habitat. Most of these new species are here as a result of human action, by either accidental or deliberate introductions, and have thrived so well that the very nature of the Great Lakes aquatic ecosystem has been significantly altered. As Ian Duggan, a biologist with the Great Lakes Institute for Environmental Research, has remarked, "Nonindigenous species pose the leading threat to the biological integrity of the lakes, and may interact with other ecosystem stresses, including climate change and toxic contaminants, potentially compounding their effects."

The massive and essentially unsolvable problem of invasive species in the Great Lakes was the focus of a congressional hearing held in Michigan's Macomb County in the fall of 2005. At the hearing, Emily Fennel, an environmental analyst with Michigan's Department of Natural Resources, noted that "the economic loss from invasive species in 2004 was $5 billion," and that "42 percent of native species are threatened by invasive species." Whereas half a century ago the Lakes provided relatively free food and water to the many communities built on its shores, today federal and local governments spend billions of dollars annually stocking and protecting native fish, controlling introduced species, and cleaning and clearing water intake valves clogged by invasive organisms—all of them introduced by us. If we have succeeded in turning the Great Lakes into a huge aquaculture experiment, it seems the experiment is running out of control.

Dandelions, an introduced species, grace a meadow interspersed with Indian paintbrush, a colorful native species.

BOLD AS BRASSICA

The highly invasive garlic mustard has been in the Great Lakes basin since settlement days but has only recently begun to take over vast areas of forest meadowland.

Garlic mustard, a European wild brassica brought over by settlers as a potherb, has suddenly become an aggressive alien. Content as an edge plant for two centuries, growing abundantly but confined to the transition zone between forest and meadow, it has recently begun invading the deep woods in the Great Lakes region, where its tenaciousness and lack of natural enemies allow it to outcompete native flora. Recent research has found that its roots produce a toxic substance that kills the fungi that form underground symbiotic relationships with other plants. It is particularly damaging to trilliums and maple seedlings: its roots can kill maple seedlings two years after the garlic mustard itself has been eradicated. Stands of garlic mustard should be cut before the plants begin to form seeds, that is, in mid-May in Ontario and mid-June in Wisconsin.

A SURFEIT OF LAMPREYS

The first nonindigenous fish species recorded in the Great Lakes has arguably been the most devastating for native fish. The sea lamprey appeared in Lake Ontario in 1835, and its subsequent conquest of all five lakes has been called "a biological legend," which puts it in the same category as the introduction of rabbits to Australia. The saga of the sea lamprey reads like a template for the many other pernicious species that have since invaded the system, from the alewife to zebra mussels.

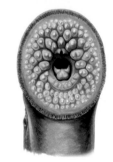

Although it looks like an eel—and is sometimes erroneously called the lamprey eel—the sea lamprey differs from the American eel in several ways. Eels have spines, with up to 111 vertebrae; sea lampreys are spineless. The dorsal, anal, and caudal fins of eels form a continuous fringe that begins a third of the way along the body and goes completely around the tail and up the lower body almost to the midpoint, while lampreys have two small dorsal fins only. Eels are catadromous—they live in freshwater and spawn in saltwater—whereas lampreys swim up freshwater streams, like salmon, to spawn. And the American eel population has declined drastically in the Great Lakes and St. Lawrence River in the past few decades despite measures to save them, whereas sea lampreys are doing very well despite our best efforts to rid the system of them.

SEA LAMPREY, (*above*) AND MOUTH CLOSE-UP

The sea lamprey is the most primitive vertebrate known to science. Fossil evidence shows it to have been around for the past 400 million years. It is little more than a leathery, cartilaginous tube and a digestive tract, with a mouth at one end and an anus at the other; it has no jaws and therefore no teeth, but rather rows of sharp, disklike protuberances on its tongue and lips. It breathes through gill pouches arranged along the length of its body, which is covered by a layer of slime. The sea lamprey feeds by attaching its mouth to the side of a fish, lacerating the fish's flank with its tongue, and then sucking the bodily fluids out of it. An anticoagulant in its saliva keeps the juices flowing freely. Fish have been found in the Great Lakes with eight or ten lamprey scars on their sides and three or four lampreys hanging off them, still sucking. A lake sturgeon was once caught in Lake Michigan with eighteen lampreys attached to it. Such fish are usually thrown back. "They cook dry," one fisherman commented.

Lampreys live for only about eighteen months as adults, spending most of that time in the shallows of the open lakes. But like salmon they swim up natal streams to spawn. The female makes a shallow nest in the streambed with her mouth, then deposits 30,000 to 50,000 eggs in the depression. The male comes along and fertilizes them, whereupon both male and female adults die. Two weeks later the eggs hatch, and the larvae burrow into the sand or silt, where, as ammocoetes, they remain for the next three to eighteen years, depending on water temperature and food supply, feeding on organic detritus. When they have reached a certain sub-adult size (slightly under 38 centimeters or 15 inches in landlocked lakes, nearly twice that in anadromous populations), having accumulated enough body fat to sustain them until they become adults, they enter a metamorphosis, developing their toothlike oral disks and functional eyes and changing color. Once this phase is complete, they emerge from their natal streambeds and move downstream to open water, where they eventually become predators.

Some believe lampreys have always been in Lake Ontario, as well as in Lake Champlain and the Finger Lakes of upper New York State. Others think they originated in the Atlantic Ocean and entered Lake Ontario via the Erie Canal, which opened in 1825. In any case, the lamprey population remained stable and confined to Lake Ontario for almost a hundred years after 1825, even though the Welland Canal opened to shipping in 1829. They caused severe damage to several Lake Ontario fish populations, including ciscoes, lake trout, and walleye, but did not migrate further upstream into Lake Erie until 1921, two years after the Welland Canal was deepened to allow larger ships into the upper Lakes, and when the supply of sizable prey species in Lake Ontario had been reduced.

In 1936, they were reported in Lake Michigan; the following year they showed up in Lake Huron; and by 1946, they were in Lake Superior. The effect of their presence on large fish is reflected in commercial fishing statistics for lake trout, once the preeminent species

FACING PAGE: Sea lampreys clamped to the flank and gill of a lake trout. Since their introduction in the 1820s, lampreys have all but extirpated native salmon stocks.

in both the commercial and sport fisheries. The total lake trout catch in Lake Huron in 1937 was 1.5 million kilograms (3.4 million pounds); ten years later it was zero. In 1946, the lake trout catch in Lake Michigan was 2.5 million kilograms (5.5 million pounds); in 1953, it was 183 kilograms (402 pounds). By the mid-1950s, the lake trout population of Lakes Michigan-Huron was no longer commercially viable. At that time, the average lake trout catch in Lake Superior was still 2 million kilograms (4.5 million pounds); by 1961, the year the lamprey population peaked in Lake Superior, the total catch was 167 kilograms (368 pounds).

Lake trout, ciscoes, and walleye were hit hard because lampreys feed only on large fish, adults greater than 43 centimeters (17 inches) long. Lake trout reach that size in about four years but do not become sexually mature until they are six or seven years old, which means most are either weakened or killed by lampreys before they are old enough to reproduce. As fish populations plummeted, lamprey numbers soared, increasing twenty- to fiftyfold per generation throughout the 1940s and '50s. The population peaked in 1961, and the following year commercial fishing of lake trout in Lake Superior was prohibited. By then there were hardly any lake trout anyway, and even the lamprey had turned to other species. Similar declines started showing up in burbot, lake whitefish, suckers, lake herring, and even large chub.

Attempts to control lampreys began in Lake Superior in the 1960s, in order to try to preserve genetic pools of lake trout that could be hatchery-reared and used to reseed populations in the other Great Lakes. Various methods were tried, including electrocution—huge electrical probes inserted into the water at dam sites along freshwater streams known to be spawning beds for lampreys—and the release of neutered males. The most successful control was a chemical larvicide called 3-trifluormethyl-4-nitrophenol (TFM) for short, developed by Vernon Applegate, a U.S. Fish and Wildlife biologist at the Hammond Bay Biological Station in Michigan. Many fish exhibit toxic responses to TFM, as do many mollusk and amphibian species, but most fish have the ability to metabolize TFM in their livers. Lampreys do not. TFM was first sprayed on lamprey spawning streambeds in 1962, and by 1966 the lamprey population had been reduced to 5 percent of its former size.

The number of lampreys declined to such an extent that the Lakes were restocked with lake trout in the hope that they would reclaim their original dominance, and in some lakes the strategy seemed to be working. By the 1990s, the lake trout population was large enough that stocking was no longer necessary; in Lake Michigan, the trout numbers were thought to be exceeding historical levels. Then sea lamprey numbers began to climb again, probably as a delayed reaction to improvements made in the 1970s to the St. Marys River, between Lake Superior and Lake Huron, to make a more hospitable habitat for lake trout and other salmonids: it also made the river more hospitable to lampreys. Today the lamprey population in the upper Lakes is nearly as large as it was in the early

1960s, and there seems no effective way of controlling it. "They duck into little streams and freshets and avoid the chemical blocks," says Jerome Keen, an analysis technician with the Great Lakes Fisheries Commission in Sault Ste. Marie, Ontario. "We hike up the smaller streams and spray, but it's hard to get them all, and it only takes a few lampreys to make a lot." Stocking lake trout in Lake Superior was halted in 1996 because it became simply an exercise in feeding lampreys: between 1995 and 1999, lampreys killed 500 tonnes (550 tons) of Lake Superior lake trout every year. In Lake Huron, only 17 percent of the lake trout population survive each year; 10 percent die naturally, 19 percent are caught by commercial and sport fisheries, and 54 percent are killed by sea lampreys. Apparently, like death and taxes, sea lampreys will always be with us.

SOME INTRODUCTIONS ARE NECESSARY

Smelts are slender, silvery fish that grow from 15 to about 30 centimeters (6 to 12 inches), depending on the species, and were once thought to be salmonids—Linnaeus named the European smelt *Salmo eperlanus*—but now have their own family, the Osmeridae. The largest, the rainbow smelt, is the anadromous Atlantic variety, introduced into Crystal Lake, near the east coast of Lake Michigan, in 1912 as food for Japanese salmon, which had been introduced earlier. The Japanese salmon disappeared, however, and the smelts escaped into Lake Michigan, where they flourished. For a while they were cursed as a nuisance, because they clogged up gill nets set for larger fish, but eventually they became an important commercial species in their own right, so much so that 1.8 million kilograms (4 million pounds) of them were taken from that lake in 1940. By that time smelts had spread into all five Great Lakes; they seem to have been introduced into Lake Ontario separately, from Cayuga Lake in northern New York.

Smelts spawn in massive numbers, surging like a wall of fish flesh up freshwater streams and into shallow, shoreline waters, much like their marine cousins on the Atlantic Coast, the similarly behaved (but not related) caplin and the (closely related) eulachon on the Pacific Coast. Like caplin, Great Lakes rainbow smelts were

The rugged coastline of Lake Superior near Rossport, east of Thunder Bay, Ontario.

literally shoveled into garbage pails by the millions in the 1950s and '60s. In 1964, the commercial catch of rainbow smelts from Lake Erie alone was 7.3 million kilograms (16 million pounds). But the population fell abruptly in the 1980s, probably because of predation by alewives, and it does not seem to have recovered its former abundance.

The increasing numbers of alewives and smelts in the Lakes led to the introduction of larger, predatorial fish to replace the Atlantic salmon and lake trout that had once kept prey species in check, but which had been nearly extirpated by the dual threats of sea lampreys and overfishing. There was also a perceived need to bolster the commercial and recreational fisheries. The first deliberate introductions were four species of Pacific salmon (of the genus *Oncorhynchus*, as distinct from the Atlantic salmon genus, *Salmo*). Although primarily a saltwater family, all salmonids (salmon, trout, char, grayling, and whitefishes) may have originated in freshwater, as suggested by their habit of returning to freshwater streams to spawn. There are no permanently saltwater salmonids, but there are several permanently freshwater species.

The kokanee, for example, introduced into Lake Michigan in 1950 with stock taken from Kootenay Lake, British Columbia, is a smaller, freshwater form of the sockeye salmon, rarely weighing more than 1.4 kilograms (3 pounds). They are now found in Lakes Huron, Michigan, and Superior, where they live on zooplankton and aquatic insect larvae such as those of the mayfly and caddisfly

A NEW TWIST

Of the 185 nonindigenous species known to have invaded the Great Lakes in the past two hundred years, the most recent is also the smallest. The virus that causes viral hemorrhagic septicemia (VHS), a disease commonly found in the Baltic Sea and the North Pacific, turned up in the Bay of Quinte on the north shore of Lake Ontario in 2005, but may have been in Lake St. Clair since 2003.

So far, VHS has killed tens of thousands of fish in Lakes Ontario, Erie, and St. Clair, affecting twelve species found in the Great Lakes, including muskellunge, northern pike, walleye, yellow perch, and rainbow trout. The disease destroys the linings of blood vessels, causing internal bleeding and liver failure; fish with VHS turn dark and have protruding eyes and pale gills. Those with the nervous form of the virus develop twisted bodies and tend to swim in circles. The virus is transmitted through bodily fluids and enters the fish's internal organs through the gills or wounds. It is not harmful to humans, but people have been advised not to eat infected fish.

Scientists don't know how the virus got into the Great Lakes, but there are two prime suspects: if it originated in Lake St. Clair, it probably arrived in the ballast tanks of a freighter that had recently sailed in the Baltic Sea; if in the Bay of Quinte, then the culprit may have been a local trout farm, since VHS is a common disease in hatchery-raised rainbow trout in Japan and in turbot farms on the Pacific Coast.

RAINBOW SMELT

CHINOOK SALMON

COHO SALMON

BROWN TROUT

until the age of four. They then spawn, late in the season, in November and December, when ice is forming on the lake, after which, as with all Pacific salmon, the adults die. The young fry emerge from the gravel in April and move down into the "nursery" lake, where they feed on zooplankton and are fed on in turn by larger fish and diving birds.

The sockeye was the first salmon to be introduced to the Lakes, in Lake Ontario in 1873. Chinook are the largest salmon, often weighing more than 13.6 kilograms (30 pounds) at which stage they are called tyee on the West Coast. Steelhead, a coastal strain of rainbow trout, were next, in 1900, and now range widely in Lakes Michigan and Huron and spawn in their tributaries, as well as migrating into tributaries of Lake Superior. In 1956, there was an accidental release of pink salmon into Lake Superior when a shipment of fertilized pink salmon eggs destined for an experimental introduction into Hudson Bay was stored temporarily at a hatchery on the Nipigon River. Somehow, 10,000 eggs were flushed down the hatchery sewer, and within a few years pink salmon were found spawning throughout Lakes Superior and Huron. A large, humpbacked salmon that feeds on alewives, the pink did very well and by 1979 had spread to all five lakes. And in 1966, the state of Michigan released 660,000 coho salmon into Lake Michigan and 192,000 into Lake Superior. Ontario planted 130,000 in Lake Ontario in 1969. Coho spawning runs now take place in many Great Lakes tributaries every eighteen months, when the adults are three or four years old.

The success of these introductions is still a matter of debate. For a long while it was not known whether these alien species were reproducing in Great Lakes waters, but it now seems fairly certain that they are, although stocking programs are still in place to keep population levels high enough to sustain a sport fishery. Since the 1960s, annual restockings have increased almost yearly. Between 1966 and 1998, 745 million hatchery-raised salmon were released into the Great Lakes. Ontario still releases 3 million exotic salmonids into Lake Ontario every year.

The brown trout is an Atlantic river species introduced into Michigan rivers in 1863 and Ontario in 1913, specifically for sport fishers. Anglers initially objected to these plantings because they thought the fish was too difficult to catch and because brown trout carry furunculosis, a disease of brook trout. But brown trout have endured in the Lakes and are now a popular species. They spawn in late autumn, using the same spawning headwaters as brook trout but later in the season. The female creates a shallow depression, or redd, in the streambed, deposits her eggs, then covers them with gravel. The adults grow to 18 kilograms (40 pounds) in their native marine environments, but only to about 6.4 kilograms (14 pounds) in freshwater lakes, down to 900 grams (2 pounds) in inland streams.

There is no doubt that such massive releases of Pacific salmonids and Atlantic trout compete with remnant populations of lake and brook trout for food and habitats, not to mention that Pacific salmonids take heavy tolls on the young of such native species as slimy sculpins, bloaters, and yellow perch. In salmon spawning streams, the larger and more aggressive Pacific species usually take over the most promising nest sites. They have been blamed for the failure of Atlantic salmon reintroduction programs in Lake Ontario, and for declines in the alewife population, the mainstay of the Lake Michigan fishery. But it is also true that their presence in the Lakes has been a boon to commercial fisheries as well as to sport fishing and tourism, upon which many formerly prosperous fishing communities have come to rely.

SOME INTRODUCTIONS ARE NOT

Other exotic species have no such benefits to recommend them. The carp was an early instance. Native to the temperate zones of Asia and Europe (the name comes from the Latin *carpum,* referring to a fish of the Danube), it was brought to England in the fifteenth century as an ornamental pond fish. It evidently found its way into the wild, since Izaak Walton, in *The Compleat Angler* (1653), refers to it as "the Queen of Rivers; a stately, good and very subtle fish." It was brought to North America in the early 1800s by Captain Henry Robinson, of Newburgh, New York, who brought six or seven dozen from France in 1832, reared them in his pond, and then released them into the Hudson River, eight years after the completion of the Erie Canal. So there may have been carp in Lake Ontario as early as 1833, although it was not until 1880, when carp were brought into Ontario as a food fish by Messrs. S. and B.F. Reesor, of Markham (no doubt to sell to the growing Asian population in the province), near Toronto, that the carp was officially recorded this far north. In 1888, carp were introduced into Sandusky Bay, on Lake Erie, and in 1892, the Ontario Fish and Game Commission reported carp in the Grand River, which runs into Lake Ontario. The next year, 286,000 kilograms (631,000 pounds) of carp were caught in Lake Erie; in 1908 the harvest was 4 million kilograms (9 million pounds), and by then carp were common in every Great Lake except Superior.

The large, brownish, heavily scaled carp is a hearty fish and a prolific breeder. A 76-centimeter (30-inch) female can release more than 2 million eggs. They spawn in June and July in warm, shallow water, when their dorsal fins can sometimes be seen protruding, sharklike, above the surface of wetlands; the eggs adhere to submerged weeds and grasses and hatch three to six days later. The young grow to 23 centimeters (9 inches) in their first year and begin to spawn in their second year. They can survive with very little oxygen, and so they do well in heavily eutrophied lakes such as Lake Erie where native species, among them yellow perch and smallmouth bass, have difficulty breathing. But they are detrimental to many species because they stir up bottom mud when they feed on aquatic roots in shallow bays and wetlands, disturbing feeding and spawning sites and killing plants that are the main food supply of other fish and diving birds.

Although carp has some value as a food fish, especially among immigrants from Asia, its introduction into the Great Lakes is not regarded as a boon. Frederick H. Wooding, in his *Book of Canadian Fishes* (1959), observed, "Although quantities are marketed each year by commercial fishermen in live, iced or smoked forms, they are not generally popular." This may be a good thing, since carp, with their high fat content and bottom-feeding ways, accumulate toxic pollutants at a great rate. A 1995 study of fish from five of the most polluted areas in the Great Lakes basin found that "the greatest carcinogenic risk for each exposure scenario resulted from consuming carp as opposed to pelagic species such as walleye or chinook salmon." People eating carp from the Saginaw River, on the western side of Lake Huron, perhaps the most contaminated

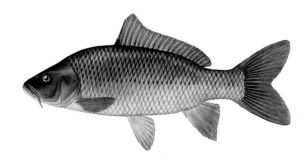

COMMON CARP

site on the Lakes, ran a 1-in-10,000 risk of developing cancer, compared with a 1-in-100,000 risk if they ate walleye. Carp from other, less contaminated areas, however, have been deemed safe for human consumption.

HITCHHIKERS FROM THE BALTIC SEA

Following the appearance of sea lampreys, alewives, carp, and Pacific salmonids in the Great Lakes, the incidence of both accidental and deliberate introductions leveled off. The first fifty years of the twentieth century saw few new species; the white perch, which entered the Lakes via the Erie Canal in 1954 and is now an abundant food fish in Lake Ontario's Bay of Quinte, is probably the most significant. With the completion of the St. Lawrence Seaway in 1959, however, allowing more and bigger saltwater vessels into the Lakes, the rate of introductions jumped significantly, from fewer than one per decade to almost one per year. In the past fifteen years, the rate of introductions has again shot up: in 2001 alone, fifteen new species were discovered to have invaded the Lakes.

THE FIRST SPIKE

Purple loosestrife *(Lythrum salicaria),* a tall, perennial, magenta-spiked bog plant that is now choking native life out of our wetlands, was one of the earliest plant invaders in North America. It was first introduced in the early 1800s, either accidentally in sheep's wool or deliberately, as a garden herb. Native to Eurasia, it is the *Lysimachia* referred to by Pliny and was highly valued as a medicinal plant by the first-century herbalist Dioscorides, who describe it as "tart and astringent...good for stanching both inward and outward bleeding." Its dried roots and leaves were made into a concoction to treat dysentery and diarrhea into the nineteenth century.

It is, however, highly invasive. Once arrived on the eastern seaboard, it quickly spread along canals and disturbed marshlands in the Great Lakes basin. Since the 1930s, it has invaded most shallow-water marshes, and now it is poised to invade deeper wetlands. With up to fifty 2-meter (6.5-foot) stems growing from a single rootstalk, purple loosestrife soon replaces native grasses, sedges, flowering plants, and bulrushes while providing no benefits to wildlife.

Some florists still sell purple loosestrife in what they call "guaranteed sterile" cultivars, but these are easily capable of hybridizing with the wild version as well as with any other of the thirteen *Lythrum* species in North America, such as thymeleaf loosestrife *(L. thymofolia)* and hyssop loosestrife *(L. hyssopifolia).* The sale of any purple loosestrife has been prohibited in Ontario, Wisconsin, Minnesota, and Illinois.

Purple loosestrife, an alien relative of the native swamp loosestrife, is known as Red-Sally in England.

There have been several vectors. Private aquariums, with their imported freshwater species, have been a major source. Approximately 10 percent of American households have aquariums and ornamental fish, and many of those—along with the snails, plants, and parasites that accompany them—end up in the Lakes, either through sewage systems or by direct dumping. Some of them do well. Goldfish, members of the carp family native to China, are now abundant in the lower Lakes. They spawn in warm, shallow waters in May, and the young are born sixty-five to seventy-six hours later, depending on the water temperature. Wild goldfish are greenish-brown, not gold, and are often mistaken for minnows and used as baitfish. Lesser-known organisms that are now common in the Lakes region and have come from private aquariums include aquatic plants such as the European frog-bit, the European water chestnut, and the Eurasian water milfoil, as well as the big-eared radix mollusk and the blue-spotted sunfish.

Most aquarium releases have not been detrimental to the Lakes ecosystem, but there is one—also a carp species—that could pose a major threat if it becomes established. A single specimen of the northern snakehead was netted by a fisher in Chicago's Burnham Harbor in 2004. Nicknamed the Frankenfish, it can grow up to 92 centimeters (3 feet) long, has a mouthful of long, needlelike teeth, is an aggressive and impatient feeder on smaller fish, and can live up to three days out of water. Importation of snakeheads or their eggs into the United States is illegal, but breeding populations have nonetheless been found in Florida, in Virginia's Potomac River, and in a tributary of the Delaware. When one was caught in a pond in Maryland, wildlife officials poisoned the pond to get rid of any others that might have lurked there. The Burnham Harbor specimen was probably an aquarium release, but electric-shock barriers have been placed across the Chicago Ship Canal in case any others decide to swim up from the Mississippi system.

A far more significant vector than aquarium releases, fishers' bait pails, or restaurant fish tanks has been the ballast water of ships entering the Great Lakes from various European and Asian seaports. Ships charge their ballast tanks with water from, say, the Baltic Sea, then discharge them after entering the Great Lakes in preparation for taking on cargo. Even ships with empty ballast tanks (called NOBOBs, meaning "no ballast on board") often clean out their tanks in Great Lakes ports, and microscopic invertebrates, protozoans, and aquatic macrophytes left over from previous trips thus enter the harbors. At the same time mollusks, algae, and crustaceans can easily adhere to ships' hulls and anchor chains and be dropped or scraped off in inland waters. Thus the propagules, or seed colonists, of marine organisms from entirely different ecosystems are systematically and repeatedly injected into the Great Lakes. That's how zebra mussels arrived.

THE DREADED DREISSENIDS

The first sighting of a zebra mussel was in Lake St. Clair in June 1985, a date that marks another tipping point in the natural history of the Great Lakes.

North America is the cradle of the world's freshwater mussel population; the upper Mississippi basin and the rivers draining into it are probably where freshwater mussels originally evolved from marine oysters and clams. There are, or were, 297 species of them, one of the richest faunal diversities for an area that size in the world. The Great Lakes hosted 23 species, covering a wide range of shell shapes and sizes, from the larger pigtoes and threeridges to the delicate ladyfingers and the smaller lilliputs and tricorns.

Mussels are members of the Mollusca, a huge phylum that includes nearly 50,000 marine, freshwater, and terrestrial species—snails and slugs, limpets, whelks, clams, oysters, and even octopuses (in which the mollusk foot has been modified into arms). Mussels, clams, and oysters belong to the class Bivalvia: soft-bodied organisms consisting of little more than a digestive system, a heart, a foot, and two hinged shells. The reduced head is a mere knot of ganglia that tell the muscular hinge when to shut the shell. North American mussels are of the family Unionidae. Unionid mussels lie half-buried on river or lake bottoms with their shells open, siphoning water over their mucus-covered gills. The gills filter out the algae, bacteria, and other organic matter suspended in the water column and propel the cleared water back into the environment. It is largely thanks to the natural filtration system of unionid mussels that, before European settlement, the Great Lakes and their tributaries were literally crystalline. Each individual mussel can filter up to 38 liters (10 gallons) of water a day, and there were millions upon millions of mussels. Wisconsin's Lake Pepin was famous for its diverse mussel population; in the 1880s, its

Zebra mussels filter phytoplankton, the food of such deepwater amphipods as *Diporeia*, from the water: before 1990, *Diporeia* formed 40 percent of the Lakes' benthic biomass, but they have now all but disappeared.

bottom was covered by an average of 50 large mussels per square meter (5 per square foot).

The shells are composed of calcium carbonate and consist of a hard, outer crust called the periostracum, and a smooth, shiny, pinkish inner surface, the nacre or mother-of-pearl. Males push themselves through the sand or sediment with their single foot, up to 3 meters (10 feet) a day, looking for females. When they are near enough to one, they exude sperm into the water, and the females siphon it onto their eggs, which they have already deposited onto their gills. The eggs hatch and the larvae, or glochidia, are ejected into the water. This is the unionid's parasitic phase, when its larvae encyst on the gill filaments of small fish (most mussel species parasitize a specific host fish), where they feed for one to twenty-five weeks before dropping onto the river or lake bottom to spend the next eight to ten years becoming sexually mature adults. Some freshwater mollusk species never grow much larger than a fingernail and are eaten, despite their shelly exteriors, by small fish with big teeth. Others live for sixty or even a hundred years, growing to 31 centimeters (12 inches) or more and as much as 1.8 kilograms (4 pounds); these are eaten by gulls, shorebirds, raccoons, and humans.

People of the Woodland culture ate a lot of mussels and wore the pearls they found in the shells as ornamental and ritual jewelry. Louis Jolliet, the first European to see the Mississippi, recorded in 1672 that native people on that river were wearing pearl ear pendants and necklaces, and burial mounds in Ohio have been found to hold thousands of bored pearls that were evidently of great religious significance, not unlike the turquoise of the Hopi. But it was another two hundred years before a shoemaker in Paterson, New Jersey, bit into his dinner of mussels from nearby Notch Brook and found a pearl that, had he not cracked it with his teeth, would have been worth a small fortune. The Great Pearl Rush was on. Over the next two years, from 1857 to 1859, Notch Creek yielded $115,000 worth of pearls, some of them perfectly round and 2.5 centimeters (1 inch) in diameter. The frenzy soon spread north to the Great Lakes, into Ohio and Wisconsin, where the Pecatonia, Sugar, Apple, and Wisconsin rivers regularly swarmed with pearl harvesters.

The introduction of cultured pearls from Japan in the early 1900s put an end to the freshwater pearl industry, but not to mussel harvesting. In 1890, an American tariff on imported mother-of-pearl drove the price of buttons up so high—to $60 per 100 pounds (45 kilograms) of oyster shell—that a German button cutter who had moved to Muscatine, Iowa, began using freshwater mussel shells, which gave new life to the declining mussel fishery. By 1900, there were two hundred button factories in the northern United States, and supplying them with mussel shells was a huge industry, employing thousands of full-time and weekend harvesters on nearly every river, lake, pond, and wetland in the upper Mississippi and Great Lakes basins. In 1899, mussels were the most valuable fishery in Wisconsin; more than 7.3 million kilograms (16 million pounds) were harvested in that state alone, selling for 60 cents per 100 pounds (45 kilograms). Shell wasn't as valuable as pearl, but there was a lot more of it.

So many mussels were taken that species began to disappear: the older, larger specimens were the best for buttons, as they had been for pearls, and since mussels don't begin to reproduce until they are old and large, most of the sexually mature mussels were soon gone and the harvest switched to younger, smaller individuals. More recently pollution has also taken its toll. Today, of the almost 300 native freshwater mussel species that existed in North America 150 years ago, 30 have become extinct, 57 are endangered, and 70 have been designated "species of concern." In Michigan, it is now illegal to possess a live unionid mussel or even a unionid shell.

It was into this underutilized unionid niche that the zebra mussel was introduced in 1985. Zebra mussels are native to the Caspian Sea but probably arrived in the Great Lakes aboard a ship from the Baltic Sea. The waters of the Ponto-Caspian basin—a three-lake system in eastern Asia that comprises the Caspian, Azov, and Black seas—are unlike those of the Great Lakes: they are high in salt content and low in oxygen in their deeper parts, having undergone rapid rates of eutrophication in the latter half of the twentieth century. Over their geological history, they have been subjected to a series of faunal invasions from the Mediterranean Sea, and many of their fish and mollusk species are therefore able to thrive in both saltwater and freshwater. When the Dnieper-Bug Canal linked the drainage basins of the Ponto-Caspian system and the Baltic Sea in the 1850s, many species, including zebra mussels, had no difficulty colonizing the latter and quickly spread into northern European rivers, lakes, and seaports. And the Baltic Sea is very much like the Great Lakes: northern, recently formed by glacial activity, oligotrophic, low in native species diversity, and with ready access to the North Atlantic. Most of the ships entering the Great Lakes come from northern European ports, and since 1959, when the St. Lawrence Seaway opened, 72 percent of the nonindigenous species introduced into the Great Lakes have been transported here in ballast tanks.

Like unionids, zebra mussels are filter-feeding bivalves; they have small (1.25-centimeter or 0.5-inch), razor-sharp shells with dark, zigzag markings, and prefer to adhere to hard substrates such as rocks, concrete piers, ships' hulls, intake pipes, and other mussels, although they can also colonize sandy or muddy substrates. Their evolutionary survival strategy is rapid reproduction: the young reach sexual maturity in their first year and are capable of producing voluminous offspring. They fuel this rapid growth by having a high filtration rate, approximately ten times that of unionid mussels relative to their body size, which allows them to ingest up to 40 percent of their body carbon per day, mostly in the form of small units of phytoplankton. As a result, zebra mussels spread rapidly from Lake St. Clair; by 1986, they were in the Detroit River, and within five years they were in both Lakes Erie and Ontario. Their numbers are almost incalculable. In 1989, zebra mussels were clogging municipal water intake facilities around Lake Erie, having reached densities of more than 750,000 mus-

sels per square meter (70,000 per square foot) of lake bottom.

Zebra mussels found a near-empty habitat and promptly began filling it, attaching themselves to rocks, cement, posts, and pipes, anywhere there was a bit of current. Because they are such efficient filterers and exist in such cosmic numbers, they have contributed greatly to clarifying the water in the lower Great Lakes. But there have been serious drawbacks, quite apart from clogged

intake valves. Clearer water has meant increased light penetration, which in turn has led to greater and deeper algal production. The mussels feed only on certain types of green algae, which is what other aquatic organisms, including unionid mussels, amphipods, insect larvae, and small fish, also eat. This allows other phytoplankton species, such as blue-green algae, which is inedible, to proliferate. Thus while they themselves are well fed, they create a phytoplankton vacuum that is quickly filled by algae that other organisms cannot consume. As a result, Great Lakes basin residents who take their drinking water from lakes—even isolated, inland lakes—have noticed a distinct swampy taste, because their intake facilities are now exposed to sunlight and filled with blue-green algae.

Within six years of the zebra mussel invasion, there were no live unionid mussels left in Lake St. Clair, and the Detroit River had undergone an 80 percent decline in unionid numbers and a 47 percent decline in unionid species. Other animals that eat phytoplankton were also adversely affected. By 1997 in Lake Ontario, the native deepwater amphipod *Diporeia hoyi*—the major food item of slimy sculpins, juvenile lake trout, bloaters, and whitefish, and a species tracked as a sentinel for lake-bottom ecosystem health—had declined from 2,100 individuals per square meter to 76 (from 1,756 per square yard to 64), with a consequent decline in those dependent fish populations. *Diporeia* had been starved out of its own pantry.

Like many ducks, this female common eider feeds on mussels—including zebra mussels—and may be helping to keep the invasive population in partial check.

Possibly the only native species to benefit from the introduction of zebra mussels are eiders. The common eider male is a handsome sea duck, black at the waterline with a white back and neck and a black cap, that breeds in the Far North but migrates south during the winter. The closely related king eider is a more familiar visitor to the Lakes; it is similar to the common eider but slightly smaller, with the male showing less white on its back and a large orange patch above its bill. Both were once popular among the down-filled parka, pillow, and mattress set; in the Arctic, eiders nest in vast colonies and line their nests with their own down. Farther south, they feed in warm, shallow bays on mollusks and other bottom life. There is also some evidence that greater and lesser scaup are feeding on zebra mussels in the Great Lakes during migration, and some concern that they are therefore bioaccumulating toxins as a result. Even if eiders and scaup were to become as common on the Lakes as cormorants, however, it is unlikely they would make a serious dent in the zebra mussel infestation. Ironically, it has been two subsequent invaders, both also from the Ponto-Caspian basin, that have kept the zebra mussel in partial check.

The first is another dreissenid mussel. The quagga mussel is native to the Black Sea but has spread to North America the same way zebra mussels did, via ships arriving from the Baltic Sea, and especially in this case from the Dnieper River. They first appeared in the St. Clair River in 1989 and immediately began ousting zebra mussels from the deeper parts of Lakes St. Clair, Erie, and Ontario. Because the Black Sea is colder than the Caspian, quagga mussels are more cold-tolerant than zebra mussels, functioning well in water that is less than 4°C (39°F), although they also prosper in warmer, shallow water. In Lake Erie they are found in water up to 23°C (73°F). They prefer softer substrates, such as sand, silt, and mud, and can exist where there is limited food.

The pattern of dreissenid invasion seems to be that zebras move in first, dominate the shallows, especially those with rocky bottoms, and spread down to a depth of about 65 meters (213 feet). There, where the water is colder and the food supply becomes limited, the quagga mussels begin. There is some mixing of zebras and quag-

gas between 65 and 85 meters (213 and 279 feet), but deeper than that it is all quaggas. In the Black and Baltic seas, quaggas are rarely found deeper than 100 meters (328 feet), but in Lake Ontario they dominate to 130 meters (426 feet) and flourish in the coldest parts of the lake.

Another problem with an overabundance of filtering dreissenid mussels is that they concentrate chemical pollutants at the bottom of the water column. As they filter-feed on polluted phytoplankton, they defecate PCB-laden matter into the sediments, where the toxins build up in the food of benthic organisms, such as worms. High concentrations of PCBs, however, remain in the mussels' body fat. Zebra mussels analyzed in 2000 were found to contain 100 parts per billion (PPB) of PCBs; small fish that ate the mussels contained up to four times that level, and larger fish such as smallmouth bass, which feed on small fish, had 1800 ppb of PCBs in their flesh. Far from blocking toxins out of the benthic environment, zebra and quagga mussels simply concentrate them in the sediments and then transfer them back into the food chain.

The lesser scaup dives to shallow lake bottoms to feed on young mussels.

The only fish that feeds on zebra mussels is another nonindigenous invader from the Ponto-Caspian basin. In 1990, the round goby was discovered in the St. Clair River near Detroit, having evidently been transported there in the ballast tanks of a transoceanic freighter. A small, aggressive, deepwater fish, the round goby grows up to 25 centimeters (10 inches) in length but is typically less than 12 centimeters (5 inches). Gobies look like sculpins, except for a black spot on their anterior dorsal fins, and their round, bullish heads and protruding eyes make them look pugnacious, which they are.

The round goby is the very model of a conquering invader: tough, resilient, and a generalist par excellence. It can live in freshwater or saltwater, can tolerate low oxygen and high pollution, exists in a wide range of temperatures, from -1°C to 33°C (30°F to 91°F), is found where the substrate is either sandy or rocky (although it prefers rocky or cobbled lake or stream beds), and enjoys a diverse diet, from young zebra mussels to zooplankton or the eggs of other fish species and even the fry of larger fish, such as smallmouth bass and perch. It has an advanced lateral line system—hair cells along its flanks that pick up anomalies in the water flow—that allows it

The female brown-headed cowbird lays her eggs in the nests of other birds, often warblers, who diligently raise her chicks at the expense of their own.

to detect predators and prey in the dark, and its fused pelvic fin forms a quasi sucker that gives it a grip on rocks and substrates where the waters are choppy. The round goby uses these gifts to aggressive advantage, chasing other small fish away from food, nesting sites, and eggs. It also hides from potential predators, such as smallmouth bass, in the spaces between rocks and cobbles on the lakebed.

ROUND GOBY

SMALLMOUTH BASS

As a result, the round goby has spread rapidly into all five Great Lakes and now exists in vast numbers. There is evidence that it has entirely taken over habitat formerly occupied by such native species as the mottled sculpin and the logperch. A 2002 study determined that there were more than 10 billion round gobies in the western end of Lake Erie alone; some researchers estimate that they now constitute as much as 50 percent of the entire fish biomass of the Lower Great Lakes.

Just as alien plant species have drastically altered the composition of the visible landscape, so too have invading nonindigenous aquatic organisms almost completely taken over the less visible realm beneath the surface of the Great Lakes themselves. Whether this change is permanent has yet to be determined; the invasions have been recent, and it takes many generations for adaptation and colonization to take hold. But there is no doubt that many native species are in a bust cycle, and many nonindigenous species are booming. To a casual observer, a typical Great Lakes landscape—acres of rolling greenery reflected in the deep blue waters of Georgian Bay, for example—might appear much the same now as it did when Étienne Brûlé and Samuel de Champlain first skimmed down the French River in search of the Orient. But a closer look would reveal that nearly half the faces in the frame weren't in the picture four hundred or even fifty years ago.

NINE

THE FUTURE OF THE GREAT LAKES

T HE **GREAT LAKES HAVE HAD** a glorious past. In 1910, when no threat to their majesty and permanence seemed possible, the poet Wilfred Campbell wrote that "there is no more beautiful, enchanting and sublime portion of the American continent" than the Great Lakes. Today, despite alterations to the cast of characters in the Great Lakes diorama, it still presents a breathtaking, mesmerizing picture.

Even in the most populous and industrialized portions of the Lakes—the south shore of Lake Erie, the western end of Lake Ontario, along the Detroit River or the southern rim of Lake Michigan—there are isolated spots so pristine, so reminiscent of bygone eras, that time seems to have passed them by as a river flows around dry, mossy boulders. On the remoter shores, around Georgian Bay, on Manitoulin Island or the north shore of Lake Superior, it is still possible to gaze out at the vast expanse of sunlit water or follow a rushing river up into the Canadian Shield and imagine oneself the first human being to set eyes on an undisturbed wilderness.

To Campbell, the Lakes region was "in many respects the most favored in North America," and that too remains true. The watershed is often cited, with the Grand Canyon and Mount Denali, as one of the natural wonders of North America. The Lakes will

FACING PAGE: A common loon and her chick. Loons build floating nests on "nursery pools," where their fledged young are taught to dive for small fish.

. . .

As a scientist, I have my own dream, that a moratorium be put on
the cutting of what is left of the global forests and that ordinary people
with an acorn and a shovel begin the long road back to nature.

DIANA BERESFORD-KROEGER, *Arboretum America*, 2003

continue to shine, in Campbell's words, "when we and all our dream-
ing lie low in dust." But the Lakes have changed, and are changing,
occasionally in ways that are beyond our control—or should be—
and very often in ways we can control—and must.

If I were to board a freighter today and sail the length of all five
Great Lakes, as I did in 1982, I doubt I would observe much difference between the Lakes as they are now and as they were twenty-
five years ago. More traffic, perhaps, more congestion in the canals.
More lights along the shorelines at night, but not many. There will
be more changes in the future, however: demographers predict that
the population of Toronto will reach 7.7 million by the year 2025,
by which time, the U.S. Census Bureau forecasts, the population in
the Great Lakes states will have soared to 73.5 million.

Environmental awareness has increased in the past three decades, and I would see more and healthier coastal wetlands, more
bald eagle nests, and more cormorants energetically beating their
wings a few feather-lengths above the waves. The water would be
cleaner. Since the International Joint Commission (IJC) introduced
its revised Great Lakes Water Quality Agreement in 1987, which
was already an improvement over the original 1972 agreement, pollution entering the lakes has declined substantially from the toxic
levels that persisted during the dark days of the 1950s and '60s.

The problem of pollution in the Lakes has not gone away, however. Estimates are that, because of the different sizes and water replacement rates of the Lakes, if we stopped dumping toxic chemicals into the lakes today, it would take six years for Lake Erie to flush itself 90 percent clean, twenty years for Lake Ontario, one hundred years for Lakes Michigan and Huron, and five hundred years for Lake Superior. Of course, we have not stopped dumping chemicals into the Lakes. Every two years since 1980, the IJC has published a report card on progress in cleaning up the Lakes, and while each report celebrates advances, the authors also point out how much work is

Lake levels lowered by increased evaporation threaten coastal habitat such as this embayment on Lake Superior's north shore.

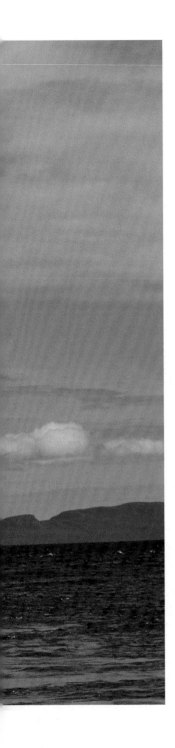

still to be done if the chemical integrity of the Lakes is to be restored. "We have made progress on that commitment," they wrote in the 2002 report, "but, with regret, we declare again, as we did in 2000, that the power of the vision captured in the Agreement has generated neither enough action nor full recovery."

Each report has focused on a different problem. The 2000 report documented the appearance of new, unidentified chemicals; scientists could name only 30 percent of the substances they found in Great Lakes salmon, snapping turtles, and herring gulls. In 2002 it was PCBs: "Concentrations of PCBs in waters of all Great Lakes are approximately 100 times higher" than was considered safe, and the most significant exposure to them was through eating fish. Signs around Lake Michigan warning people not to eat fish caught in the lake had been removed in 1997, but two years later they went back up when carp, walleye, and perch from Saginaw Bay tested high for PCBs and dioxin. The signs are still there.

In 2004, the IJC focused on mercury. Although mercury discharges from paper mills in the United States and Canada "dropped substantially" from 1990 to 1999, the United States was still emitting 105 tonnes (116 tons) of it each year, Canada was adding another 11 tonnes (12 tons), and much of it was ending up in the Lakes through airborne emissions from coal-fired power plants. Following warnings from the EPA and the FDA, the report recommended

If water levels in the canals continue to decline, bulk carriers like the *Cartiercliffe Hall* may disappear from the Lakes, as more grain will be shipped through Churchill, Manitoba.

that we not eat the organs, fat, or skin of any fish caught in any of the Great Lakes, and that we consume the flesh of only small species such as bass, pike, walleye, or perch, in quantities no greater than 170 grams (6 ounces) a week. These local advisories, the report stated, were "expected to exist for decades to come." And indeed, more recent studies have extended that warning to the oceans: in 2007, Health Canada suggested that children and pregnant women avoid eating canned albacore tuna and shark more than twice a week because of high mercury levels worldwide, another reminder of the close links between the Great Lakes ecosystem and the larger world.

But the longest-lasting and most perplexing pollution problem lies hidden in the lakebeds. Since it is too soon for most of the pollution that was in the Lakes in the 1970s to have flushed out, reduced contaminant levels in the upper waters of the Lakes means that most of the pollutants have settled into the sediments. "The persistent toxic substances found in contaminated sediment," the IJC wrote in its *Tenth Biennial Report*, released in 2000, "are the dominant issue" in those basin areas targeted by the commission for particular attention. Bottom-feeding fish and mollusks ingest them, and disturbances of the lake bottom rerelease them into the water. Either way, the toxins return to the food chain. In its 2002 report, the IJC warned again that "without sediment cleanup, injury to the health of humans, fish and wildlife will continue."

It is difficult to avoid disturbing sediment. Zebra and quagga mussels drag themselves about on the lake bottom, insect larvae burrow into the mud, currents and ice stir the benthic soup, lake freighters churn the beds with their prop wash. And how do you dredge a canal without literally agitating the sediments that line its lowest depths? In the late 1970s, the U.S. Army Corps of Engineers (USACE) announced a plan to deepen and widen the St. Lawrence Seaway from stem to stern, to permit the passage of oceangoing vessels with a draft of 9.8 meters (32 feet). The USACE also wanted to open the seaway to winter navigation, which would require the Coast Guards of both countries to keep the canals and shipping lanes ice-free. This was before the days of environmental assessments, and no one knew what effect year-round shipping and reduced ice cover would have on aquatic organisms in the Lakes and along the shores. Nonetheless, the proposal met with immense opposition, especially from residents of the Thousand Islands, and even attracted the involvement of the infamous peace activist Abbie Hoffman. In 1984, the U.S. Congress rejected winter navigation, but the upper Lakes were granted an extended season: the locks at Sault Ste. Marie, which had been operating from April 1 to December 14, were allowed to remain open until January 7, plus or minus two weeks.

In 2002, the USACE again announced a plan to deepen and widen the St. Lawrence Seaway—including the complete removal of two of the Thousand Islands—and to build longer locks that would accommodate for the first time 305-meter (1,000-foot) oceangoing Panamax vessels all the way to Duluth and Thunder Bay. Apart from the impact this development would have on wildlife habitat, such a massive disturbance of lake sediments would have put hundreds of millions of tonnes or tons of sequestered PCBs and other pollutants back into circulation, as the USACE's own "reconnaissance"

study pointed out. (Part of its plan was to dredge canals and harbors to 15.3 meters, or 50 feet, and dump the contaminated sediment in deeper water at the center of each lake.) Again, opposition from a coalition of fifty environmental groups put the proposed dredging on hold, at least temporarily. The scheme has not been rejected, merely shelved until the cost-sharing governmental partners decide whether to go ahead with the funding. Meanwhile, projections are that the seaway, especially the Welland Canal, will reach carrying capacity around the year 2030. It's not unlikely that some time before then, the USACE will be back in Washington and Ottawa with another plan to improve and extend seaway navigation. The USACE did receive authorization to build a new lock long enough to accommodate the Panamax vessels at Sault Ste. Marie, Michigan, in anticipation of the expected onrush of oceangoing traffic.

The organisms most affected by polluted sediments are those that live in deep water. In fact, the true legacy of the postwar years in the Great Lakes is the number of deepwater species that have disappeared as a result of contaminants. As well as the blue pike, three of the five species of ciscoes (closely related to the lake whitefish) that once thrived deep in the Great Lakes have become extinct: the last of the deepwater ciscoes, which occurred only in Lakes Huron and Michigan, was caught in 1951; the blackfin cisco, which inhabited all the Lakes except Erie, has not been reported since the 1960s; and the longjaw cisco, another deepwater fish found only in Lakes Huron and Michigan, vanished in the 1970s. The deepwater sculpin is also extinct, leaving the slimy sculpin as the only remaining indigenous deepwater prey fish in the Great Lakes, and it is rarely found deeper than 92 meters (300 feet).

The IJC continues to monitor water quality, and many improvements have been made. Lake Erie has been restored to oxygenated health once more, and although phosphorus levels seem to be creeping up again, laws and inspection processes are in place. Increased vigilance will eventually identify the sources and halt the increase. Like DDT and PCBs, phosphorus is a manageable problem. The same cannot be said, however, for some of the other threats to the physical integrity of the Lakes.

A WHOLE NEW FOOD CHAIN

As we have seen, many of the native species that dominated the Lakes ecoregions for the past 10,000 years have disappeared or been crowded out by alien invaders. More than 185 nonindigenous aquatic species have already found a permanent home in Great Lakes waters, and today most of the links in the Lakes' food chain are dominated by exotic species. In the benthic mud of Lake Ontario, native gastropod snails have been replaced by the New Zealand mud snail. The most common alga in Lake Ontario phytoplankton now is *Thalassiosira baltica*, an import from the Baltic Sea. The dominant organisms in zooplankton are the spiny waterflea and the fishhook water flea, which turned up in the Lakes in 1982 and 1998 respectively, predators that feed on other zooplankton, including native copepods. These are eaten by round gobies, alewives, and Pacific salmon, all introduced species, and their fingerlings are snatched up by double-crested cormorants, which have recently invaded the Great Lakes in unprecedented numbers.

There is currently no effective mechanism in place to control the introduction of new species into the Lakes. The most common method of entry—and the focus of the IJC's concern—is via the ballast tanks of ships arriving from foreign ports. Measures to prevent new introductions have been taken. Since 1993, for example, ships leaving ports in Europe or Asia have been required to empty their ballast tanks in mid-ocean and refill them with saltwater before entering the Lakes. But since then the rate of nonindigenous species coming into the Lakes has actually increased. Larger species are not getting in, but new, smaller organisms have begun showing up. The fishhook water flea was detected in Lake Ontario in 1998 and has rapidly ousted native types; it spread into Lake Michigan the next year, probably in ballast water taken on by a freighter in Lake Ontario. Obviously, stricter regulations are required, forcing all ships to manage their ballast water in all lakes to prevent the inadvertent introduction of alien species.

Regulations are also being proposed by the IJC for ships entering the Great Lakes without ballast in their tanks—the so-called NOBOBs—which until now have been exempted from the rules

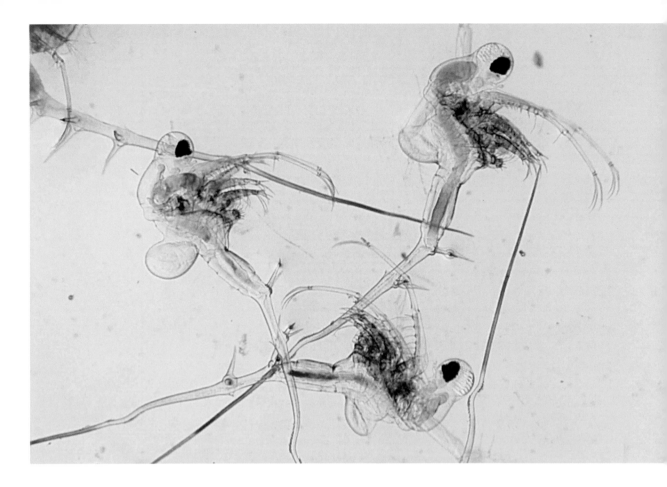

applied to ballasted ships. NOBOBs, which make up nearly 70 percent of Great Lakes traffic, have been allowed to flush out their "empty" ballast tanks in Great Lakes ports. But ballast tanks are never completely empty: deposits accumulate in the tanks below the pump level and may contain seeds, eggs, and larvae of invasive species that are then released into the Lakes. The IJC is calling for controls that apply to all ships coming into the Great Lakes, whether they contain freshwater or saltwater ballast or no ballast at all.

Before such regulations can be passed, there is much work to be done. Funding has to be found, research conducted, technology perfected, and inspection routines established. Even if the required legislation were passed today, the IJC calculates that it would take five to eight years for it to come into force. At the rate new nonindigenous organisms are entering the Lakes, there could be a dozen new species inhabiting Great Lakes waters before measures are in place to prevent or control them. And each one could be as devastating to native species and habitat as sea lampreys and zebra mussels have been in the past.

PIPE DREAMS

Since the beginning of European settlement around the Great Lakes, our idea of water—like that of nature itself—has undergone a fundamental change. As a society, we no longer see water as simply part of the landscape, a passive natural element; increasingly, we view it as a resource to be harnessed and exploited. We have become like timber merchants who regard a tree not as a living member of a forest ecosystem but as so many board feet of lumber. Water has always been important for drinking and as a means of transportation, just as trees have long provided wood for fuel and building. But until the early 1800s, transportation was dependent on the location of water; by the end of the nineteenth century, engineers were relocating water to provide transportation where it was needed, and the Age of Canals was under way.

Engineers also moved water for purposes other than transportation. Municipalities around the Lakes began withdrawing massive amounts of water, not only for drinking but also for industrial use. The amount taken from the Lakes increased at an incredible rate: in 1985, cities, industries, and power generators took 75 billion cubic meters (2.65 trillion cubic feet) of water from the Lakes per year. About 9.3 percent, or 7 billion cubic meters (247 billion cubic feet) per year, was for household use; the rest went to manufacturing, which soaked up 24.6 billion cubic meters (868.7 million cubic feet) of water a year, and power production (water used to cool nuclear reactors, or passed through turbines to create electricity), which used 43.8 billion cubic meters (1.54 billion cubic feet) a year. By 2002, power production alone accounted for 95 percent of all withdrawals—3 billion cubic meters (106 billion cubic feet) *per day*—and total water withdrawals had jumped to 1169 billion cubic meters (41.3 trillion cubic feet) a year. It has been estimated that not a drop of water leaves the Lakes without having passed through

FACING PAGE: The spiny waterflea, one of the latest in a long series of invasive species now making their homes in the Great Lakes.

the cooling system of a nuclear reactor somewhere along its journey from Duluth. Most of that water is eventually returned to the lake it was drawn from. But returned water often comes back at a higher temperature, and it is drawn from the lake's bottom waters and returned to the lake's surface.

At least the water was used in the Great Lakes basin. In recent years, numerous proposals have been put forward to divert water out of the basin, for use as far away as Texas. The Ogallala Aquifer is a subterranean body of water underlying nearly 1.5 million square kilometers (600,000 square miles) of the American Midwest, stretching roughly from western Texas, Oklahoma, and New Mexico all the way north to South Dakota. It was formed at the same time as the Great Lakes from glacial meltwater that originated in the Rocky Mountains. Historically it has been tapped by ranchers of the High Plains for crop irrigation, but in many places a century of continuous pumping has depleted the store of fossil water beyond the aquifer's ability to replenish itself. The Ogallala is drying up. As early as 1982, a U.S. federal study predicted that within half a century the aquifer would no longer sustain the 5.2 million hectares (12.8 million acres) of cropland that had come to depend on it. By 2020, 40 percent of the farmers drawing from the Ogallala would have to look for their water from some other source or else decommission their land. More recent studies, undertaken in the increasingly dry years of the late 1990s, suggest that 2020 was an optimistic date. As Marq de Villiers notes in his book *Water*, "If there is not to be a large-scale collapse—if three hundred thousand people are not going to be destitute, and a substantial American industry consigned to the trash can of history—something will have to be done. But what?"

When the Ogallala Aquifer was full, it contained as much water as Lake Huron, a fact that has not escaped the attention of High Plains farmers, nor of the USACE. In 1983, the USACE investigated the feasibility of building a pipeline to divert 24 million cubic meters (848 million cubic feet) of water a day from Lake Superior into the Missouri River, a distance of about 965 kilometers (600 miles), from somewhere around Duluth, Minnesota, to somewhere in South

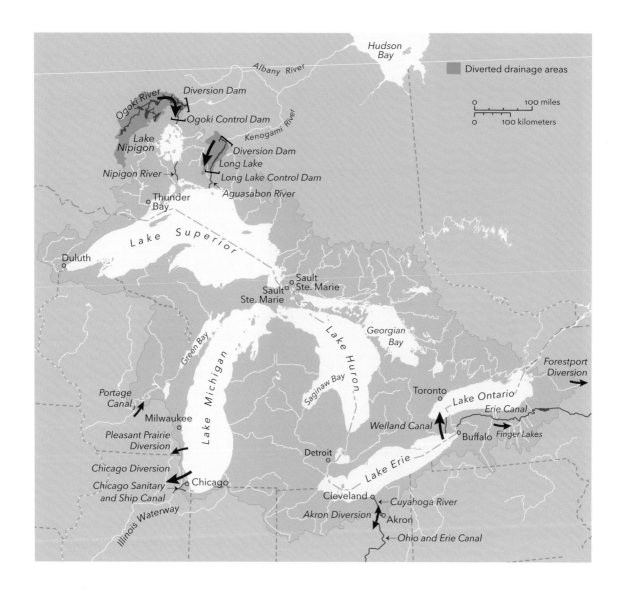

Dakota. The project was abandoned when the USACE determined it would require seven 1,000-megawatt nuclear power plants to run the pumps that would move the water uphill onto the Great Plains. In other words, the decision not to take water from the Great Lakes was made for economic, not logistical or environmental, reasons.

Similarly, and almost simultaneously, the province of Quebec under Premier Robert Bourassa came up with an even more harebrained scheme. Named the GRAND Canal (for Great Recycling and Northern Development Canal) and expected to cost C$100 billion, the proposal called for the construction of a dyke across the top of James Bay, separating it from Hudson Bay. When all the rivers emptying into James Bay had turned it into a huge freshwater reservoir, the water would be diverted south into Lake Superior—so that water taken by the USACE from the American side would be replenished on the Canadian side. The project was officially cancelled by Bourassa's successor Jacques Parizeau, after much public outcry, but fears remain that the dreams of the Grand Canal Co. Ltd. have simply been put on hold until the political climate warms to the idea of selling engineered water to the drought-stricken American Southwest. (A former president of the Grand Canal consortium, Simon Reisman, was the chief Canadian negotiator of the North American Free Trade Agreement.) Once again, a dubious scheme was shelved not because of the disastrous effect it would have on the James Bay ecosystem—on the fish, plants, and other organisms that for millennia have relied on specific salt levels in James Bay water—but because of the absence of a market for Canadian water when the Missouri River project fell through. When the economics of such megaprojects begin to make sense, as some day they may, the blueprints for them could be dusted off and propped back up on the NAFTA partners' drawing boards.

It's not as though such proposals are without precedent. The idea that water is a commodity, and a highly mobile one at that, has made the Great Lakes the focus of diversion projects since the middle of the nineteenth century. They seem to stem in part from our apparently compulsive need to push water around like children playing in a roadside ditch during spring runoff. Most of these projects, which involve irreversible tampering with Great Lakes water levels, are still worrisome from an environmental point of view. If the Great Lakes basin is a holding tank for most of North America's freshwater supply, it is a tank that has, over the years, sprung a lot of leaks.

The New York State Canal System, for example, which includes the Erie and Oswego canals, allows up to 433,000 cubic meters (15.3 million cubic feet) of Lake Ontario water per day to drain into the Hudson River watershed, and has done so since the canal opened in the early 1800s. During periods of drought in New York City, such as occurred in the 1960s and again in the mid-1980s, city officials suggested that that amount be vastly increased, rather like opening a gigantic fire hydrant when New Yorkers want to beat the heat. So far these proposals have met with such resistance from Great Lakes basin residents that they have been dropped. Dropped, that is, until the next heat wave.

When high levels of radium were found in two wells in Pleasant Prairie, Wisconsin, in 1982, the village council decided to divert water from nearby Lake Michigan and discharge it into the Mississippi basin. They received approval from the state to take 12,000 cubic meters (424,000 cubic feet) a day, with the proviso that by 2010 they will have built a pipeline that would return the water to Lake Michigan. Great Lakes United, a citizens' environmental group that monitors water diversion projects, has expressed alarm at this solution, stating that new housing developments in Pleasant Prairie are placing heavier demands than expected on the diverted

FACING PAGE: Pitcher plants are native to sphagnum bogs throughout the basin. Bristles lining the curled leaves help trap insects, which are then ingested.

water, and that two versions of the agreement between the village and the state exist, a signed version and an unsigned version. The proviso to return the water to Lake Michigan by 2010, it claims, is in the unsigned version.

Then there is the Chicago Sanitary and Ship Canal, stretching 48 kilometers (30 miles) between Lake Michigan and the Illinois and Des Plaines rivers. Work began in 1848 on its prototype, the Illinois and Michigan Canal, which cut across the narrow divide separating the Chicago River, a small, sluggish stream that meandered through Chicago and drained into Lake Michigan, from the larger Illinois River, which flowed south into the upper Mississippi Valley. In 1860, deaths in Chicago from typhoid fever, cholera, and dysentery began to soar, and by 1900, they had reached 65 per 100,000 population, the highest toll in the country, because the city's sewage was dumped directly into the Chicago River, which emptied into Lake Michigan close to where the city took its drinking water. The first section of the Chicago Sanitary and Ship Canal was dug in 1905, a short, 8-kilometer (5-mile) ditch that linked the Chicago River with the Des Plaines River, also part of the Mississippi system. Since Lake Michigan is higher than the Des Plaines, water in the Chicago River began flowing backward, draining water and sewage from Lake Michigan into the Mississippi system at the rate of about 283 cubic meters (10,000 cubic feet) per second. The engineers had in fact reopened the ancient Chicago Outlet through which the upper Lakes once drained into the Gulf of Mexico. Residents on Lake Michigan grew alarmed when water levels on the lake began to decline, and in 1929 the U.S. Supreme Court limited the diversion to 42.5 cubic meters (1,500 cubic feet) per second, or nearly 3.7 million cubic meters (130 million cubic feet) of water daily. That amount has crept up over the years; in 1967, the Supreme Court adjusted the allowable discharge drastically, and today Chicago's sewage still ends up in the Gulf of Mexico, washed there by 8 million cubic meters (281 million cubic feet) of Lake Michigan water every day.

In 1995, the state of Michigan claimed that Illinois was violating the 1967 ruling by allowing an extra 756,000 cubic meters (26.7 million cubic feet) of water a day to flow out of Lake Michigan.

Illinois countered that the locks and flow meters maintained by the Corps of Engineers were old and leaking. By this time an agreement had been signed among the eight states bordering the Great Lakes which stipulated that no one state could divert water from the Lakes without the agreement of the other seven: Illinois was allowed to repair its locks and reduce the outflow to 1967 levels, and Michigan agreed not to prosecute over the violations that had already occurred.

The diversion of Lake Michigan water through the Chicago canal has dropped the lake level by 5 centimeters (2 inches), not an alarming amount. But if the USACE plan to deepen the existing shipping channels and connecting linkages goes ahead, lake levels will drop

further: dredging the St. Clair River to accommodate larger ships has already lowered both Lake Michigan and Lake Huron by a further 40 centimeters (16 inches). And, as urban centers continue to grow in the Great Lakes region and suburbs and industries require greater infusions of lake water, many new diversion proposals are certain to emerge.

Not all water diversions remove water from the Great Lakes. The Portage Canal, for example, completed in 1876 and linking the Wisconsin River to the Fox to provide a commercial route for ships between the Mississippi and the Great Lakes, diverts 240,000 cubic meters (8.5 million cubic feet) of water a day from the Mississippi watershed into Lake Michigan. (Although the canal was never used commercially and has long lain in disuse, plans were announced in July 2006 for a US$2.75 million "rehabilitation" of the canal for pleasure craft.)

In 1940, work commenced on a megaproject north of Lake Superior that since 1950 has diverted roughly 142 cubic meters (5,000 cubic feet) per second of water into Lake Superior that would normally flow into James Bay. The intention was to increase Ontario's capacity to generate electricity at Niagara by diverting water into the turbines without lowering lake levels or reducing the amount of water flowing over Niagara Falls. Because of the size of Lake Superior, the diversion has raised Superior's level by only 5 centimeters (2 inches). But diversions into the Lakes do not offset the effects of diversions out of them.

Lowered lake levels severely affect the human economy of the Great Lakes. When surface levels drop, either the lake bottoms have to be dredged deeper to accommodate shipping, or ships have to carry less cargo. Since 1997, coal and grain freighters on the Lakes have had to lighten their loads in order to navigate some of the shallower channels and locks; it takes 245 tonnes (270 tons) of cargo to lower a 229-meter (750-foot) ship 2.5 centimeters (1 inch) into the water, and so ships have to sail 245 tonnes (270 tons) lighter every time the lake level is lowered by that much. Low water levels also influence air quality by exposing contaminated sediments at the shoreline, which then dry out and evaporate into the atmosphere.

FACING PAGE: Island white pines in Bing Inlet, Georgian Bay, Ontario.

And they threaten shorebird and fish communities by reducing the amount of water in coastal wetlands and other fish spawning areas.

Demands for Great Lakes water will rise in the coming decades. According to Adele Hurley, director of water issues at the University of Toronto's Munk Centre for International Studies, water stress in the Missouri River, and therefore in the Mississippi, due to decreased snow melt in the Rockies, "will sooner or later affect every single water drinker around the Great Lakes." Diversion projects added to increased local household and commercial use have already put tremendous stress on lake levels. As early as 1981, the IJC predicted that water consumption from the Great Lakes would grow fivefold by the year 2035. Continuing increases in population within the basin will further increase withdrawals. But the biggest challenge to Great Lakes water levels, and therefore water quality, is going to come from a different source: global warming.

CHANGING CLIMATE, CHANGING LAKES

According to the Nature Conservancy of Canada and Environment Canada, global warming is expected to cause a rise in temperatures in the Great Lakes region of between 3°C and 7°C (5.4°F and 12.6°F) in winter and between 3°C and 10°C (5.4°F and 18°F) in the summer when the atmospheric carbon dioxide level reaches 360 parts per million, double that of pre-industrial-revolution days. Many scientists suggest that level will be reached by the year 2050, perhaps even by 2030. Such dramatic changes will lead to increased evaporation, which, along with reduced ice cover, water diversion and current dredging projects, will bring water levels in the Great Lakes much lower than historical levels. Experts with the U.S. Global Change Research Program predict that increased evaporation due to higher temperatures could drop lake levels by as much as 1.5 meters (5 feet) by mid-century.

Such a decrease in the depth of canals and shipping lanes would necessitate additional and widespread dredging of the St. Lawrence Seaway in places where supertankers are barely clearing the bottom now. The resulting disturbance of toxic sediments could bring back the pollution levels of the 1960s. Similarly, the Chicago Sanitary and Ship Canal would have to be deepened to prevent the Chicago River from reverting to its initial flow back into Lake Michigan. This would require engineers to lower the channel bed by 1.2 meters (4 feet) through solid rock for a distance of 48 kilometers (30 miles) to get the water flowing into the Illinois River again.

But the consequences of lower lake levels for commercial traffic and contaminated sediments are not the only worrisome aspects of global climate change. Perhaps the most serious long-term effects will be to the region's natural ecosystems, to the animals and plants that have, over the past 10,000 years, adapted to the historic climate in and around the Lakes. Global warming is a planet-wide, all-inclusive phenomenon, and it's difficult to predict exactly what it will mean to a particular region. But scientists are giving us a general idea of what we have to look forward to.

Since the late 1980s, when the NASA physicist James Hansen sounded the first alarm to the U.S. Senate that global warming was

Reintroduction of the massasauga rattler, the basin's only venomous snake, has been successful but contentious in southwestern Ontario.

Poison ivy, with its shiny, trifoliate leaves, is found throughout the Great Lakes basin as a shrub, a tree or sometimes a vine.

DON'T TOUCH

Poison ivy accounts for more than 350,000 reported cases of dermatitis every year. The plant's toxic ingredient, urushiol, a resin that can be transferred only by touch, suffuses the entire plant, including stems, leaves, and roots. Because it does not evaporate in air, the resin can remain potent on clothes, pets, and even door handles for years. Furthermore, since poison ivy is a member of the cashew family, along with mangoes, cashews, and pistachios, eating those foods can bring on a renewed bout of dermatitis.

Recent studies suggest that global warming will cause poison ivy to become an even greater menace. In controlled-environment experiments, plant scientists at Duke University increased carbon dioxide levels by 54 percent—the amount atmospheric carbon dioxide is expected to increase by 2050 if we continue to burn today's amount of fossil fuels—and found that poison ivy grew larger and three times faster than normal. Its urushiol level soared by as much as 33 percent. By mid-century, experts warn, giant poison ivy plants could be shading or choking out smaller shrubs on the forest floor, and cases of toxic reaction to it could triple to more than 1 million cases annually.

a reality (one member of that Senate committee was Al Gore), the effects of climate change have become increasingly evident: consistently rising temperatures, especially in the inner cities of Chicago and Toronto, have carried with them increased health hazards for the elderly, the homeless, and people with respiratory problems, higher demands on power facilities for air conditioning, rising rates of evaporation not only from the Lakes but also from forests and agricultural croplands, more demand for water for irrigation and cooling, and spikes in the amount of water vapor, an extremely potent greenhouse gas, entering the atmosphere.

A year after Hansen's wake-up call, Canadian scientists told the House of Commons Standing Committee on the Environment that an average global temperature increase of 2°C (3.6°F)—which they expected, at the time, would be reached by the end of the twentieth century—would have significant effects in the Great Lakes region. More recent studies have refined that analysis. The IJC's report *Climate Change and Water Quality in the Great Lakes Region*, published in 2003, and the most recent report from the Intergovernmental Panel on Climate Change, published in 2007, found that higher summer and winter temperatures would greatly affect the boreal forest north of Lake Superior by increasing the risk of forest fires, creating more favorable conditions for insects such as the spruce budworm, and causing some northern tree species to move farther north. According to the House of Commons report, "local extinctions" can be expected to occur. Increased evaporation would lower water levels in all five lakes; severe drought would cause extensive crop failures in Ontario's agricultural heartland, especially for such crops as potatoes, corn, and soybeans, which require large amounts of water. One study, conducted by the University of Guelph, predicted agricultural losses of C$170 million a year in Ontario alone.

The recent dramatic increase in hurricanes and tropical storms coming from the American South is a direct consequence of higher surface temperatures in the mid-Atlantic. Although people living in the Great Lakes basin might be tempted to think that tropical storms don't affect them, intense storm activity in the South alters weather patterns in the Great Lakes region in weird and unpredictable ways.

September 2005—when Hurricane Katrina destroyed much of New Orleans—was one of the warmest Septembers on record throughout the Great Lakes basin, and water temperatures were also at record highs. November, however, was one of the coldest; more snow fell on Michigan's Upper Peninsula that month than during any previous November in recorded weather history. A recent study in New York State found that there has been a significant increase in snowfall within the Great Lakes region since the 1930s, an increase not found outside the watershed. The city of Syracuse, New York, for example, experienced its four heaviest snowfalls ever in the 1990s, which was also the warmest decade of the century. The study, published in the *Journal of Climate*, blamed the contradictory phenomenon on global warming: "Recent increases in water temperature are consistent with global warming. Such increases widen the gap between water temperature and air temperature—the ideal condition for snowfall."

In some areas of the Great Lakes, winter ice is melting much earlier than usual; in other areas, it's not forming at all. Ice duration and extent have been slowly declining for at least a century. One study, conducted in 2000 at Lake Mendota near Madison, Wisconsin, showed that between 1856 and 1998 ice duration decreased by thirty days, with a record low in the winter of 1997–98. One result of

Snow squall at Indian Head, on Ontario's Bruce Peninsula. As lake surfaces warm, reduced ice cover in winter could mean more shore erosion and a faster rate of evaporation.

reduced ice cover is a longer shipping season, with consequent increases in shore erosion (ice cover reduces waves and protects shorelines from being washed away) and increased evaporation, since surface water can evaporate year-round. Another is a change in the amount of light radiation, or the albedo, in the region. When the Lakes are covered with ice, they reflect more of the sun's heat away from the earth's surface. Open water, being darker, absorbs solar energy and contributes to already rising water temperatures.

The U.S. Environmental Protection Agency (EPA) points to other possible consequences of global warming. Fish spawning streams around the Lakes will become warmer, reducing habitat for cold-water species such as trout and salmon by as much as 86 percent. Although spawning times are determined by the number of hours of daylight, which does not change, the success of the spawning—the number of hatchlings that survive to become adults and perhaps the ratio of male hatchlings to female—depends to a great extent on water temperature. A variation of a fraction of a degree above or below normal can make a huge difference in a given year's fish populations. Fishers know that if there is especially cold weather at spawning time, there will be a bumper harvest of lake trout or whitefish the following summer, since those are cold-water-spawning species. Fishers want "a cold fall and a dirty winter."

The smallmouth bass, originally restricted to the Great Lakes, is now one of the most popular sport fishes in North America and is found in England, Russia, and Africa.

Warm falls and mild winters, on the other hand, are disastrous. Cool-water species, such as pike, walleye, or alewives (which spawn in midsummer), will also be adversely affected by warmer temperatures. John Casselman, a fish biologist with the Ontario Ministry of Natural Resources who has been tracking water temperatures and correlating them with fish growth patterns in Lake Ontario for the past three decades, estimates that with a water-temperature rise of 1°C (1.8°F), cool-water fish populations will decline by a factor of 2. In other words, only half the fish will survive to adulthood. After that the numbers soar off the chart: with a 2°C (3.6°F) rise, the populations will decline by a factor of 18, "and I won't even predict what would happen if the temperature rises more than that," he adds, although he mentions that a factor of 36 has been touted for a 4°C (7.2°F) rise.

Warm-water fish, however, such as largemouth and smallmouth bass and most exotics, "will explode," says Casselman. An increase of 1°C (1.8°F) will raise fish production by a factor of 2.4; a 2°C (3.6°F) increase produces a sixfold increase; and a 3°C (5.4°F) rise yields a fifteenfold increase. Because of global warming, he adds, water temperatures in Lake Ontario have already gone up by almost 1°C (1.8°F)—more than that in some shallow embayments, such as the Bay of Quinte, where warm-water fish tend to spawn. This might explain why nonindigenous species such as the round goby have done so well in the Great Lakes: they spawn prodigiously in warm water, while the populations of their major native predator—walleye—plummet. It also suggests why such cold-water fish as lake trout are doing so poorly and have to be restocked every year. Salmonids spawn successfully in warmer water, but their principal food species—alewives and walleye—do not, and so young salmon have less food. Salmon do not eat round gobies.

Migrating birds could also find their favorite ponds or wetlands suddenly dry, or their migration dates out of sync with insect hatching times; they could arrive at their Great Lakes resting areas too late for the larval stages of the insects they rely on to fuel their migration. Even resident birds may find themselves feeling less at home. In Pennsylvania, for instance, the EPA's Mid-Atlantic States Regional Global Warming Assessment has noted that an increase of 2°C (3.6°F) could mean that nine of the state's native breeding bird species would no longer breed that far south. As southern grasslands and Carolinian tree species such as black walnut and black cherry slowly advance north, pushing the Great Lakes–St. Lawrence forest into northwestern Ontario and the boreal forest farther toward Hudson Bay, out of the Great Lakes basin, bird, mammal, and insect species will move with them. A 1997 study of the bobolink, the black and white songbird with a bright yellow patch on the back of its neck, now common in summer meadows throughout the region, found that during extremely warm summers the species did not nest as far south as it did in cooler summers; the report predicted that with a climate change such as is expected by mid-century, the bobolink would no longer be found breeding south of the Great Lakes.

Other birds might not be found at all. As a result of global warming, certain tree species now native to the Great Lakes basin, including quaking aspen, yellow birch, red pine, white pine, and jack pine, may decline by 50 to 70 percent. This would seriously affect species that depend on these trees for their survival. The endangered Kirtland's warbler is an example. Between 1900 and 1986, the species was seen in Ontario only thirty-seven times. In the 1970s, bird counts indicated that there were fewer than 250 breeding pairs of Kirtland's warblers left in North America. Kirtland's warblers breed almost exclusively in the northern portion of Michigan's Lower Peninsula, in small stands of immature jack pine growing on sandy ground. Habitat restoration by selective fires and forest regeneration in the 1990s helped to increase the number of breeding warblers: in 2005, there were 1,300 males in the Lower Peninsula. The disappearance of half that region's jack pine stands because of global warming would put the Kirtland's warbler back in peril of extinction.

The IJC's 2003 report on climate change outlined some likely scenarios, based on studies of alterations that were already taking place. The boreal forest, where climate changes are slightly accelerated because of the northern latitude, offers an indication of what lies ahead. Between 1970 and 1990, the average temperature in the boreal region increased by 0.55°C (1°F), precipitation decreased by 60 percent, and evaporation increased by 50 percent. Evapotranspiration—the loss of water vapor from plants—also increased. The Great Lakes basin already loses 65 percent of the water that falls on it through evapotranspiration. A significant increase in moisture loss would have serious consequences for the boreal ecosystem, which depends on damp soil and bogs for its continued health.

FACING PAGE: One of the rarest birds in the Great Lakes basin, the Kirtland's warbler breeds in only a small area of Michigan's Upper Peninsula.

It's not a hopeful picture. Less ice, more evaporation, more shore erosion, less precipitation. Fewer native species, more alien plants, unstoppable aquatic organisms. These are enormous transformations to an ecosystem that has been trying to stabilize for more than ten millennia. The IJC report implied that rather than try to prevent these changes—it may be too late for that—we should learn to anticipate and adapt to them. Develop new crops that can tolerate a drier climate; shift the economic bases of certain communities from winter recreation to less climate-dependent industries; build more confined disposal facilities to accept toxic sediments from dredged harbors and channelways.

These measures may help humans adjust to an altered climate, but what about the rest of the ecosystem? Most species can accommodate radical modifications in their habitats if those modifications take effect over sufficiently long periods of time. But if the schedules suggested by the most recent predictions are valid, the organisms most likely to thrive will be those that arrive here from a region that is already warm.

THE RISING TIDE

The governments of the states and provinces within the Great Lakes basin have gradually come to terms with the alarming news about the state of its ecosystem, and are aware of the threats that water diversion, global warming, and invasive species pose to its preservation. Organizations such as the International Joint Commission and the Great Lakes Commission, backed by citizens' groups demanding more and better habitat protection and restoration, and supported by government-funded, scientific research, are taking positive steps toward returning the Lakes to something resembling their natural

The turkey vulture can smell decaying carrion from 300 meters (1,000 feet) and is often used by other opportunists to locate food. Natural gas workers also follow turkey vultures to locate pipeline leaks.

VULTURE CULTURE

The turkey vulture is the only vulture species found regularly in the Great Lakes basin, and it has been migrating this far north only since the 1920s. A large, completely black-feathered bird with a bald, red head and a 2-meter (6.5-foot) wingspan, the turkey vulture looks like a large hawk when seen from the ground; like the hawk, it rides warm air currents, circling high overhead until prey is sighted or— in the case of the vulture—smelled (turkey and black vultures are two of the very few species of birds with a sense of smell). Unlike hawks, vultures hold their wings in a distinct V, or dihedral, shape.

Their expansion into the Great Lakes region has been attributed to a number of factors: more roads mean more roadkills, the turkey vultures' main source of food, and the ban on DDT spraying has improved their reproductive rate. Global warming has also made northern areas more hospitable. Whatever the reasons, counts conducted by Bird Studies Canada at the Long Point Bird Observatory show that over the past fifty years, the turkey vulture population in the Great Lakes basin has increased by 15 percent annually, compared with only 2 percent in the rest of the continent.

Commenting on the near extinction of the California condor in the American West, the environmentalist David Brower remarked, "You know your society is in trouble when the vultures start dying." In the Great Lakes region, the vultures are doing just fine.

beauty and abundance. All acknowledge that future generations dwelling within the Great Lakes basin deserve to enjoy the same health and other, less tangible benefits as their ancestors did.

In the revised Water Quality Agreement of 1987 and later reports, the IJC identified forty-three Areas of Concern, or AOCs—specific harbors, wetlands, and stretches of shoreline on both sides of the border that had been so degraded by pollution or urban development that they were barely able to support aquatic life—and earmarked them for immediate restoration. Each AOC was mandated to come up with a plan for cleaning up its site and given a time limit within which to implement the necessary measures. Since then, some advances have been made, and precedents have been set to ensure that future restorations will be accomplished more easily.

Proof that aquatic ecosystems are changing for the better can be seen on the lakeshores of many of the major urban areas surrounding the Lakes. Waterfronts that once were functional but unsightly conglomerations of train tracks, warehouses, and factories are being transformed into parkland, residential developments, nature trails, and wildlife habitats. Windsor, Toronto, Detroit, Chicago, and Milwaukee have all transformed sections of their shorelines into attractive parks in which native wildlife species are returning. Even Ohio's Cuyahoga River, which in the 1960s was so polluted that it famously caught fire, now flows through Cuyahoga Valley National Park, where recent surveys show that great blue heron nests are increasing at the rate of 5.6 percent per year.

In Waukegan Harbor, Illinois, one of the 26 Areas of Concern in the United States, 448 tonnes (494 tons) of PCB-laden sediments dredged from the harbor bottom were thermally treated and stored in confined disposal facilities. Similarly, Hamilton Harbour, at the western end of Lake Ontario, was one of 17 Canadian AOCs and has now been cleaned up to a great extent. Once 2,150 hectares (5,300 acres) of the most toxic water in the Lakes, the site of Canada's largest concentration of industry and shipping, the harbor received not only industrial waste but also Hamilton's raw sewage. Herring gulls from the harbor were found to contain 57 different toxic contaminants and had a reproductive rate of only 18.6 percent.

After the 1987 revisions to the Water Quality Agreement committed the federal governments of both Canada and the United States to clean up the AOCs, citizens' coalitions in Hamilton began to work with government and industry representatives, scientists, and environmentalists to return the harbor to a healthier state while still maintaining it as an important industrial lakeport. Within five years, there was a plan calling for public access to the harbor, removal of contaminated soil, and the creation of Bayfront Park; by 1997, public access to the harbor had more than tripled, and the water was deemed safe for swimming. In addition, restoration of the Cootes Paradise marsh had begun, and C$13 million had been raised to add 63 hectares (156 acres) to the wetlands. New wastewater treatment facilities were built and existing plants upgraded, phosphorus discharges were lowered to federally mandated targets, and in many places fish habitat was brought back to preindustrial conditions.

The IJC wants to see cleanup work begin on two AOCs a year, and cleanups completed on two others, which would mean that all contaminated hot spots on the Great Lakes could be gone by 2030. This will require coordinated efforts from every level of government and an engaged citizenry, and the commission is confident that, given such cooperation, its goals can be achieved.

The Great Lakes can never be returned to the pristine condition in which Europeans found them three centuries ago, but with luck and much work we may once again be able to eat the fish, breathe the air, and drink the water. One bright sign for the future of the Great Lakes is the extent to which awareness of the many problems the basin faces is growing among politicians and citizens' groups. Threats to the Lakes' integrity are increasingly met with resistance.

Polls conducted in 2002 found that 55 percent of Great Lakes basin residents oppose the degradation of their environment because of the Lakes' natural beauty; 54 percent cited the Lakes' role in maintaining the balance of nature that sustains them; 52 percent felt the Lakes form part of their regional identity; and 64 percent accept a responsibility to preserve the Lakes for future generations. Politicians respond to such findings. Every lake and river, every bay,

FACING PAGE: Canada geese stage for southern migration near Oshawa, on Lake Ontario. Their return each spring has become a symbol of conservation and renewal.

every ecosystem, every endangered or threatened species around the basin has its champions.

Dave Dempsey, author of *On the Brink: The Great Lakes in the 21st Century*, is perhaps more aware than most of the range and complexity of the challenges, but he is encouraged by the public's growing engagement with the Great Lakes and their multifaceted issues. "If there's good news," he says, "it's the slowly rising tide of consciousness. Somehow we have to get back to the idea that this is our home and we can't afford to destroy it."

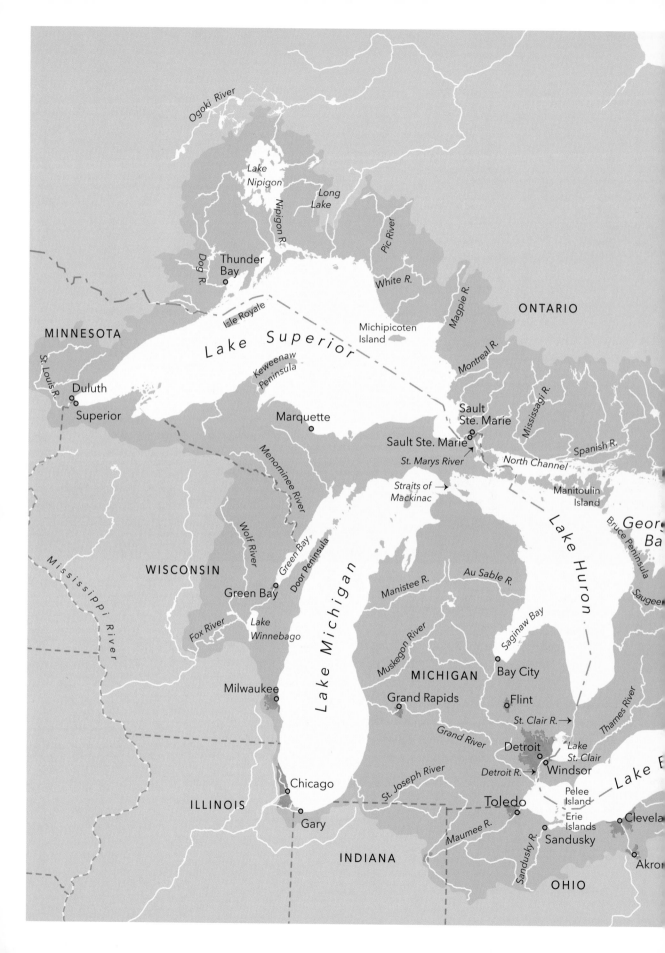

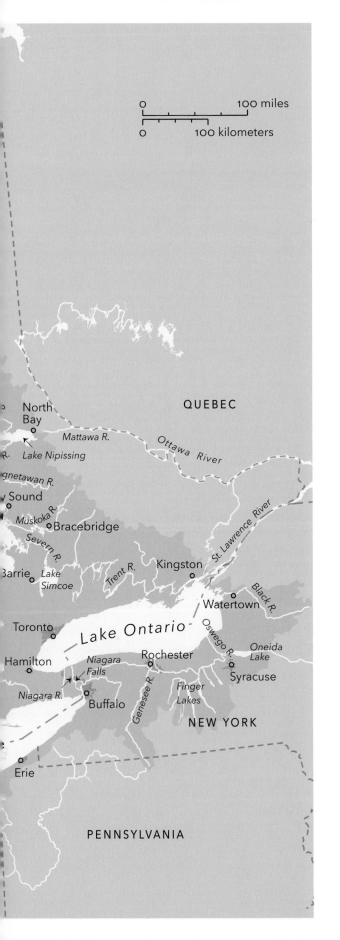

FURTHER READING

THE GREAT LAKES AND THEIR BASIN

Ahern, Frank. *Algonquin Park through Time and Space.* Toronto: Warwick, 2006.

Ashworth, William. *The Late, Great Lakes: An Environmental History.* Toronto: Collins, 1986.

Beck, Gregor Gilpin, and Bruce Litteljohn, eds. *Voices for the Watershed: Environmental Issues in the Great Lakes—St Lawrence Drainage Basin.* Montreal: McGill-Queen's University Press, 2000.

Brehm, Victoria, ed. *The Women's Great Lakes Reader.* Tustin, MI: Ladyslipper Press, 2000.

Campbell, Wilfred. *The Beauty, History, Romance and Mystery of the Canadian Lake Region.* Toronto: Musson, 1910.

Dempsey, Dave. *On the Brink: The Great Lakes in the 21st Century.* East Lansing: Michigan State University Press, 2004.

Dennis, Jerry. *The Living Great Lakes: Searching for the Heart of the Inland Seas.* New York: St. Martin's, 2003.

Downing, Elliot Rowland. *A Naturalist in the Great Lakes Region.* Chicago: University of Chicago Press, 1922.

Havighurst, Walter. *The Long Ships Passing: The Story of the Great Lakes.* New York: Macmillan, 1961.

Lewis, J.C., ed. *Guide to the Natural History of the Niagara Region.* St. Catharines, ON: published by the editor, 1991.

Rousmaniere, John, ed. *The Enduring Great Lakes: A Natural History Book.* New York: W.W. Norton and American Museum of Natural History, 1979.

Unwin, Peter. *The Wolf's Head: Writing Lake Superior.* Toronto: Viking Canada, 2003.

Waters, Thomas F. *The Superior North Shore: A Natural History of Lake Superior's Northern Lands and Waters.* Minneapolis: University of Minnesota Press, 1987.

Weller, Phil. *Fresh Water Seas: Saving the Great Lakes.* Toronto: Between the Lines, 1990.

WATER, FISH, AND RELATED THEMES

Bogue, Margaret Beattie. *Fishing the Great Lakes: An Environmental History, 1783–1933.* Madison: University of Wisconsin Press, 2000.

Casselman, John M. "Effects of Temperature, Global Extremes, and Climate Change on Year-Class Production of Warmwater, Coolwater, and Coldwater Fishes in the Great Lakes Basin." *American Fisheries Society Symposium* 32 (2002): 39–60.

———. "Dynamics of Resources of the American Eel, Anguilla Rostrata: Declining Abundance in the 1990s." In *Eel Biology*, edited by K. Aida, K. Tsukamoto, and K. Yamauchi. Tokyo: Springer-Verlag, 2003.

Casselman, John M., and K.A. Scott. "Fish-Community Dynamics of Lake Ontario: Long-Term Trends in the Fish Populations of Eastern Lake Ontario and the Bay of Quinte." In *State of Lake Ontario: Past, Present and Future*, edited by M. Munawar. New Delhi: Goodword Books, 2003.

Casselman, John M., et al. "Changes in Relative Abundance, Variability, and Stability of Fish Assemblages of Eastern Lake Ontario and the Bay of Quinte—The Value of Long-Term Community Sampling." *Aquatic Ecosystem Health and Management* 2 (1999): 255–69.

De Vault, David S., et al. "Contaminant Trends in Lake Trout and Walleye from the Laurentian Lakes." *Journal of Great Lakes Research* 22, no. 4 (1996): 884–95.

De Villiers, Marq. *Water: The Fate of Our Most Precious Resource*. 2nd ed. Toronto: McClelland & Stewart, 2003.

Dobiesz, Norine E., et al. "Ecology of the Lake Huron Fish Community, 1970–1999." *Canadian Journal of Fisheries and Aquatic Science* 62 (2005): 1432–51.

Eshenroder, Randy L., et al. "Lake Trout Rehabilitation in the Great Lakes: An Evolutionary, Ecological and Ethical Perspective." *Journal of Great Lakes Research* 21, supplement I (1995): 518–29.

Gunn, John M. "Spawning Behavior of Lake Trout: Effects on Colonization Ability." *Journal of Great Lakes Research* 21, supplement I (1995): 323–29.

Hoyle, J.A., et al. "Resurgence and Decline of Lake Whitefish (Coregonus Clupeaformis) Stocks in Eastern Lake Ontario, 1972 to 1999." In *State of Lake Ontario: Past, Present and Future*, edited by M. Munawar. New Delhi: Goodword Books, 2003.

Hubbs, Carl L., and Karl F. Lagler. *Fishes of the Great Lakes Region*. Rev. ed. Ann Arbor: University of Michigan Press, 2004.

Kandel, Robert. *Water from Heaven: The Story of Water from the Big Bang to the Rise of Civilization and Beyond*. New York: Columbia University Press, 2003.

MacIsaac, H.J., and T.C. Lewis. "Modeling Aquatic Species Invasions." *Canadian Journal of Fisheries and Aquatic Science* 59 (2002): 1245–56.

Pielou, E.C. *Fresh Water*. Chicago: University of Chicago Press, 1998.

Ricciardi, A., and J.B. Rasmussin. "Predicting the Identity and Impact of Future Biological Invaders." *Canadian Journal of Fisheries and Aquatic Science* 55 (1998): 1759–65.

Scott, W.B., and E.J. Grossman. *Freshwater Fishes of Canada*. Ottawa: Fisheries Research Board of Canada, 1973.

MAMMALS IN THE GREAT LAKES REGION

Baker, Rollin H. *Michigan Mammals*. Lansing: Michigan State University Press, 1983.

Boer, Arnold H., ed. *Ecology and Management of the Eastern Coyote*. Fredericton: University of New Brunswick, 1992.

Dearborn, Ned. *Foods of Some Predatory Fur-Bearing Animals in Michigan*. Ann Arbor: University of Michigan Press, 1932.

Geist, Valerius. *Moose: Behavior, Ecology, Conservation*. Stillwater, MN: Voyageur Press, 1999.

Grady, Wayne. *The Nature of Coyotes: Voice of the Wilderness*. Vancouver: Greystone, 1994.

Grambo, Rebecca L. *The Nature of Foxes: Hunters of the Shadows*. Vancouver: Greystone, 1995.

Hazzard, Evan B. *The Mammals of Minnesota*. Minneapolis: Bell Museum of Natural History, 1982.

Jackson, Hartley H.T. *Mammals of Wisconsin*. Madison: University of Wisconsin Press, 1961.

Mech, L. David. *The Wolf: The Ecology and Behavior of an Endangered Species*. Minneapolis: University of Minnesota Press, 1970.

Parker, Gerry. *Eastern Coyote: The Story of Its Success*. Halifax: Nimbus, 1995.

Theberge, John B., and Mary Theberge. *Wolf Country: Eleven Years Tracking the Algonquin Wolves*. Toronto: McClelland & Stewart, 1998.

Westcott, Frank. *The Beaver: Nature's Master Builder*. Willowdale, ON: Hounslow, 1989.

Woods, S.E., Jr. *The Squirrels of Canada*. Ottawa: National Museums of Canada, 1980.

PLANTS, INCLUDING TREES, WILDFLOWERS, FUNGI, AND LICHENS

Armson, K.A. *Ontario Forests: A Historical Perspective.* Toronto: Fitzhenry & Whiteside, 2001.

Barron, George. *Mushrooms of Ontario and Eastern Canada.* Edmonton: Lone Pine, 1999.

Beresford-Kroeger, Diana. *Arboretum America: A Philosophy of the Forest.* Ann Arbor: University of Michigan Press, 2003.

Brodo, Irwin M., Sylvia Duran Sharnoff, and Stephen Sharnoff. *Lichens of North America.* New Haven: Yale University Press, 2001.

Celestino, Mary. *Wildflowers of the Canadian Erie Islands.* Windsor, ON: Essex County Field Naturalists, 2002.

Dobbs, David, and Richard Ober. *The Northern Forest.* White River Junction, VT: Chelsea Green, 1995.

Groves, J. Walton. *Edible and Poisonous Mushrooms of Canada.* Ottawa: Canada, Department of Agriculture, 1962.

Kendrick, Bryce. *The Fifth Kingdom.* 3rd ed. Newburyport, MA: Focus Publishing, 2000.

Morsink, Willem. *Ontario Urban Forests—Scrapbook II: Growing Interest and Concern.* Toronto: Ontario Urban Forest Council, 2006.

Morton, J.K., and Joan M. Venn. *The Flora of Manitoulin Island.* Waterloo, ON: University of Waterloo, 2000.

Phillips, H. Wayne. *Plants of the Lewis & Clark Expedition.* Missoula, MT: Mountain Press, 2003.

Pratt, Rutherford. *The Great American Forest.* Englewood Cliffs, NJ: Prentice-Hall, 1965.

Scott, Geoffrey A.J. *Canada's Vegetation: A World Perspective.* Montreal and Kingston: McGill-Queen's University Press, 1995.

Traill, Catherine Parr. *Studies of Plant Life in Canada.* Toronto: William Briggs, 1906.

Voss, Edward G. *Michigan Flora.* 2 vols. Bloomfield Hills, MI: Cranbrook Institute of Science, 1972, 1979.

Waldron, Gerry. *Trees of the Carolinian Forest: A Guide to Species, Their Ecology and Uses.* Erin, ON: Boston Mills Press, 2003.

Wells, James R., et al. *Wildflowers of the Western Great Lakes Region.* Detroit: Wayne State University Press, 1999.

Yahner, Richard H. *Eastern Deciduous Forest: Ecology and Wildlife Conservation.* Minneapolis: University of Minnesota Press, 2000.

Zichmanis, Zile, and James Hodgins. *Flowers of the Wild: Ontario and the Great Lakes Region.* Toronto: Oxford University Press, 1982.

AMPHIBIANS AND REPTILES

Ditmars, Raymond L. *The Reptiles of North America: A Review of the Crocodilians, Lizards, Snakes, Turtles and Tortoises Inhabiting the United States and Mexico.* New York: Doubleday, 1936.

Johnson, Bob. *Familiar Amphibians and Reptiles of Ontario.* Toronto: Natural Heritage Press, 1989.

Logier, E.B.S. *The Snakes of Ontario.* Toronto: University of Toronto Press, 1958.

INSECTS

Angier, Natalie. *The Beauty of the Beastly: New Views of the Nature of Life.* Boston: Houghton Mifflin, 1995.

Dunn, Gary A. *Insects of the Great Lakes Region.* Ann Arbor: University of Michigan Press, 1996.

Evans, Howard Ensign. *Life on a Little Known Planet: A Biologist's View of Insects and Their World.* New York: Dutton, 1968.

Hubbell, Sue. *Broadsides from the Other Orders: A Book of Bugs.* New York: Random House, 1993.

GEOLOGY

Coniglio, Mario, Paul Karrow, and Peter Russell. *Manitoulin Rocks: Rocks, Fossils and Landforms of Manitoulin Island.* Waterloo, ON: University of Waterloo, 2006.

Dorr, John, Jr., and Donald Eschman. *Geology of Michigan.* Ann Arbor: University of Michigan Press, 1970.

Dott, Robert J., and John W. Attig. *Roadside Geology of Wisconsin.* Missoula, MT: Mountain Press, 2004.

Eyles, Nick. *Ontario Rocks: Three Billion Years of Environmental Change.* Toronto: Fitzhenry & Whiteside, 2002.

Holcombe, Troy L., et al. "Small Rimmed Depression in Lake Ontario: An Impact Crater?" *Journal of Great Lakes Research* 27, no. 4 (2001): 510–17.

Hough, Jack L. *Geology of the Great Lakes.* Urbana: University of Illinois Press, 1958.

LaBerge, Gene. *Geology of the Lake Superior Region.* Missoula, MT: Mountain Press, 2003.

Wiggers, Raymond. *Geology Underfoot in Illinois.* Missoula, MT: Mountain Press, 1997.

SCIENTIFIC NAMES

Common names for plants and animals are given in the text without their scientific names, which are provided here. The entries are listed alphabetically by their common names, which means that not all species will be found with the other members of their families: for example, black oak will be in the Bs and white oak in the Ws. To find the scientific name of organisms mentioned in the text, look under the full common name.

alewife, *Alosa pseudoharengus*
alpine woodsia fern, *Woodsia alpina*
American basswood, *Tilia americana*
American beach grass, *Ammophila brevigulata*
American beech, *Fagus grandifolia*
American black duck, *Anas rubripes*
American coot, *Fulica americana*
American eel, *Anguilla rostrata*
American elm, *Ulmus americana*
American lotus. *See* yellow lotus
aquatic buckbean, *Menyanthes trifoliata*
arethusa, *Arethusa bulbosa*
arrow-leaved violet, *Viola sagittata*

bald eagle, *Haliaeetus leucocephalus*
balm of Gilead, *Populus candicans*
balsam fir, *Abies balsamea*
balsam poplar, *Populus balsamifera*
beard lichen, *Usnea hirta*
beaver, *Castor canadensis*
bellflower, *Campanula americana*
big-eared radix mollusk, *Radix auricularia*
bigtooth aspen, *Populus grandidentata*
black-backed gull, *Larus marinus*
black-backed woodpecker, *Picoïdes arcticus*
black bear, *Ursus americanus*
Blackburnian warbler, *Dendroica fusca*
black-capped chickadee, *Parus atricapillus*
black-crowned night heron, *Nycticorax nycticorax*
blackfin cisco, *Coregonus nigripinnis*
black-footed reindeer lichen, *Cladina stygia*
black morel, *Morchella angusticeps*

black oak, *Quercus velutina*
black rat snake, *Elaphe obsoleta*
black spruce, *Picea mariana*
Blanding's turtle, *Emys blandingii*
blue ash, *Fraxinus quadrangulata*
blue jay, *Cyanocitta cristata*
blue pike, *Stizostedion vitreum glaucum*
blue racer, *Coluber constrictor foxi*
blue-spotted sunfish, *Enneacanthus gloriosus*
blue-winged warbler, *Vermivora pinus*
bobcat, *Lynx rufus*
bobolink, *Dolichonyx oryzivorus*
bog bilberry, *Vaccinium uliginosum*
bog buckbean, *Menyanthes trifoliata*
Bonaparte's gull, *Larus philadelphia*
book louse, *Liposcelis bostrycophila*
boreal chickadee, *Poecile hudsonica*
boreal chorus frog, *Pseudacris maculata*
boreal owl, *Aegolius funereus*
bracken fern, *Pteridium aquilinum*
brassy minnow, *Hybognathus hankinsoni*
broad-leaved arrowhead, *Sagittaria latifolia*
brown-headed cowbird, *Molothrus ater*
brown trout, *Salmo trutta*
bullfrog, *Rana catesbeiana*
bullhead lily, *Nuphar variegatum*
bur oak, *Quercus macrocarpa*
burred horsehair lichen, *Bryoria furcellata*
butterfly weed, *Asclepias tuberosa*

California condor, *Gymnogyps californianus*
Canada goose, *Branta canadensis*
Canada lynx, *Lynx canadensis*
Canada violet, *Viola canadensis*
Canada warbler, *Wilsonia canadensis*
Canterbury bells, *Campanula medium*
capelin, *Mallotus villosus*
cardinal flower, *Lobelia cardinalis*
Carolina wren, *Thryothorus ludovicianus*
carp, *Cyprinus carpio*
Caspian tern, *Sterna caspia*
cedar waxwing, *Bombycilla cedrorum*
cerulean warbler, *Dendroica cerulean*
chestnut-sided warbler, *Dendroica pensylvanica*
chinquapin oak, *Quercus muehlenbergii*
cliff fern, *Woodsia alpina*
coho salmon, *Oncorhynchus kisutch*
common dandelion, *Taraxacum officinale*
common eider, *Somateria mollissima*

common goldeneye, *Bucephala clangula*
common horsehair lichen, *Bryoria trichodes*
common juniper, *Juniperus communis*
common loon, *Gavia immer*
common merganser, *Mergus merganser*
common milkweed, *Asclepias syriaca*
common morel, *Morchella esculenta*
common snapping turtle, *Chelydra serpentina*
corn salad, *Valerianella umbilicata*
corn speedwell, *Veronica arvensis*
cougar, *Felis concolor*
coyote, *Canis latrans*
cucumber tree, *Magnolia acuminata*
cutlips minnow, *Exoglossum maxillingua*
cylindric blazing star, *Liatris cylindracea*

death angel (mushroom), *Amanita phaloides*
death cap (mushroom), *Amanita virosa*
deepwater cisco, *Coregonus johannae*
deepwater sculpin, *Myoxocephalus quadricornis*
dense button snakeroot or dense blazing star, *Liatris spicata*
dodder, *Cuscula gronovii*
double-crested cormorant, *Phalacrocorax auritus*
downy false foxglove, *Gerardia virginica*
downy wood mint, *Blephilia ciliata*
dragon's mouth. See arethusa
duck potato, *Sagittaria rigida*
dwarf dandelion, *Krigia virginica*
dwarf lake iris, *Iris lacustris*

eastern fox snake, *Elaphe vulpina gloydi*
eastern hemlock, *Tsuga canadensis*
eastern massasauga rattlesnake, *Sistrurus catenatus*
eastern red cedar, *Juniperus virginiana*
eastern tamarack, *Larix laricina*
eastern towhee. *See* rufous-sided towhee
eastern white cedar, *Thuja occidentalis*
eastern white pine, *Pinus strobus*
emerald shiner, *Nortopis atherinoides*
Eurasian water milfoil, *Myriophyllum spicatum*
European frog-bit, *Hydrocharis morsus-ranae*
European water chestnut, *Trapa natans*
evening grosbeak, *Coccothraustes vespertinus*

fall dandelion, *Leontodon autumnalis*
false pennyroyal, *Trichostema brachiatum*
fern-leaved false foxglove, *Gerardia pedicularia*
fishhook water flea, *Cercopagis pengoi*
flowering spurge, *Euphorbia corollata*
fly agaric (mushroom), *Amanita muscaria*
fox snake, *Elaphe vulpina*
fox squirrel, *Sciurus niger*
fragrant water lily. *See* white water lily

gadwall, *Anas strepera*
garlic mustard, *Alliaria petiolata*
Gattinger's agalinis, *Agalinis gattingeri*
goldfish, *Carassius auratus*
gray birch, *Betula populifolia*
gray fox, *Urocyon cinereoargenteus*
gray hair lichen, *Bryoria capillaris*
gray jay, *Perisoreus canadensis*
gray reindeer lichen, *Cladina rangiferina*
gray squirrel, *Sciurus carolinensis*
gray wolf, *Canis lupus*
great blue heron, *Ardea herodias*
great egret, *Casmerodius albus*
greater sandhill crane, *Grus canadensis tabida*
great gray owl, *Strix nebulosa*
great horned owl, *Bubo virginianus*
Great Lakes wheatgrass, *Agropyron psammophilum*
green milkweed, *Asclepias viridiflora*

hackberry, *Celtis occidentalis*
herring gull, *Larus argentatus*
Hill's thistle, *Cirsium hillii*
hooded warbler, *Wilsonia citrina*
Hooker's orchid, *Habenaria hookeri*
hoptree, *Ptelea trifoliata*
horsehair lichen, *Bryoria lanestris*
Houghton's goldenrod, *Senecio houghtonii*

indigo bunting, *Passerina cyanea*

jack pine, *Pinus banksiana*

Kentucky coffee tree, *Gymnocladus dioicus*
king eider, *Somateria spectabilis*
king rail, *Rallus elegans*
Kirtland's warbler, *Dendroica kirtlandii*

Labrador tea, *Ledum groenlandicum*
ladyfinger mussel, *Elliptio dilatatus*
lake chub, *Couesius plumbeus*
Lakeside daisy, *Hymenoxys herbacea*
lake sturgeon, *Acipenser fulvescens*
lake trout, *Salvelinus namaycush*
lake whitefish, *Coregonus clupeaformis*
lance-leaved coreopsis, *Coreopsis lanceolata*
lanceolate milkweed, *Asclepias lanceolata*
larch sawfly, *Pristiphora erichsonii*
largemouth bass, *Micropterus salmoide*
larger pigtoe mussels, *Fusconia flava*
least bittern, *Ixobrychus exilis*
lesser scaup, *Aythya affinis*
lilliput mussel, *Carunculina parva*
loggerhead shrike, *Lanius ludovicianus*

logperch, *Percina caprodes*
longjaw cisco, *Coregonus alpenae*
long-leaved reed grass, *Calamovilfa longifolia*
Louisiana waterthrush, *Seiurus motacilla*
lowbush cranberry, *Viburnum edule*
low sweet blueberry bush, *Vaccinium angustifolium*

mallard, *Anas platyrhynchos*
marram grass. *See* American
    beach grass
marsh marigold, *Caltha palustris*
marsh wren, *Telmatodytes palustris*
mayapple, *Podophyllum peltatum*
mayfly, order Ephemeroptera
meningeal worm, *Parelaphostrongylus tenuis*
moccasin flower. *See* pink
    lady's-slipper
monarch butterfly, *Danaus plexippus*
monk's-hood lichen, *Hypogymnia physodes*
moose, *Alces alces*
mottled sculpin, *Cottus bairdi*
mountain cranberry, *Vaccinium*
    vitis-idaea
mountain maple, *Acer spicatum*
mourning dove, *Zenaida macroura*
muskellunge, *Esox masquinongy*
muskrat, *Ondatra zibethicus*

narrow-capped morel. *See* black morel
New Zealand mud snail, *Potamopyrgus antipodarum*
nodding trillium, *Trillium cernuum*
northern cardinal, *Cardinalis cardinalis*
northern flying squirrel, *Glaucomys sabrinus*
northern harrier, *Circus cyaneus*
northern leopard frog, *Rana pipiens*
northern parula, *Parula americana*
northern pike, *Esox lucius*
northern pintail, *Aras acuta*
northern redbelly dace, *Phoxinus eos*
northern saw-whet owl, *Aegolius acadicus*
northern snakehead, *Channa argus*
northern three-toed woodpecker, *Picoïdes tridactylus*
northern waterthrush, *Seiurus noveboracensis*
northern white violet, *Viola pallens*

old man's beard lichen, *Usnea spp.*
olive-sided flycatcher, *Contopus cooperi*
one-flowered wintergreen, *Moneses uniflora*
opossum, *Didelphis virginiana*
osprey, *Pandion haliaetus*
ovenbird, *Seiurus aurocapillus*

pale-footed horsehair lichen, *Bryoria fuscescens*
paper birch. *See* white birch
pawpaw, *Asimina triloba*

pignut hickory, *Carya glabra*
pileated woodpecker, *Dryocopus pileatus*
pine grosbeak, *Pinicola enucleator*
pine siskin, *Spinus pinus*
pine warbler, *Dendroica pinus*
pink lady's-slipper, *Cypripedium reginae*
pink salmon, *Oncorhynchus gorbuscha*
piping plover, *Charadrius melodus*
pitcher plant, *Sarracenia purpurea*
Pitcher's thistle, *Cirsium pitcheri*
pitted beard lichen, *Usnea covernosa*
poison ivy, *Rhus radicans*
poke milkweed, *Asclepias exaltata*
polypody fern, *Polypodium virginianum*
porcupine, *Erethizon dorsatum*
powdered beard lichen, *Usnea laricina*
powder-headed tube lichen, *Hypogymnia tubulosa*
prairie dropseed grass, *Sporobolus heterolepis*
prairie milkweed, *Asclepias hirtella*
prairie white-fringed orchid, *Habenaria leucophaea*
prothonotary warbler, *Prothonotaria citrea*
puma. *See* cougar
purple finch, *Carpodacus purpureus*
purple foxglove, *Digitalis purpurea*
purple loosestrife, *Lythrum salicaria*
purple milkweed, *Asclepias purpurascens*
purple trillium, *Trillium erectum*

quagga mussel, *Dreissena bugensis*
quaking aspen, *Populus tremuloides*

raccoon, *Procyon lotor*
rainbow smelt, *Osmerus mordax*
rainbow trout, *Oncorhynchus mykiss*
red crossbill, *Loxia curvirostra*
red fox, *Vulpes fulva*
red-headed woodpecker, *Melanerpes erythrocephalus*
red pine, *Pinus resinosa*
red-seeded dandelion, *Taraxacum crythrosphermum*
red spruce, *Picea rubens*
red squirrel, *Tamiasciurus hudsonicus*
red-tailed hawk, *Buteo jamaicensis*
red wolf, *Canis rufus*
ring-billed gull, *Larus delawarensis*
robin, *Turdus migratorius*
round goby, *Neogobius melanostomus*
ruffed grouse, *Bonasa umbellus*
rufous-sided towhee, *Pipilo erythrophthalmus*
rusty blackbird, *Euphagus carolinus*

sand cherry, *Prunus pumila*
sandhill crane, *Grus canadensis*
sassafras, *Sassafras albidum*
savanna sparrow, *Passerculus sandwichensis*
Scotch pine, *Pinus sylvestris*

sea lamprey, *Petromyzon marinus*
sedge wren, *Cistothorus platensis*
shagbark hickory, *Carya ovata*
sharp-shinned hawk, *Accipiter striatus*
sharp-tailed grouse, *Tympanuchus phasianellus*
shellbark hickory, *Carya laciniosa*
shield fern, *Dryoptera fragrans*
silver maple, *Acer saccharinum*
slate-colored junco, *Junco hyemalis*
slimy sculpin, *Cottus cognatus*
smallmouth bass, *Micropterus dolomieui*
small purple-fringed orchid, *Habenaria psycodes*
small skullcap, *Scutellaria parvula*
snowshoe hare, *Lepus americanus*
sockeye salmon, *Oncorhynchus nerka*
solitary sandpiper, *Tringa solitaria*
sora, *Porzana carolina*
southern flying squirrel, *Glaucomys volans*
spatterdock, *Nuphar advena*
speckled alder, *Alnus rugosa*
sphagnum moss, *Sphagnum andersonianum*
spiny waterflea, *Bythotrephes longimanus*
spoonhead sculpin, *Cottus ricei*
spottail shiner, *Notopis hudsonius*
spotted sandpiper, *Actitis macularia*
spotted turtle, *Clemmys guttata*
spotted wintergreen, *Chimaphila maculata*
spring peeper, *Pseudacris crucifer*
springtails, *order Collembola*
spruce budworm, *Choristoneura fumiferana*
starflower, *Trientalis borealis*
star-tipped reindeer lichen, *Cladina stellaris*
sugar maple, *Acer saccharum*
Sullivant's milkweed, *Asclepias sullivantii*
swamp cottonwood, *Populus heterophylla*
swamp milkweed, *Asclepias incarnata*
swamp white oak, *Quercus bicolor*
sycamore, *Platanus occidentalis*

tamarack, *Larix laricina*
threeridge mussel, *Amblema costata*
trembling aspen. *See* quaking aspen
tricorn mussel, *Dysnomia triquetra*
tulip tree, *Liriodendron tulipifera*
turkey vulture, *Cathartes aura*
twinflower, *Linnaea borealis*

velvet-leaf blueberry, *Vaccinium myrtilloides*

walleye, *Stizostedion vitreus*
water arum, *Calla palustris*
white ash, *Fraximus americana*
white birch, *Betula papyrifera*
white oak, *Quercus alba*
white perch, *Morone americana*

white spruce, *Picea glauca*
white-tailed deer, *Odocoileus virginianus*
white trillium, *Trillium grandiflorum*
white violet, *Viola blanda*
white water lily, *Nymphaea odorata*
white-winged crossbill, *Loxia leucoptera*
whooping crane, *Grus americana*
whorled milkweed, *Asclepias verticillata*
wild calla. *See* water arum
wild turkey, *Meleagris gallopavo*
winterberry, *Ilex verticillata*
winter tick, *Dermacentor albipictus*
wood duck, *Aix sponsa*
wood frog, *Rana sylvatica*
woodland caribou, *Rangifer tarandus caribou*
wood terrapin or wood turtle, *Clemmys insculpta*
wood violet, *Viola palmata*
wormwood, *Artemisia campestris*

yellow-billed cuckoo, *Coccyzus americanus*
yellow birch, *Betula lutea* in Canada,
    Betula alleghaniensis in the United States
yellow horse gentian, *Triosteum angustifolium*
yellow lotus, *Nelumbo lutea*
yellow morel, *Morchella esculenta*
yellow perch, *Perca flavescens*
yellow-spotted salamander, *Ambystoma maculatum*
yellow warbler, *Dendroica petechia*

zebra mussel, *Dreissena polymorpha*

ILLUSTRATION CREDITS

PHOTOGRAPHS

David Barbour: p. 49

George Barron: pp. 10, 154, 155

Stephen Doggett/KlixPix: p. 257

Great Lakes Fishery Commission: p. 279

Troy L. Holcombe and the *Journal of Great Lakes Research*: p. 48

Pete Janes/KlixPix: p. 220

Linda Kershaw/KlixPix: pp. 70, 133

Phil Kor, Ontario Parks: pp. 61, 65, 208

Lori Labatt: pp. 41, 52, 87, 108, 193, 222, 226–227, 270–271, 305

Diane Lackie: p. 131

Bruce Litteljohn: pp. ii, vi–vii, viii, 4, 9, 15, 20, 31, 38, 46, 62, 68, 78–79, 91, 99, 100–101, 104, 116, 119, 127, 140–141, 167, 176, 179, 207, 211, 232, 258–259, 262–263, 275, 282–283, 288–289, 306–307, 320, 324, 335

Janet Longhurst: pp. 212–213

Robert McCaw: p. 164

Bev McMullen: p. 24, 26–27

Ethan Meleg: pp. 35, 36, 156, 163, 173, 180, 184, 187, 200, 204–205, 276, 296–297, 309, 316, 326–327

Phil Meyer/KlixPix: p. 168

Dawn M Photography: p. 217

NASA/Goddard Space Flight Center Scientific Visualization Studio: p. 80

National Oceanic and Atmospheric Administration, Great Lakes Environmental Research Laboratory: pp. 244–245, 272, 292, 295, 312 (NOAA/GLERL/KlixPix)

Natural Resources Canada/KlixPix: p. 92

Jon Nelson: pp. 66–67

Pelee Island Winery: p. 159

Scot Stewart: pp. 16, 19, 42, 57, 74–75, 84, 89, 94–95, 103, 107, 112, 122–123, 137, 144–145, 146, 152, 160, 166, 170, 171, 190–191, 194, 196–197, 219, 225, 238–239, 242, 251, 268, 299, 300, 302, 319, 328, 331

Eleanor Kee Wellman: pp. 115, 128, 132, 151, 172, 252–253, 256, 264, 267, 323, 332

MAPS

Except for the sources noted below, the maps are based on information in the public domain.

P. 14: Ecoregions of the Great Lakes Basin, adapted from Taylor H. Ricketts, et al., *Terrestrial Ecoregions of North America: A Conservation Assessment* (Washington, D.C.: Island Press, 1999).

P. 32: Great Lakes Basin in Relief, adapted from United States Environmental Protection Agency and Government of Canada, *The Great Lakes: An Environmental Atlas and Resource Book* (Chicago, IL, and Downsview, ON, 1995).

P. 51: Great Lakes Geology, adapted from Antony R. Orme, editor, Physical Geography of North America (New York, Oxford University Press, 2002).

P. 73: Isostatic Uplift, adapted from *Canadian Geographic*, 2000 Annual, Volume 120, Issue 1.

P. 76: Summer and Winter Temperatures, adapted from United States Environmental Protection Agency and Government of Canada, *The Great Lakes: An Environmental Atlas and Resource Book* (Chicago, IL, and Downsview, ON, 1995).

P. 81: Precipitation and Snowbelt Areas, adapted from United States Environmental Protection Agency and Government of Canada, *The Great Lakes: An Environmental Atlas and Resource Book* (Chicago, IL, and Downsview, ON, 1995).

P. 183: Major Wetlands of the Great Lakes Basin, adapted from United States Environmental Protection Agency and Government of Canada, *The Great Lakes: An Environmental Atlas and Resource Book* (Chicago, IL, and Downsview, ON, 1995).

P. 203: Alvar Communities in the Great Lakes Basin, adapted from International Alvar Conservation Initiative, *Conserving Great Lakes Alvars* (Chicago, The Nature Conservancy, 1999).

INDEX

Italicized page numbers refer to figure captions.

THE DAVID SUZUKI FOUNDATION

THE DAVID SUZUKI FOUNDATION WORKS through science and education to protect the diversity of nature and our quality of life, now and for the future.

With a goal of achieving sustainability within a generation, the Foundation collaborates with scientists, business and industry, academia, government and non-governmental organizations. We seek the best research to provide innovative solutions that will help build a clean, competitive economy that does not threaten the natural services that support all life.

The Foundation is a federally registered independent charity, which is supported with the help of over 50,000 individual donors across Canada and around the world.

We invite you to become a member. For more information on how you can support our work, please contact us:

THE DAVID SUZUKI FOUNDATION
219–2211 West 4th Avenue
Vancouver, BC
Canada V6K 4S2
www.davidsuzuki.org
contact@davidsuzuki.org
Tel: 604-732-4228
Fax: 604-732-0752

Checks can be made payable to The David Suzuki Foundation. All donations are tax-deductible.

Canadian charitable registration: (BN) 12775 6716 RR0001

U.S. charitable registration: #94-3204049